ORGANIZATIONAL CAPITAL

ORGANIZATIONAL CAPITAL

The Path to Higher Productivity and Well-being

JOHN F. TOMER

 PRAEGER

New York
Westport, Connecticut
London

Library of Congress Cataloging-in-Publication Data

Tomer, John F.
  Organizational capital : the path to higher productivity and
well-being / John F. Tomer.
  p. cm.
  Bibliography: p.
  Includes index.
  ISBN 0-275-92582-X (alk. paper)
  1. Industrial organization. 2. Industrial management.
3. Industrial productivity. 4. Business enterprises. I. Title.
HD31.T635   1987
338.5—dc19   87-16828
                CIP

Library of Congress Catalog Card Number: 87-16828
ISBN 0-275-92582-X

First published in 1987

Praeger Publishers, One Madison Avenue, New York, NY 10010
A division of Greenwood Press, Inc.

Printed in the United States of America

(∞)™

The paper used in this book complies with the
Permanent Paper Standard issued by the National
Information Standards Organization (Z39.48-1984).

10 9 8 7 6 5 4 3 2 1

Dedicated to
Doris, my wife
and
Geraldine, my mother

Contents

CREDITS

Chapters 2 and 3:
John F. Tomer, "Productivity and Organizational Behavior: Where Human Capital Theory Fails" in Benny Gilad and Stanley Kaish, eds. *Handbook of Behavioral Economics* (Greenwich, CT: Jai Press, 1986). Reprinted by permission of the publisher.

Chapter 4:
John F. Tomer, "Organizational Change, Organizational Capital and Economic Growth," *Eastern Economic Journal* 7 (January 1981): 1–14. Reprinted by permission.

Chapter 5:
John F. Tomer, "Worker Motivation: A Neglected Element in Micro-Micro Theory," *Journal of Economic Issues* 15 (June 1981); 351–362. Reprinted from the *Journal of Economic Issues* by special permission of the copyright holder, the Association for Evolutionary Economics.

Chapter 7:
John F. Tomer, "Working Smarter the Japanese Way: The X-Efficiency of Theory Z Management" in Paul Kleindorfer, ed. *The Management of Productivity and Technology in Manufacturing* (Philadelphia: Plenum, 1985). Reprinted by permission of publisher.

Chapter 9:
John F. Tomer, "Developing Organizational Comparative Advantage Via Industrial Policy," *Journal of Post Keynesian Economics* 9(Spring 1987), 455–472.

Foreword

There is a steady and growing interest among economists in prying open the black box of standard microeconomic theory and attempting to analyze its insides. This seems to be part of a long swing in intellectual activity where initially the firm was stripped of its recognizable features in the interest of simplicity and rigor, and then gradually, as if the process had gone too far, a return was made to building up our image of the firm into something more recognizable to those who know firms in reality.

From approximately the early 1870s to the 1950s, the firm was gradually denuded of recognizable characteristics so that it fit neatly into the needs of a formalized hypothetico-deductive system of the market, the modern Walrasian general equilibrium model. The end result was that the firm turned out to be no more than a production function, that is, a translation device between inputs and outputs. This enabled theorists to reduce economic activity entirely to questions of exchange.

In recent decades there has been some movement in the other direction, that is, an attempt to see the firm as a functioning organization with internal activities, problems, and controls. This general process has been carried out along various lines and has gradually been developed across the political spectrum of economists. If we must generalize, it appears that conservatives have taken a property-rights approach; they view the firm as a locus of contracts in which property rights solve essentially property-rights conflicts. Those in the middle such as Tomer and myself are sometimes viewed as taking a Hobbesian view, within which there is a recognition of the conflict between the need to cooperate and the desire to pursue personal interests. The Marxists seem to have taken, for the most part, a class-war view of the enterprise. But of course such capsule descriptions understate the great deal of work and thought that has really gone on in these efforts. Unfortunately they stress differences rather than the overlapping insights contained in the various approaches.

A related development appears to be the recognition by economists of the value in connecting their work with that of organization theorists found in schools of business administration. Tomer, to his credit, draws on various strands, although for the most part he seems to be in the middle-of-the-road school. Viewing the firm as a locus of both conflicting and possibly cooperative behavior naturally leads, so it seems to me and to Tomer, to a theory-of-games approach, and especially to the Prisoner's Dilemma paradigm. To my mind this view gives the organizational picture a necessary realism, because these conflicting tendencies are, of essence, important aspects of the reality of life in the enterprise, since firm members cannot always reconcile group objectives and personal objectives.

To try to understand economic organization in general is a difficult problem. A good deal could be said for the notion that it would help if the basic unit possessed some recognizable degrees of realism, such as the conflict-cooperation dichotomy, even if the needs of scientific work force us to reduce the complexity of reality to something much simpler. There is clearly no need to work with something quite as simple and unrealistic as the neoclassical black box. To find a unifying concept around which to build the overall structure, Tomer has hit upon the useful idea of attempting to relate everything to the concept of organizational capital. This has the advantage of drawing on a counterpart concept of human capital, which has now been written about for several decades. This approach permits a degree of coherence to the entire enterprise that would otherwise be absent. On the whole, Tomer's approach helps to solve some of the puzzles surrounding the nature of the firm, and of normal economic life, while like all good research it raises questions and opens avenues of research for others to follow. This is a critical area of economic research. Tomer has made a useful contribution which deserves careful reading and assimilation.

Harvey Leibenstein
Harvard University

Acknowledgments

Writing a book is of necessity a somewhat lonely task. This is why an author needs the support, encouragement, and feedback of others. I feel a special appreciation for the people that have helped me, and thus made my task less onerous and more rewarding. Of course, I alone bear the responsibility for the virtues and defects of the final product. Mentioned below are some of the people who have been most helpful. I apologize to the helpful people I may have neglected to mention.

Zoltan Acs deserves special mention. It was on a beautiful June day in 1984 when Zoltan and I were having an intellectual discussion and strolling around Manhattan College that the idea for this book crystallized. It was a pleasant coincidence then that I was able to follow in Zoltan's footsteps because his book, which preceded mine, was published by Praeger. I appreciate very much our stimulating conversations over the years and regret the circumstances that led to his departure from Manhattan College.

I can not say enough about how helpful and supportive Romesh Diwan has been. On many occasions he invited me to make presentations at various conferences and at seminars held at the Rensselaer Polytechnic Institute. The papers presented on these occasions were in many cases early versions of the chapters of this book. These presentations provided an opportunity for me to try out my ideas and meet fellow researchers with similar interests. I am grateful for Romesh's humanism, his appreciation of my work and his role in creating a positive intellectual atmosphere in the Economics Department at Rensselaer Polytechnic Institute.

Because my ideas diverged greatly from economic orthodoxy, I was fortunate to complete my Ph.D. thesis under the supervision of Robert J. Alexander at Rutgers University. He allowed me a great deal of latitude in developing my ideas and following my instincts wherever they led. He did not object when I first wrote about the organizational capital idea in one of the chapters of my thesis, even though the idea was not well developed at that point. This support was crucial for me.

The most important direct intellectual influence on my work is undoubtedly that of Harvey Leibenstein. My writings have built on his X-efficiency theory in a number of different ways. After I sent Harvey a copy of my article on worker motivation he invited me to talk with him in January 1981 at his Harvard office. I was very grateful for that opportunity to meet him, and I am glad our paths have continued to cross over the years. Harvey is a quiet man and a true scholar whose life's work has coherence and purpose. I admire him because he uses economic theory creatively to capture aspects of human behavior that orthodox theory ignores.

Two economic journal editors deserve special note. First, William Waters, Editor of the *Review of Social Economy,* saw merit in my article, "Community Control and the Theory of the Firm." This article was especially important to me because it was my first full-fledged effort in the economics of organizational behavior. Its publication gave me the encouragement I needed to continue. I thank him also for his invitation that led to my participation in the 1984 Marquette University Conference, which related to community, solidarity and cooperative enterprise. Second, the decision by Ingrid Rima to publish my article "Organizational Change, Organizational Capital and Economic Growth" in the *Eastern Economic Journal* was a very important one for me. It validated my growing belief that my preoccupation with the organizational capital concept was a legitimate activity with real potential, and not an abnormal obsession. I am appreciative of the breadth of scholarship that Ingrid brings to bear in her editorship of the *Eastern Economic Journal.*

Three associations have been especially important to me; the Association for Social Economics, the Association for Evolutionary Economics, and the Society for the Advancement of Behavioral Economics. The Association for Social Economics is notable for its congenial, compassionate membership whose concerns are unfailingly humanistic. I particularly appreciate the opportunity I had to present my article, "Working Smarter the Japanese Way," at their December 1982 meeting. Second, my association with the Association for Evolutionary Economics has provided me with important opportunities to interact with a larger, more diverse group of institutionally minded scholars.

My participation in the Society for the Advancement of Behavioral Economics has been particularly exciting because I was one of the founding members of this group and because I share much in terms of aspiration, outlook and research style with its members. It has been a pleasure to be associated with Benjamin Gilad and Stanley Kaish of Rutgers University at Newark; Shlomo Maital of Technion, Israel; Richard Hatwick of Western Illinois University; and many of the others who have played significant roles in the birth and growth of the Society for the Advancement of Behavioral Economics.

Klaus Weiermair of York University and Peter Birckmayer of Empire State College both read the manuscript when the book was nearly finished and provided useful feedback. Klaus is especially noteworthy because he has independently developed ideas quite similar to mine with respect to Japanese management and internal organizational relationships. Also, I appreciate the encouragement and friendship shown to me by Kurt Dopfer of St. Gallen University, Switzerland.

I am grateful for the appreciation that Mark Lutz of the University of Maine at Orono has shown for my work, and I hope that I can do as much as he is doing to try to make economics a more humanistic subject of study. In 1982, Roy Rotheim of Skidmore College suggested that I write a review essay on Rodney Clark's *The Japanese Company*. This timely suggestion gave me the first opportunity to try out some of my developing ideas on Japanese management. Roy has also been very supportive and has listened sympathetically to my career tales of woe.

Both Jim Orr of Manhattan College and Dan Orne of Rensselaer Polytechnic Institute read earlier versions of several of my chapters; I am grateful for their comments and my stimulating discussions with them regarding labor economics, Japanese management and managerial trends. Also, I appreciate the members of the economics departments at Manhattan College and Rensselaer Polytechnic Institute who have taken the trouble to attend my presentations and have shared their observations with me.

Chapters 2 and 3 were originally prepared for presentation at the first Behavioral Economics Conference at Princeton University on May 22, 1984. Benjamin Gilad is notable for his conference invitation and initial suggestions that led to the writing of that paper. Comments by Amyra Grossbard-Shechtman of San Diego State University and my discussion with her led to a marked improvement in the economic analysis. A later version of that paper appears as a chapter entitled "Productivity and Organizational Behavior: Where Human Capital Theory Fails" in *Handbook of Behavioral Economics* edited by Benjamin Gilad and Stanley Kaish (Greenwich, CT: Jai Press, 1986). This work is reprinted by permission of the publisher.

Chapter 4 is developed from my paper "Organizational Change, Organizational Capital and Economic Growth," which appeared in *Eastern Economic Journal* 7 (January 1981), 1–14. It is reprinted by permission.

Chapter 5 is an adaptation of "Worker Motivation: A Neglected Element in Micro-Micro Theory," *Journal of Economic Issues* 15 (June 1981), 351–362. It is reprinted from the *Journal of Economic Issues* by special permission of the copyright holder, the Association for Evolutionary Economics.

Chapter 7 benefited from the presentation of earlier versions at the Second United States-Japan Business Conference and at the Wharton Conference on Productivity, Technology, and Organizational Innovation sponsored by the Center for the Study of Organizational Innovation. Benjamin Gilad of Rutgers University at Newark, Jeremiah Sullivan and Thomas Roehl of the University of Washington, and Jay B. Barney of the University of California, Los Angeles, are noteworthy for their constructive criticism and comments on the paper. A slightly different version of this chapter, entitled "Working Smarter the Japanese Way: The X-Efficiency of Theory Z Management," appears in *The Management of Productivity and Technology in Manufacturing* (Philadelphia: Plenum, 1985) edited by Paul Kleindorfer. It appears by permission of the publisher. I am indebted to Paul Kleindorfer for his skillful editing and his equally skillful conference organizing.

Chapter 9 was developed from my paper entitled "Developing Organizational Comparative Advantage via Industrial Policy," which appeared in the *Journal of Post Keynesian Economics* 9 (Spring 1987), 455–472.

I am especially appreciative of the support given to me by a number of my noneconomist friends: Thomas McGuire, Donald Pangburn, and Michael O'Rourke are notable in this respect. They have on occasion listened patiently to my ideas and sympathized with my problems.

Betty Jean Kaufmann typed a number of my chapters and along with Cathy Keenan was helpful in dealing with my software conversion problems. She has been unfailing in her friendliness. Mary Salo also helped by typing drafts of several chapters.

Barbara Leffel, Catherine Woods and Michael Fisher, my three editors at Praeger, were all very helpful. Barbara Leffel is noteworthy for her belief in my project and for her cheerful, patient efforts to encourage me to sign up with Praeger. Michael Fisher has been extremely diligent in working with me to put the manuscript in final shape and to get the production process rolling. On the occasions when I have needed advice, he has never failed to provide valuable guidance.

Last but not least is my wife, Doris, who has been my partner in this endeavor. Somehow she has not only managed her career, our home and our two sons, Russell and Jeffrey, but she has found time to advise me on my career decisions and to occasionally read my chapters. She has managed all this despite my occasional grumpiness and the fact that for the last three and a half years my job has required me to be out of town for three to four days a week. Certainly without her assistance, encouragement and caring, it would have been difficult to complete this project.

ORGANIZATIONAL CAPITAL

1

Introduction

Organization is being increasingly appreciated as an important influence on both the productivity of economic enterprises and the worker's ability to satisfy their individual needs. Not only do we suspect organization to be a key factor in the successes of Japanese companies like Toyota, Sony, and Matsushita, but it seems related to the successes of U.S. institutions like 3M, IBM, Hewlett-Packard and even the Los Angeles Raiders and the Boston Celtics. Nevertheless, this factor has seemed to defy scholarly analysis, especially for economists. Internal organizational relationships simply don't fit into the orthodox theory of the firm; and in explanations of the sources of economic growth, the organization factor has at best been lumped unceremoniously with the rest of the residual, the unexplained and the unmeasured part of the growth rate.

Therefore, this book proposes a new economic concept, organizational capital, which holds great promise as: 1) an explanation of a neglected source of economic growth; 2) an explanation for the behavior and productivity of the firm; 3) an explanation of how productivity is related to interorganizational behavior; 4) a guide to formulating better governmental policies with respect to economic growth and development; and 5) a vehicle for achieving overall a better appreciation of how institutional arrangements contribute to economic as well as social outcomes.

The book's analysis is explicitly part of the emerging field of behavioral economics. That is, it borrows from noneconomic behavioral disciplines, in this case organizational behavior, and integrates these insights with economic theory. The book is also humanistic in that it views organizing efforts as well as all other economic activities as the means by which people achieve their ultimate ends; becoming all that they are capable of becoming. To the extent that organizational investment enables people to obtain greater satisfaction of their higher needs, it enables greater human well-being. Thus, the organizational capital analysis is suggestive of an alternative approach to orthodox welfare analysis.

Investment in organizational capital refers to the using up of resources in order to bring about lasting improvement in productivity as well as worker well-being through changes in the functioning of the organization. Organizational capital formation could involve 1) changing the formal and informal social relationships and patterns of activity within the enterprise or 2) changing individual attributes important to organizational functioning, or 3) the accumulation of information useful in matching workers with organization situations. Organizational capital is human capital in which the attribute is embodied in either the organizational relationships, particular organization members, the organization's repositories of information, or some combination of the above in order to improve the functioning of the organization.

The key organizational behavior insight is that the behavior, personality, and motivation of an individual in an organization cannot be explained simply by personal attributes. For a firm with given tangible capital goods and technology, individual behavior, and thus organizational productivity, is the result of an interaction between the characteristics of the organization and the individual. Individual behavior and productivity will be determined by the organizational climate, the structure of the organization, and the organization's socialization processes as well as by individual attributes. In the case of an investment in "pure" organizational capital such as a change in organizational structure or climate, organizational functioning and productivity improve because the changed organization evokes new and better worker behavior. For completeness, two "hybrid" types of organizational capital should be mentioned; these types contribute to the functioning of the organization but may be embodied in employees in the form of information or behavioral attributes inculcated, perhaps, as a result of the organization's socialization process. Information relevant to matching employees with other employees and organization positions may also be embodied in the organization's formal files in a way that makes it available to decision makers.

The vast and growing literature on organizational behavior contains many insights, case histories and empirical analyses related to the features of organizations that make for high productivity. These insights have undoubtedly been underutilized by U.S. companies, and they have been virtually ignored by economists. If organizational relationships do much to shape and motivate the individual actions that are ultimately responsible for society's productivity, it is incumbent upon economists to do more to incorporate these insights into their theoretical framework. Otherwise, economists' advice to policy makers on the range of options available for increasing productivity and well-being will be woefully inadequate.

AN EXAMPLE

The story of Springfield Remanufacturing Center Corporation (SRC) of Springfield, Missouri, a small company whose main business is rebuilding diesel engines and engine components, provides a good example of organizational investment (Rhodes 1986). In early 1983, SRC's president, Jack Stack, and 12 other employees bought the business, which had formerly been a division of International Harvester Company. In 1979 SRC's fortunes were at a low ebb, with a loss of $2 million on sales of $26 million. Although SRC began a rebound once Stack arrived as plant manager in 1979, its prospects seemed dim again in 1982–1983 as its parent, International Harvester, was failing. Since then SRC has achieved an amazing turnaround for which its approach to management is largely responsible. "Since the leveraged buyout, SRC's sales have grown 40% per year and are expected to reach $42 million in fiscal 1986; net operating income has risen to 11% [of sales[; the debt-to-equity ratio has been cut from 89-to-1 to 5.1-to-1" (p. 43).

The "Stack" approach to management combines a rigorous preoccupation with data and a very people-oriented approach. Under Stack's leadership, "they developed a meticulously detailed reporting system that at one point had them calculating a full-blown income statement every day" (Rhodes 1986, 43). SRC focuses not only on the income statement but on performance data in relation to standards; other data collected relate to product quality, safety, productivity, and employee turnover. The problem that SRC has apparently solved is how to utilize these data for managing without destroying the creative energies of its workers. Stack's approach to getting employee involvement was to make using the data a good game, one with fun, action, and excitement, and that anyone could learn to play. The SRC game is won when performance data reach target levels; this triggers various individual and group awards as well as celebrations, such as the plant close-down for a "beer bust" which marked 100,000 hours without a recordable accident. To get everyone involved in these games, it was first necessary to educate all 200 workers in a full range of business courses, especially accounting, so that they would know what the numbers meant. Second, everyone had to become involved in setting standards and goals. The result is that Springfield's employees work hard and have fun playing the "Great Game of Business." SRC's nonmanagement people share indirectly in ownership through an employee stock option plan (ESOP), and the atmosphere is egalitarian. According to one employee, "The barriers between management and employees just don't exist here" (p. 42).

Clearly, SRC has initiated changes in organization and management that have succeeded admirably in eliciting high motivation, cooperation and performance from its employees. A basic premise of this book is that it is useful to view the resources used for making such organizational changes as investments that bring into existence increases in productive capacity because of improved organizational functioning. In the SRC case, these human capital investments seem to be spread across the spectrum from pure human capital to pure organizational capital. SRC may be different from other firms in the extent of its success with organizational change and the extent of its use of financial and operational data, but it is certainly not alone in attempting a significant organizational change as a way to improve business performance. Nor is its situation as the target of a leveraged buy-out unique. For example, a similar organizational transformation occurred in 1982 when Rexworks Inc., a Milwaukee-based manufacturer of heavy construction machinery, was bought from Rexnord by nine of its managers including chief executive officer, James Stollenwerk (Stollenwerk 1984). Nevertheless, this path to greater productivity and greater worker well-being is important. The lack of understanding of this phenomenon by economists in particular is an important reason for this book.

KEY ORGANIZATIONAL BEHAVIORAL CONCEPTS

To appreciate the organizational capital concept, it needs to be related to a few key organizational behavior concepts, and these, in turn, must be linked to several important economic concepts. To begin, let's consider one of the most basic notions of organizational behavior. This is the idea that organizations shape the behavior of individual members. It follows that a "badly shaped" organization, one of poor quality, can lead to counterproductive or low productivity individual behavior even when the individual members have highly productive attributes.

Second, it has been observed that young corporations frequently are dominated by a single entrepreneur and characterized by a lack of explicit organization and organizing activity. If things go well, chances are it is because of the vision, drive and determination of the entrepreneur, not because of the organization. Despite early success, the expansion potential of such a corporation will be very limited unless it can structure its expanding activities. In other words, further growth requires that the corporation create a hierarchy and take on the characteristics of a bureaucracy. This means introducing formal chains of command, standard operating procedures and such systematic business practices as budgeting, forecasting, goal setting, and planning, all with the goal of achieving greater predictability and control. While this introduction of systematic practice is necessary and undoubtedly leads to increased efficiency, it is not without problems.

The problems occur because the systems that control may simultaneously stifle, lowering motivation and creativity and producing tension, frustration and antagonism. Furthermore, a corporation's attachment to systematic procedure may inhibit it from making needed changes in response to environmental novelty and uncertainty. The answer to these problems is, however, not to do away with all structures and systems; it lies in finding ways to invigorate the organization's members and to counter the deadening influences of bureaucracy. The answer lies in creating dynamic corporations that are managed in a way that taps the energies of its members and channels and coordinates them in order to achieve common goals. While there is no uniformity of opinion, there is growing agreement among human resource management professionals on the characteristics of management that make corporations dynamic. The essence, according to Chris Argyris (1960, 21–23), is that organization members who are able to satisfy their higher needs, especially their need for self-actualization, will have considerably more energy available for organization tasks. Moreover, these members' decision-making effectiveness, creativity and ability to play an effective role in groups will also be related to their ability to satisfy their needs in the organization. Thus, Argyris and many others have sought ways to create the organizational conditions conducive to this need satisfaction. Among the leaders in this task of organization development are Robert Blake and Jane Mouton (1985), who have written extensively on how to create the kind of organizational climate and interpersonal styles which result in good team work, conflict resolution and problem solving, as well as in high achievement.

Despite this growing knowledge of organizational behavior, many attempts at organization development (particularly in the 1960s and 1970s) have been failures. Managers, thus, have experienced both a growing awareness of the possibilities of organizational revitalization and the realization that creating a dynamic corporation is not a trivial task. Because managers are naturally interested in how to accomplish this, much attention in the 1980s has focused on concrete organizational models of well-functioning business enterprises. The search is on to discover examples of dynamic organizations in order to learn the keys to their success.

Ezra Vogel (1979) has led the way by pointing to Japan; he believes that Japan is number one in social relations both within the corporation and without. He found, for example, that "the large modern Japanese company is committed to the whole individual, not simply to the task-related part of the individual. . . . [Its] primary commitment . . . is not to its stockholders but to its employees. Japanese workers reciprocate this commitment" (pp. 151–152). William Ouchi (1981) delved deeper into the organizational reasons for the success of Japanese companies. One of his most important findings relates to the difference between Japanese and U.S. companies in the way that employees are controlled. Ouchi explains that, "The basic mechanism of control in a Japanese company is embodied in a philosophy of management" which provides implicit control in contrast with the explicit control mechanisms typical in American firms (p. 41). Thus, Japanese employees' efforts are guided to a great degree by the values and shared beliefs of the company they belong to and identify with. Ouchi also pointed to a number of successful U.S. corporations that function similarly.

Thomas Peters and Robert Waterman (1982) started their search for management excellence in the United States. They found eight important attributes among corporations which ranked high on both management excellence and long-term financial performance measures. Among these, the most notable are the tendency for excellent corporations to 1) foster leaders and innovators throughout the organization (letting people be "champions" of new ideas), 2) consider "the rank and file as the root source of quality and productivity gain," not fostering adversarial labor relations or regarding "capital investment as the fundamental source of efficiency improvement," 3) consider the basic philosophy of the business as an extremely important influence on its achievements, and 4) have simple organizational forms and relatively small top-level staffs (pp. 14–15).

Producer cooperatives provide another model of good organization, and the Mondragon Cooperatives in the Basque region of Spain are far and away the most productive and most distinctively cooperative in their organization (see, for example, Bradley and Gelb 1981 and 1982, Thomas and Logan 1982, Thomas 1982, and Jones 1980). While it is clear that Mondragon has benefited from good leadership and a strong, clear philosophy, David Ellerman (for instance, 1984) has emphasized that their formal legal structure 1) insures the continuation of worker self-management insofar as voting and economic profit rights are made personal or nontransferable rights and 2) provides desirable collective and individual incentives, which tend to be lacking in other cooperatives.

While each is different, the organizational models explicit or implicit in the writings referred to above share one fundamental idea: organizations that are less controlling and more participative in a variety of ways will be more vital, efficient and satisfying places to work. The literature on human resource management makes this point over and over again in a variety of different ways. Walton (1985a) calls the move to greater participation a move from a control to a commitment strategy. He finds that

research generally supports the hypothesis of a net advantage in moving toward the commitment strategy. That is, the average effectiveness of these units appears to be higher than the average of more conventionally organized but otherwise comparable units. Poorly conceived or badly implemented commitment-oriented systems are undoubtedly less effective than the better-managed conventional ones. (Walton 1985a, 53)

KEY ECONOMIC CONCEPTS

The concept of human capital, which states that capacity for production as well as human satisfaction can be embodied in people, was developed first by Gary Becker and Theodore W. Schultz (see, for example, Becker 1964). In their view, people could add to their human capital endowments through the acquisition of skills and knowledge; this generally increased their own productivity and income-earning ability and that of the enterprise in which they worked. Multiplied many times these investments in human capital taking place within firms and educational institutions have become an important source for total output growth in many nations. Whereas explanations of economic growth used to focus largely on processes that created tangible and financial assets, the key role played by intangible capital formation is now being recognized. Organizational capital is perhaps the least tangible and least marketable of these intangible assets. Maybe this has something to do with the fact that it has been least analyzed by economists.

Another key economic concept is X-efficiency (and its opposite X-inefficiency), developed by Harvey Leibenstein (1966, 1976). The degree of X-inefficiency refers "to the degree to which actual output is less than maximum output (for given inputs)" (1966, 95); X-inefficiency is considered to be the normal state of affairs. In Leibenstein's analysis, an important reason for the omnipresence of X-inefficiency is that individuals taking into account their own interests and organizational incentives generally choose to exert less effort than would be optimal from the organization's point of view. This means that the organization's costs are greater than the minimum or, conversely, its productivity is less than potential. If we interpret this situation as Leibenstein has, such a firm is operating *within* its production possibility frontier. But now let's suppose that these workers' effort levels are as high as they could be given the character of the firm's organization and management. My view is that it is useful to think of this as a position *on* a firm's production possibility frontier given the firm's investment in organizational capital. If this firm uses up resources in the effort to improve its organizational attributes, to the extent that it is successful, this organizational investment makes it possible for the given inputs to achieve a greater output. In other words, investment in organizational capital by virtue of the changed organizational incentives experienced by workers results in higher effort and, correspondingly, the realization of higher output. Organizational capital formation thus involves an improvement in X-efficiency. It is, of course, also possible to increase X-efficiency by moving from within the production possibility frontier to its surface, as when a firm simply takes up some slack, perhaps because management puts additional pressure on workers. The latter is consistent with Leibenstein's usage, and doesn't involve any investment in organizational capital. It should also be noted that X-inefficiency in a dynamic context implies less innovation and growth than are possible. Accordingly, a firm's organizational investment would be expected to lead to faster growth and more innovation.

THE LINK BETWEEN ORGANIZATIONAL BEHAVIOR AND ECONOMICS

The link between the organizational behavior and economics concepts is by now, I suspect, apparent to many readers. In essence, when managers attempt to revitalize their corporations through changes, for example, in organizational structure and culture, they are making investments in organizational capital, which is a kind of human capital. If such investments are in "pure" organizational capital, that is, changes in structure, climate or interpersonal patterns of interaction, it is the changed organizational attributes that evoke improved worker behavior, and thus higher productivity and worker well-being. In this pure case, the firm's productivity would be unchanged should one worker be replaced by another one with an equal human capital endowment. The firm's organizational capital investment, which is embodied in the organization and not the workers, determines how productive workers and other inputs are. Of course, ordinarily things are not so clear; workers' productivity may be affected by their firm-specific attributes (which could be related to organizational functioning), and the replacement of a worker who has made such investments by one who hasn't would certainly affect the firm's productivity. Regardless, the main point is that initiation of organizational change by a business can be expected to raise its X-efficiency and add to its stock of intangible capital.

It should be noted that as with other types of capital, an investment in organizational capital is no guarantee that a business will realize the potential inherent in this investment. Moreover, there is no guarantee that the existing level of a firm's organizational capital stock will be maintained. In other words, organizational capital is subject to depreciation, obsolescence, inefficient utilization and disuse. Just because the Boston Celtics have a good organization and have the potential to win next year's National Basketball Association Championship doesn't mean that they will win it; nor does it mean that they will always have a good organization. Just because Peters and Waterman have identified Hewlett-Packard as having excellence in management doesn't mean that Hewlett-Packard's managers won't make errors leading to lower economic performance or drift away from excellent managerial principles and practices. Finally, a highly participative and much praised organization hasn't prevented the problems that have befallen People's Express Airlines. The existence of organizational capital, like other types of capital, implies capacity and potential. It does not determine performance, it only enables it.

ECONOMISTS' NEGLECT OF ORGANIZATION

Economists' neglect of the study of organization is well known. Consider a few of the reasons: understanding organizational behavior requires sensitivity to sociological and psychological modes of thinking that are quite different from the way economists typically reason. Economists' arguments are generally framed in a very closely reasoned, abstract, and quantifiable way, whereas organizational behavior practitioners favor qualitative, less abstract explanations that are more likely based on their observations of actual behavior than derived from deductions. Generally speaking, economists and organizational behavior professionals are not familiar with each other's literature. Thus, the distinct differences between the two disciplines has been an important barrier to the interdisciplinary activity necessary to incorporate more organizational insight into economics. This barrier may be breaking down to some degree as an increasing number of economists (such as members of the Society for the Advancement of Behavioral Economics) are becoming interested in behavioral economics, and a growing number of psychologists (such as members of the International Association for Research in Psychological Economics) and sociologists are becoming interested in economic questions. Nevertheless, the economic realm involving analysis of markets and contracts has continued to resist penetration by the "softer" disciplines.

To the extent that organizational considerations have been incorporated into economics, they have usually been in the "harder" or structural aspects like the shape of the hierarchy, or the locus of authority and power in making major decisions. Very little attention has been paid to such softer organizational considerations as managerial style, organizational culture and interpersonal communication patterns. My suspicion is that most economists, if they have thought about these matters at all, have considered them 1) unimportant, 2) intangible outcomes not separable from the role of the entrepreneur, 3) not measurable, 4) not lasting (unstable, changeable factors), or 5) factors safely ignored because either they vary so little from one firm to the next or differences among firms are random. These beliefs are no longer tenable. It has become clear that the difference between managerial success and failure is crucially dependent on these very intangible organizational considerations. In the future this is even more likely to be true. It should be noted that recent analyses of the deficiencies of U.S. management have focused more on these softer aspects of organization than on deficiencies in structure. Thus, because of economists' neglect of these increasingly important matters, this book focuses more on the softer aspects of organization than on the structural elements. Moreover, the organizational capital concept is extremely valuable since it provides a way to integrate the softer elements into economic analysis.

ORGANIZATIONAL CAPITAL AT THE SOCIETAL LEVEL

Another desirable feature of the organizational capital concept is that it can refer to capacity embodied in relationships between organizations as well as relationships within organizations. The former includes relationships between businesses and relationships between businesses and government. The functioning of these interorganizational relationships also reflects the magnitude and quality of the organizational investments made. To develop economically and socially a society must improve its inter- as well as intraorganizational functioning via appropriate organizational investment. Relatedly, the more one focuses on organizational matters, the easier it becomes to see that the roots of some of society's worst social problems lie in failed relationships. Thus, a social-critical point of view is fostered when the functioning of organizations is made an explicit part of economic analysis. Conversely, the organizational focus helps one envision ideal societal functioning and corporate behavior. Finally, because the organizational capital concept helps us see the gap between existing social relationships and what is possible, it helps us to think about the processes for closing the gap, including the role that government might play.

PLAN OF THE BOOK

Chapter 2 provides a systematic review of the organizational behavior ideas that are most important for understanding the organizational capital concept. The focus is on explaining how productivity potential is related to organizational attitudes. Depending on a corporation's evolutionary stage, (whether entrepreneurial, mechanistic or dynamic) different organizational features will be more or less important. To become dynamic, a corporation must develop its organization along three dimensions: the psychological, structural, and individual.

Beginning in chapter 3, the organizational behavior insights are integrated with economic theory. Here the concept of organizational capital is carefully developed and related to human capital and X-efficiency theory. It is useful to think in terms of a spectrum of human capital types from pure human to pure organizational in order to understand the roles of the four types of firm-specific human/organizational capital in organizational functioning.

Chapter 4 utilizes the organizational capital concept to explain economic growth. More specifically, organizational capital formation is related to entrepreneurial behavior and technological change, and a production function approach is utilized to indicate how to measure that part of a nation's economic growth attributable to organizational investment. The final part of chapter 4 involves an estimate of the management consultant contribution to the annual rate of growth in the United States using a "growth accounting" approach.

Chapter 5 begins with X-efficiency theory, in particular Leibenstein's theory of work effort determination. In order to integrate this theory with the organizational capital approach and utilize the findings of industrial psychologists on worker motivation, a revised theory of effort determination is developed. The added variables, including characteristics of the work environment and personality, enable the theory to explain how particular improvements in organization and management will lead workers to choose higher effort levels and be more motivated. The model also indicates how excessive pressure on workers might lead to a deterioration of organizational functioning (destruction of organizational capital), and thus lower work effort.

Cooperative behavior within firms and its relationship to productivity is the subject of chapter 6. Not surprisingly, the basic "Prisoner's Dilemma" model is used to explain both the benefits of cooperation and the tendency for cooperation to break down. A number of authors have made revisions to this model that explain why the worst noncooperative scenarios occur infrequently, but even these revised versions are limited in their ability to explain how interemployee relationships and their development affect cooperation. This is because the softer sociological and psychological dimensions of behavior have not been included. To add this element and to indicate how greater cooperation can be developed in organizations, it is necessary to link the organizational capital approach with the prisoner's dilemma model.

Are companies managed the Japanese way more X-efficient than their typical American counterparts? Chapter 7 draws on X-efficiency theory, transaction cost economics and organizational behavior to explain why the answer is yes. In particular, the analysis leads to the conclusion that in comparison to American management, the Japanese management ideal reduces labor market transaction costs, increases cooperation and worker effort, improves membership behavior including absenteeism and labor turnover, and reduces organizational inertia. These benefits follow from the nature of the employer-employee relationships that have been developed in Japanese companies, especially the large, internationally competing firms.

Chapter 8 develops the view that increasing worker participation leads to higher productivity and worker well-being. On the one hand, worker participation may be increased by the introduction of organizational forms providing workers with formal channels and activities through which participation in decision making can be steered. On the other hand, increased worker participation may come about through changing the organization's culture and patterns of interpersonal interaction. Organizations that do the most to develop increased worker participation in both senses are the ones expected to be the most dynamic, with the highest productivity, productivity growth and worker well-being. Theory Z organizations are the ones that have developed their full potential in these respects. The final part of chapter 8 provides a review of empirical studies of the relationship between worker participation and economic performance. The evidence supports the view that increasing worker participation improves economic performance.

Developing cooperative relationships between business and government is another way to improve productivity and well-being. Chapter 9, like chapter 6, uses the prisoner's dilemma model as a starting point in developing this theme. The prisoner's dilemma model in conjunction with different concepts of externalities provides an interesting view of the benefits of interorganizational cooperation and the reasons for noncooperative outcomes. The second section develops the implications of this analysis for industrial policy. The basic idea is that organizational policy as one component of an industrial policy would involve governmental efforts to foster intra- and interorganizational cooperation in order to increase the competitiveness of business enterprises and increase the nation's organizational comparative advantage. The key question is: how can government foster the formation of desired organizational capital?

Is a fundamental, irreversible wave of change occurring as a post-industrial society starts to emerge from our present industrial one? If this is so, what does this imply about future organizational forms? Chapter 10 explores the implications of new technology, changed demographic patterns and increased global competition for the organization of the future. One clear conclusion emerges: To take full advantage of the potential inherent in new technology and in the attributes of young workers will require a managerial shift from strategies of control to participative human resource strategies that elicit high motivation and commitment. While there are reasons for believing that this shift has begun, it is not clear to what extent U.S. management will successfully relinquish past patterns.

2

Productivity and Organizational Behavior

Whether it's at Honda, the Boston Celtics, Procter and Gamble, or Springfield Remanufacturing Center Corporation, the correspondence between "good organization" and high productivity is increasingly being recognized. Moreover, the vast and growing literature on organizational behavior contains many insights on the features of organizations that make for high productivity. These insights have largely been disregarded or overlooked by economists. If organizations do much to shape the individual behaviors that are responsible for firm productivity, it is incumbent upon economists to do more to incorporate these factors into their theoretical framework. The purpose of this chapter is to review a number of the most important ideas of organizational behavior writers, selecting the ideas with implications for changing economic theory, notably human capital theory. This review is designed to indicate how productivity potential i. related to the characteristics of the organization and not to the attributes of individuals or to tangible capital.

THREE STAGES OF CORPORATE EVOLUTION

Insights about organizational productivity can be put into perspective by considering a theory of the stages of corporate evolution known as "Corporate Darwinisn" (Blake, Avis, and Mouton 1966). In this view, there are three stages of corporate evolution: entrepreneurial, mechanistic and dynamic. The "entrepreneurial" corporation is dominated by the drive and determination of a single entrepreneur who directs and controls the activities of subordinates bound to him out of fear and loyalty. While the entrepreneurial company may achieve success and grow, its expansion potential is restricted by the entrepreneur's ability to personally control a large and growing organization (p. 10).

At this point, unless the organization can take on a mechanistic character, the company's growth will peter out. The mechanistic stage is reached when the corporation introduces systematic business practices involving such things as budgeting, job descriptions, formal organizational charts, procedures manuals, forecasting, and so on, to achieve greater predictability, and control. While these systematic practices do introduce elements of efficiency and control which are necessary in large corporations, they also cause problems to the extent that the "system" saps rather than taps human energies, leading to "frustrations, tensions, strife, sacrificed creativity, and reduction of meaningful accomplishment" (Blake, Avis, and Mouton 1966, 11).

Due to these problems, some corporations have looked for ways to break out of the mechanistic stage into the dynamic stage.

In the dynamic stage of corporate evolution, systematic business practices are retained, even strengthened, but initiative and vigor are restored to the very heart of the organization—its people. The method of restoring this vigor and initiative makes use of behavioral science knowledge of leadership and motivation, management by objectives, involvement and commitment, confronting conflict, teamwork, and so on. (Blake, Avis, and Mouton 1966, 12)[1]

THE ENTREPRENEURIAL CORPORATION

The entrepreneurial corporation with its single head and relatively undeveloped organization is recognizable in skeleton form as the firm depicted in much of orthodox microeconomic theory. The entrepreneur's role as innovator has also received much attention from economists such as Joseph Schumpeter (see, for example, 1961) who have analyzed the important contribution of innovation to economic growth. Although the entrepreneur is generally viewed as organizing (and compensating) the factors of production, there is little room here for viewing organization as a distinct factor of production. Later economists who have analyzed corporate organization have, however, pointed to particular organizational features which are related to productivity, and thus have implicitly treated organizations as such. Therefore, we need to consider the most significant organizational characteristics of mechanistic and dynamic corporations and how they contribute to productivity.

THE MECHANISTIC CORPORATION

In the view of Max Weber, the modern or mechanistic corporation is one which applies the principles of bureaucracy in order to achieve "rational efficiency, continuity of operation, speed, precision, and calculation of results" (Gerth and Mills 1958, 49). For Weber, bureaucratic organization was not only technically superior, but it and the rationalization which accompanied it were also historically inevitable.

An organization, regardless of type, can be thought of as an intricate human strategy designed to achieve certain objectives. The key element of the mechanistic organization is the formal organization structure or organization chart which "represents the intended rational strategy of the organization, . . . [i.e., an attempt] . . . to create a logically ordered world" (Argyris 1960, 10–11). Among the common principles used as a guide in designing this hierarchy of authority are specialization, unity of command and span of control (Simon 1957, chapter 2). When a large group of workers is necessary to accomplish a task, the task will inevitably be divided into subtasks and assigned to individuals or groups specializing in these functions. To accomplish the task, the subtasks must be coordinated with each other using integrative mechanisms that do not allow for face-to-face communication. Following Jay Galbraith,

the simplest method of coordinating interdependent subtasks is to specify the necessary behavior in advance of their execution in the form of rules or programs. . . . If everyone adopts the appropriate behavior the resultant aggregate response is an integrated or coordinated pattern of behavior . . . [without] further communication. (1973, 10)

When an organization encounters new situations, the old rules and programs are likely to be unsatisfactory; thus, additional integrating devices are needed. A satisfactory response to the new situation must consider all the affected subtasks, and this involves substantial information collection and problem solving. A hierarchy emerges when subtask managerial positions are created to handle these information collection and decision-making tasks necessitated by uncertainty, and higher positions are created to handle those aspects which can't be handled at the lowest managerial level. "In addition, the hierarchy is also a hierarchy of authority and reward power, so that the decisions of [managerial] role occupants are effective determinants of the behavior of the task performers" (Galbraith 1973, 11). The use of hierarchy as an integrating mechanism adds to but does not replace the use of rules and other mechanisms such as targets and goal setting. Thus, the hierarchy has an important function for the organization; how well it is tailored to the organization's purposes will determine how effective and efficient the organization is. Further, the formal organization structure, including rules and hierarchy, provides for the reliable completion of tasks and goal achieve-ment through the channeling of communications and work activities.

In addition to hierarchy and rules, the mechanistic corporation has drawn greatly on the scientific management tradition of thought stemming from Frederick Taylor (1911) and his disciples. The essence of this tradition is the systematic analysis of work by managers who are responsible for planning the flow of work and the content of jobs in order to increase productivity. Scientific management principles emphasize simplifying work and mini-mizing worker discretion, thereby reducing the skills required of the worker.

THE DYNAMIC CORPORATION

In the dynamic corporation, the human energies dormant in the mecha-nistic stage are "unleashed and funneled into finding creative and effective solutions to problems of production, many of which may have plagued the company for years" (Blake, Avis, and Mouton 1966, 12). The problems of the mechanistic corporation which keep productivity below potential are inherent in its hierarchy and scientific management. First, its requirement that the system operate like a well-ordered machine leaves the individual in the position of a cog feeling demoralized. Second, when novelty and uncer-tainty are high, the straightforward application of hierarchy and scientific management will fail to achieve potential productivity as its integrating mechanisms will be inadequate for the magnitude of information processing and problem solving involved. Third, the mechanistic organization may fail to achieve potential productivity because of a lack of fit between the organi-zation and its members' attributes. The dynamic corporation is superior to the mechanistic one along all three dimensions: the psychological, the struc-tural and the individual.

THE PSYCHOLOGICAL DIMENSION

Chris Argyris (1960) has led the way in pointing out that "there is a lack of congruency between the needs of healthy individuals and the demands of the . . .[mechanistic] organization" (p. 14). On the one hand, healthy ma-ture individuals are "predisposed toward relative independence, activeness, use of their important abilities, [and] control over their immediate work world," while mechanistic organizations tend "to require the agents to work in situations where they are dependent, passive, use few and unim-portant abilities, etc." (p. 14). As a result, mature individuals will experi-ence frustration, psychological failure, short time perspective, and internal conflict in this environment (p. 15). Further, subordinates in a mechanistic organization are likely to experience rivalry and intersubordinate hostility due to the competition for a limited number of positions at the higher levels in the hierarchy and a tendency "to develop an orientation toward their own particular part rather than towards the whole" (p. 16) due to being rewarded only for doing their subtask well. Employees will also react to the formal organization by creating informal activities, which on the one hand may enable them to defend themselves from the negative psychological aspect of organizational experience but on the other hand may run counter to the purposes of the organization and consume substantial energy and other resources (pp. 16–18). Adaptive informal activities include absenteeism, turnover, quota restriction, slowdowns, trade unions, increasing emphasis on material factors and decreasing emphasis on human factors, noninvolvement, withdrawal from work, and alienation.

Thus, in Argyris's view, motivation is lower than potential in a mechanistic organization, and the same is true for productivity. "It is simply impossible to say that the motivation resides 'in' the individual or 'in' the organization. . . . The motivation of the participant is best understood as a resultant of the *transactions* between the individual and the organization" (Argyris 1960, 21). When the organization enables a member to satisfy his higher needs (especially his need for self-actualization), the amount of psychological energy the member has for organization tasks will be considerably higher (pp. 22–23). Moreover, there is reason to believe that members' decision-making effectiveness, creativity and ability to play an effective role in their group are also related to the degree to which the organization satisfies their needs (p. 23).

Becoming a dynamic organization in the psychological sense requires not the elimination of hierarchy but the creation of conditions where healthy individuals can have high motivation and psychological energy due to their ability to satisfy their needs while working toward the organization's purposes. Transforming an organization in this sense has been called organizational development (OD), the essence of which is changing the organizational climate and interpersonal style. According to Porter, Lawler and Hackman (1975, chapter 15), there are two main approaches to OD:

1. Helping organizations build more effective *teams* of organization members, with special attention to issues of participation and leadership within teams.

2. Helping organizations find new and better means of managing interpersonal and intergroup (e.g., department-department or line-staff) *conflict,* with special attention to creating a climate of collaboration throughout the organization. (p. 458)

OD specialists or consultants have used many different means to help organizations become more dynamic. However, some of the most dynamic organizations (both Japanese and U.S.) do not owe their success to the use of OD experts. Rather, it seems due to a combination of the use of superior leadership and the evolution of a clearly articulated set of convictions (superordinate goals) supported by the company's actions and which employees find motivating and relevant for their work behavior (see, for example, Ouchi 1981; Pascale and Athos 1981; Peters and Waterman 1982).[2] Undoubtedly, an organizational climate which fosters trust and self expression will be one where harmful conflicts will be kept to a minimum and energetic cooperation will be encouraged.

THE STRUCTURAL DIMENSION

When uncertainty is high, the mechanistic organization (at least in the simple form outlined above) will fail to achieve potential productivity because of its inadequate information processing capacity. Uncertainty refers to "the lack of or absence of information about what will occur in the future" (Nadler, Hackman and Lawler 1979). Uncertainty derives from the degree of unpredictability of the work tasks, the instability or rate of change of the work environment, and the degree to which different task elements making up the larger task are interdependent on each other (pp. 190–191). In the presence of greater uncertainty, more information processing and problem solving must be done to insure the successful completion of tasks. Given the organization of the basic work units and their internal relationships, dealing with uncertainty means either developing coordination and control mechanisms so that the organization's information processing capacity meets its requirements or reducing its information processing needs by manipulating its external environment or settling for lower performance (chapter 11). Let's consider coordination and control mechanisms in more detail.

It is useful to think of these mechanisms on a continuum with hierarchy and rules at the low end and vertical information systems and lateral relations on the high end (Nadler, Hackman and Lawler 1979, 216). Vertical information systems "are mechanisms that collect data about organizational functioning and distribute these data to a predetermined network of organizational members" (p. 207). The creation of lateral relations is a way to exchange information and achieve coordination directly between work units rather than by moving information up and down the hierarchy (p. 208). Among the processes for achieving the desired lateral relations are:

1. direct contact between managers,

2. creation of a liaison role,

3. creation of task forces,

4. use of teams,

5. creation of an integrating role,

6. change to managerial linking role, and

7. establishing the matrix organizational form. (Galbraith 1973, 110)

Organizations typically face a trade-off in deciding upon the appropriate coordination and control mechanism since the superior information processing of these mechanisms typically involves greater cost and complexity. Another alternative open to the organization is to create new, self-contained units which contain all the resources (including types of personnel) necessary for task accomplishment, thereby eliminating the interdependency with other units. An example of this is the change from a functional organizational form to more or less independent groups based on product lines, geographical areas or markets (p. 16) as is done in multidivisional corporations.[3] In sum, the dynamic organization will be able to survive, grow and be more efficient than the mechanistic organization in industries and environments characterized by high uncertainty and novelty, because they have been tailored with many of the above considerations in mind.

One other structural consideration deserves mention here, the structure of jobs. Recall that in the mechanistic ideal, a la Taylor, job design involves simplification, specialization, and standardization. However, the debilitating effects of these jobs on individuals is well known. To counteract these nonmotivating and unsatisfying effects, the job enrichment approach was developed. The general theory is that work will become more satisfying for healthy, mature individuals when jobs are characterized by increased variety, skill requirements, autonomy and performance feedback for the worker, and when the job is more meaningful overall compared to jobs designed according to "scientific management" (Nadler, Hackman and Lawler 1979, chapter 5). Another alternative to scientific management job design is to design work for interacting groups or work teams, an approach which also promises to increase motivation and satisfaction (pp. 86–88).

THE INDIVIDUAL DIMENSION

Organizational behavior can also be improved by changing the attributes of individuals, in particular their skills and attitudes. Of course, change in either the organizational climate or the organizational structure could alter individual attributes, especially change in the climate. However, the focus here is on activities designed to change individuals directly in order to attain the desired organizational result.

On-the-job training is designed to improve work skills and thereby aid worker productivity. According to Herbert Simon,

training is applicable to the process of decision wherever the same elements are involved in a large number of decisions. Training may supply the trainee with the facts necessary in dealing with these decisions; it may provide him a frame of reference for his thinking; it may teach him "approved" solutions; or it may indoctrinate him with the values in terms of which his decisions are to be made. (1957, 170)

Besides improving performance by improving ability in these ways, training may lead to better performance via higher motivation as suggested by Peters and Waterman's analysis of the effect of seemingly excessive training sessions for teenage ticket takers and other "cast members" at Disney World in Florida (1982, 167–168).

Training, as Simon points out, as an "influence upon decisions has its greatest value in those situations where the exercise of formal authority through commands proves difficult. . . . Training permits a higher degree of decentralization of the decision-making process by bringing the necessary competence into the very lowest levels of the organizational hierarchy" (1957, 170–171). Thus it substitutes for rules and programs as a control mechanism and lowers the need for hierarchy as individuals working responsibly and knowledgeably are able in many cases to deal with uncertainty and novelty without resort to managers (Galbraith 1973, 12–13).

Training within the firm is part of the larger process known as socialization.

Socialization . . . refers to the whole process by which an individual, born with behavioral potentialities of an enormously wide range, is led to develop actual behavior which is confined within a much narrower range—the range of what is customary and acceptable for him according to the standards of his group. (Child 1954, 655, quoted in Porter, Lawler, and Hackman 1975, 162)

In this process of "learning the ropes," the individual faces demands from the organization, and typically experiences a counter process, individualization, in which the member attempts to exert influence on the organization (Porter, Lawler, and Hackman, 161–162). Whereas training tends to be a formal process, much of socialization consists of informal social interactions through which members acquire new expectations, beliefs and attitudes and learn about group norms. It is useful to refer to many of these latter aspects as social learning, as contrasted with technical learning. According to Karl-Olof Faxen, social learning is

learning about other people and groups in the work organization, about their motives, reactions, values and ambitions. It also relates to the way in which one perceives oneself and one's role in the organization in such matters as responsibility and authority, operating methods and specific expertise (1978, 132).

According to Edgar Schein, organizational effectiveness depends on socialization. "The speed and effectiveness of socialization determine employee loyalty, commitment, productivity and turnover" (Schein, 1968, 2, quoted in Porter, Lawler, and Hackman, 162). John Kotter's research on the joining-up process of new employees confirms Shein's view. Kotter finds that when joining-up is managed well the new member's expectations about what is desired from the organization and what the individual is able to offer will match the organization's expectations about what it can give and what it wants. When this type of "psychological contract" between the individual and the organization has been established, the outcomes are generally higher job satisfaction, higher productivity and longer tenure with the organization (Kotter, 1973). Another aspect of socialization occurs when an organization desires to change itself by changing the "types" of people who are members. Organizations can do this by systematically selecting people with the desired characteristics and terminating people who are not the right type (Porter, Lawler, and Hackman 1975, 441–442). Another approach is to use special types of experiential training outside the firm in the hope that when the members return to the organization their attitudes, beliefs and values will be closer to what the organization desires. Along this line, many corporations have tried programs as diverse as encounter groups and human relations training (for example, the courses offered by the Dale Carnegie Institute). The presumption of firms using these approaches is that a new group of employees or a group of old employees with new attitudes will increase productivity by enabling the organization to function closer to the desired manner. Dynamic corporations seem more likely to use these approaches.

Clearly, the organizational insights of this chapter need to be integrated into economic theory. Chapter 3 takes a number of important steps in this direction.

3

Organizational Capital and Economic Theory

The purpose of this chapter and the following one is to integrate the insights of organizational behavior concerning productivity (as discussed in the previous chapter) with economic theory. This involves (1) defining and developing the concept of organizational capital, (2) integrating it with human capital theory, and (3) showing its usefulness, particularly as an explanation of economic growth. The latter task is undertaken in chapter 4.

THE KEY INSIGHT

An individual's organizational behavior and productivity cannot be explained simply by one's personal attributes and the tangible capital used; organizational relationships have much to do with shaping these behaviors (Argyris, 1960, 21). As the previous chapter indicated, the individual's behavior and productivity will be determined by the organizational climate, the structure of the organization and the organization's socialization processes as well as by individual attributes. Utilization of the organizational capital concept helps in understanding this interaction by providing explicit recognition that at least a part of productive capacity is directly related to these organizational attributes. In other words, when the organization is treated as a productive asset, the insight that organizations are more than the sum of their members is incorporated into economic theory.

ANTICIPATIONS OF ORGANIZATIONAL CAPITAL

Economists

A number of writers have recognized the asset-quality of modern business organizations but have not made formal attempts to introduce a concept of organizational capital into economic theory. Economists such as Alfred Marshall, Frank Knight, and Simon Kuznets are notable in this regard. Marshall (1961, 138) states that "capital consists in a great part of knowledge and organization," and he includes the organization of a business in his list of types of nonmaterial wealth (pp. 54–57). Furthermore, "the organization of a free and well-ordered state is to be regarded as an important element of national wealth" (p. 59). Thus, in Marshall's view, it is "best sometimes to reckon Organization as a distinct agent of production" (p. 139). Knight clearly realized that when it comes to increasing productivity there are competing investment alternatives. For example, "One may invest . . . in creating new equipment goods . . . or in finding and developing new material resources, or in developing his own natural powers . . . or *in improving business organization,* or in creating new social tastes or wants" (Knight 1921, 371; emphasis mine). According to Knight:

Organized effort enables a social group to produce more of the means of want-satisfaction than it could by working as individuals. During the course of history, the possibility of increased efficiency has led to an ever greater degree of specialization, which in turn has constantly called for a more elaborate and effective mechanism of coordination and control. . . . (1967, 15)

Moreover, "There is no mechanical solution of the human social problem, as in the case of the animal organism or even of insect societies; human beings have to form themselves into an organization as well as to control and operate it when constructed" (p. 17). Kuznets also argues for a broad concept of capital (Kuznets 1965, 100) and recognizes explicitly that organizational behavior within the modern, impersonal, limited-liability corporation is very different from the older, more personal types of organization and "results in a capacity to cooperate that would hardly have been expected of their elders and ancestors, accustomed to entirely different economic relations" (Kuznets 1965, 102).

Managerial Authors

A number of managerial authors also recognize that organization is a productive asset. For example, Peter Drucker advises managers that "economic performance that is being achieved by mismanaging managers is illusory and actually destructive of capital" (Drucker 1965, 16). He is more explicit about the importance of organization when he states that "a poor organization structure makes good performance impossible no matter how good the individual manager may be" (Drucker 1965, 223). Selwyn Becker and Gerald Gordon consider the formal business organization to be a form of property.

> The person(s) who by virtue of his rights to the organization's resources has the right to shape and mold (as well as to dissolve, sell, or otherwise transfer) the organization to attain his goal is, in essence, the owner(s) of the organization. The assertion that formal organizations are owned means that formal organizations can be treated as property. (Becker and Gordon 1966, 317)

Rensis Likert (1973) has gone beyond mere recognition of the asset-quality of organizations; he has proposed a system of "human resource accounting" which would enable a firm to determine the value of its human organization. He believes that the use of such an accounting system would lead initially to better management and decision making and ultimately to greater productive efficiency. This would come with the recognition of the way different management actions influence the functioning of the organization and how that, in turn, influences the economic achievements of the enterprise. Likert, in essence, proposes that the accounting or information systems of business should reflect what social scientists have learned about organizations. His proposal represents a marked departure from present accounting practices even though the "good will" item on some firms' balance sheets may reflect the extra profits they have been realizing as a result of a well-functioning organization.

THE ORGANIZATIONAL CAPITAL CONCEPT

Definition

Investment in organizational capital refers to the using up of resources in order to bring about lasting improvement in productivity and/or worker well-being through changes in the functioning of the organization. Organizational capital formation could involve 1) changing the formal and informal social relationships and patterns of activity within the enterprise or 2) changing individual attributes important to organizational functioning, or 3) the accumulation of information useful in matching workers with organization situations.[1] Organizational capital is human capital in which the attribute is embodied in either the organizational relationship, particular organization members, the organization's repositories of information, or some combination of the above in order to improve the functioning of the organization.[2]

A Factor of Production

It follows that organizational capital is a factor of production and, accordingly, is an element in the production function along with labor, tangible capital, human capital that is unrelated to organizational functioning, and other types of intangible capital (Tomer 1981a, 6–7). A number of prominent economists have used closely related concepts in their writings. For example, Michael Jensen and William Meckling (1979, 471) use a production function which includes a "generalized index describing the range of choice of 'organizational forms' or internal rules of the game available to the firm." In their view, this variable plays "an important role in motivating self-interested and maximizing individuals to achieve the physically possible output." Armen Alchian and Harold Demsetz (1972) have developed the view that the productivity of a team may be greater than the sum of the separable productive contributions of individual team members. Presumably, in many circumstances the realization of the productivity potential of this team work requires considerable time and effort, that is, it requires a substantial investment in organizational capital. When organizational investment allows the other inputs to achieve an output closer to potential, one can speak of an increase in X-efficiency following the usage of Harvey Leibenstein (for example, 1976).[3] Such an increase in X-efficiency, in my view, represents an outward movement of the production possibility frontier. Leibenstein (1976, 46), however, views X-efficiency improvements as a movement from within the frontier to its outer boundary.[4]

The Human–Organizational Capital Spectrum

The Spectrum. Gary Becker (1964, 1) defined human capital formation as "activities that influence future monetary and psychic income by increasing the resources in people." Since organizations are undeniably composed of people, and because an organizational investment will lose value should a sufficient number of people leave the enterprise, organizational capital is clearly a type of human capital. In my previous writing (1973, 1981) I have juxtaposed only two very different types of human capital: the type vested only in individuals (pure human capital) and the type vested only in organizational relationships (pure organizational capital). However, on further consideration of the realities involved in organizing to achieve higher productivity, it seems appropriate to think of a spectrum of human–organizational capital with the pure human type on the far left, the pure organizational type on the far right, and two human–organizational capital hybrids, H-O and O-H, in the middle (see Table 3.1).

Focus on Firm-Specific Capital. The focus of this section's analysis is on firm-specific human capital. Consider first pure human capital formation due to training. According to Becker (1962, 17), "training that increases

Table 3.1
The Human-Organizational Capital Spectrum

Pure Human Capital	Human-Organizational Capital Hybrids		Pure Organizational Capital
H-H Capital	H-O Capital	O-H Capital	O-O Capital

productivity [of laborers], more in firms providing it" than in firms that do not is firm-specific. More generally, firm-specific investment increases productivity more in the firm doing it than in others. A firm-specific factor of production is one which is specific to another factor of production, that is, it is a more flexible factor which is capable of being adapted to one or more other factors through investment which thereby raises its productivity when the other factor or factors are present. For the purpose of this analysis, the factors of production are (1) technology, (2) employees and (3) organizations (or organizational capital). Technology refers to the firm's particular tangible capital or technical activities embodying the current state of technical knowledge. Employees refers to the particular workers in the firm along with their different human capital endowments. Organization refers to the particular features of the firm's organizational relationships which reflect investments in organizational capital. Table 3.2 shows six possible classifications, A through F, which are used to explain the functioning of the four types of human capital in the spectrum. As shown, human capital may be vested or embodied in employees or the organization, and it may be specific to one or more of the three factors of production.

Pure Human Capital. Pure human or H-H capital formation is probably best illustrated by training during which the student-worker learns a technical skill such as operating a particular type of machinery. Clearly, the attribute acquired and vested in the employee is related to the worker's

Table 3.2
Classification of Human-Organizational Capital Types According to Function in the Firm

			Vested In	
			Employees	Organization
Specific To	Factors of Production	Technology	A	D
		Employees	B	E
		Organization	C	F

productivity, and if the worker should quit, the firm's productivity will decrease until they can hire and train someone else. This is pure human capital because this attribute does not contribute to the functioning of the organization. It is specific to the firm's technology but not to the firm's organization, so it is classified in box A of the classification.[5]

Pure Organizational Capital. Pure organizational or O-O capital formation, on the other hand, may be illustrated by a change in the formal organizational structure in which the channels of communication and formal relationships between several work groups are altered. Assume for the purposes of analysis that these structural changes improve productivity by changing workers' organizational behavior in ways that improve the functioning of the organization; also assume that workers (regardless of their attributes) adapt immediately to the new behavioral patterns so that the orientation time and cost are negligible. This is pure organizational capital formation because only the characteristics of the organization have evoked the desired worker behavior. This is not due to any change in workers' attributes, such as would be the case if orientation involving some training or socialization were necessary. Clearly, O-O capital is embodied in the organization. Moreover, since the changed characteristics must be adapted to other (unchanging) organizational characteristics, O-O capital is organization-specific, and thus is classified in box F of the human–organizational capital classification. Of course, if these organizational characteristics have, in turn, been adapted to the firm's technology and employees, the O-O capital is also specific to those factors. In this case, boxes D and E are also correct classifications of O-O capital. Also note that the loss of an individual worker will not change the productivity stemming from the structural change since it derives from and is vested in the organization and does not come from an individual attribute. Of course, it might be true that if a high fraction of the organization's members left, the investment in organizational capital would be destroyed or substantially reduced in productive value.

H-O Capital. On the left side of the spectrum, but not the far left, is a type of capital which is part human capital and part organizational capital. H-O capital relates to individual attributes which contribute to the behaviors important for the functioning of the organization. Most organizational change, for example, will require a significant amount of social learning to acquaint organization members with the new roles required of them.[6] This orientation process may involve changing the attitudes, values or expectations of individuals who adjust to the new social requirements explicit and implicit in the new situation. Such social learning is likely to be much longer lasting than technical learning (Faxen 1978, 133). To the extent that individual attributes such as attitudes and knowledge change, an investment is embodied in the employees. However, to the extent that the attributes acquired are specific to the organization's characteristics and functional requirements, the investment is organization-specific, and thereby a type of organizational capital. Thus, H–O capital is classified in box C; it could also be classified in box A if the organization were, in turn, adapted to the firm's technology.[7]

As Shein (1968) and Kotter (1973) have pointed out, organizational effectiveness depends on socialization. By influencing individuals' values, attitudes and behavioral norms, socialization determines individual responsiveness to organization stimuli. Most organizational changes will require additional socialization. Once the new organization with its new social knowledge and attitudes are created, there will be many members who can orient individuals who subsequently enter the organization. The orientation process involves a use of resources in the sense that the orienter's and the orientee's attention would be focused on some other productive contribution, if the orientation were not occurring.

Education and training, even if occurring outside the organization, may have an organizational capital aspect to the extent that the individual acquires attributes directly related to his functioning in an organization rather than related to his technical task performance. Presumably, most such education or training will be general and not firm- or organization-specific.[8] Consider again the training of a machine operator. If it includes elements related to the worker's responsibilities for maintaining the machine, ensuring safety to himself and others, reporting malfunctions and waste, communicating information on productivity, and other aspects of proper social behavior on the job, these notions will undoubtedly influence his organizational behavior (and the productivity of the organization) more than his technical task performance. Some of the attributes inculcated by education may have a negative effect on organizational productivity. For example, many business organizations hesitate to hire people with Ph.D degrees (except of course where they are necessary, such as in research and development) because the typical Ph.D. is thought too independent, cognitive and theoretical in orientation. Recently, there has been an increasing reluctance to hire MBAs from elite academic institutions because the typical MBA is thought too ambitious, impatient about mundane tasks and likely to leave the firm in a few years. On the other hand, education may develop qualities of logical reasoning, and good communication and work habits, which are extremely valuable to organizations (Reynolds 1982, 118).

O-H Capital. Between pure organizational capital and H–O capital on the spectrum is O–H capital, which resembles pure organizational capital more than human capital. O–H capital derives from the firm's investment in information about the actual and desired characteristics of current and prospective employees. Employees' desired characteristics presumably follow from the characteristics of the whole organization as well as the particular organizational settings in which employees are placed. A good part of this information comes to be embodied in the formal repositories of the organization's memory, that is, it is documented in the organization's files and available to decision makers (Simon 1957, 166). The other part is the subtle and less quantifiable information retained in the memories of managers, personnel people and coworkers. The latter information is an attribute of these people while the former is an attribute of the organization.[9]

What I refer to as O-H capital is called organizational capital by Prescott and Visscher (1980).[10] They point out how the organization's information on employee abilities and the characteristics of tasks enables it to lower production costs by improving the match between people and jobs (pp. 447–449). Firms can also improve productivity by utilizing information regarding how an employee's attributes complement those of others in team work situations (pp. 448, 456).[11] Another similar source of productivity improvement stems from the use of knowledge about what types of individuals are most compatible with the overall purposes and values of the organization. Such information can be used, as in many of the leading Japanese companies, to guide the selection of entry level recruits (Clark 1979, 156–167). While Alchian and Demsetz (1972) do not refer to this information as capital, they recognize that the employer through his monitoring of employees acquires "special superior information about their productive talents" and that "efficient production with heterogeneous resources is a result not of having *better* resources but in *knowing more accurately* the relative productive performances of those resources" (p. 793).

While O-H capital may be embodied in either its employees or in the organization (for example, in formal files), it is invariably organization-specific since the information on worker's desired characteristics almost always derives from some of the features of the organization. Thus, O-H capital is generally classified in both boxes C and F of the human–organizational capital classification. To the extent that the information on worker's desired characteristics follows from the characteristics of other employees or the technology in the firm, O-H may be classified in the A, B, D or E boxes as well.

Summary. The preceding analysis has focused on four types of firm-specific capital along the human–organizational capital spectrum: pure human (H-H), H-O, O-H, and pure organizational (O-O). Table 3.3 contrasts these types. First, pure human capital such as results from training a machine operator or bookkeeper is specific to the technology of the firm and is an attribute of an individual. Second, H-O capital such as results from the formal and informal socialization of a new member of the organization is specific to the firm's organization and perhaps to its technology but is an attribute of the employee. Third, O-H capital is formed when the firm acquires information that aids in the utilization of their employees; it is specific to the firm's organization and perhaps to its technology and employees, and is an attribute either of the organization or of certain members. Lastly, pure organization capital resulting, for example, from a change in the formal organizational structure is specific to the firm's organization and

Table 3.3
The Human–Organizational Capital Spectrum

	Pure Human Capital	Human–Organizational Capital Hybrids		Pure Organizational Capital
	H-H Capital	H-O Capital	O-H Capital	O-O Capital
Examples	Machine Operator Training, Bookkeeping Training	Formal Socialization of new member of organization	Acquiring information about employees' abilities, compatibility	Changing formal organizational structure
Attribute of (Vested in)	Employee	Employee	Organization and/or certain employees	Organization
Specific to	Technology	Organization	Organization	Organization
May also be specific to	—	Technology	Technology, Employees	Technology, Employees

perhaps its technology and employees, and is an attribute of the organization.

This perspective is highly suggestive about what organizational changes a firm would have to make in order to achieve its labor productivity potential. It would have to adapt the formal and informal aspects of its organization to its overall purposes, develop and utilize information on employees' suitability for tasks and organizational situations, and facilitate the employee socialization processes to help members adjust to the social and technical demands of the organization. In other words, the firm must make investments in pure organizational capital, O-H capital and H-O capital in order to get the most out of its tangible capital and its laborers with their pure human capital endowments. Any time a firm decides on a productivity improvement program with an organizational aspect, it is likely that the organizational investments involved will fall along several points of the human-organizational capital spectrum. Consider some examples.

EXAMPLES OF ORGANIZATIONAL INVESTMENT

On January 10, 1984, General Motors announced

the most extensive restructuring of its U.S. auto operations ever. . . . The reorganization is . . . designed to: 1) help GM launch its new models on schedule, 2) provide more cost control, 3) boost quality control . . . and 4) make its divisions build more distinctive models.(*Business Week*, January 23, 1984, 32–33)

The reorganization involved changes in the formal organization structure and changes in the organizational climate. The changes in organizational climate are indicated by planned changes in their management style which are intended to make them "less bureaucratic and more team-oriented." The formal organization structure change involves dividing all its operations into two groups: small cars, and intermediate and large cars. Further, "GM's engineering will be consolidated, not spread throughout the sprawling corporation, and . . . product development and manufacturing will be more centralized" (*Business Week,* January 23, 1984, 32–33). Although the *Business Week* article does not mention it, it would be very surprising if these relatively pure organizational capital investments were accomplished without substantial investments in H-O and O-H capital so that employees were able to adjust to and be properly utilized in their new organization settings.

While reorganization of the size and scope of GM's may be rare, organizational change is common and important. According to Kotter and Schlesinger, "most companies or divisions of major corporations find that they must undertake moderate organizational changes at least once a year and major changes every four or five" (1979, 106). Recently my cousin, an auto assembly line worker at a New Jersey plant of Ford Motor Company, told me how Ford has introduced a major organizational change which involves an imitation of the assembly procedures pioneered by the Japanese auto companies, most notably Toyota.[12] Under the new approach, workers are held responsible for the quality and not just the quantity of their assembly efforts, and are expected to push a button to stop the assembly line if problems develop which can't be dealt with in the allotted time. In the event of a problem, correction efforts are initiated by this worker or by others. The expected result of the increased worker responsibility and autonomy is not only a higher quality product but also cost savings as it reduces the need for quality inspectors.

According to my cousin, Ford has substantially reduced the number of inspectors. He went on to suggest, however, that the new system has some "bugs" in it. For example, if workers press the button too many times they are liable to be yelled at, and if they fail to press the button when there is a problem, they are similarly liable. My cousin clearly felt ambivalent about this. In his view, this situation stems from a lack of resolution as to whether quantity of production or quality takes precedence, and reflects the organizational conflict between the production and quality managers. My suspicion is that these feelings are likely to be reflected in lower than potential productivity and that resolution of this organizational matter would therefore have great importance to Ford. To achieve such a resolution would mean making an additional investment in organizational capital.

It should also be noted that the Ford assembly workers involved were treated to a special luncheon during which the proposed organizational change was first explained and that prior to the implementation they attended several question and answer sessions.

Consider the types of investment involved in Ford's productivity improvement program. To begin, there's a tangible capital investment in the push button system and an investment in new organizational knowledge, information about the Japanese approach. The latter is quite similar to an investment in new technological knowledge. Then there's the basic organizational change, an investment in pure organizational capital, vested in the organization and specific to both the preexisting aspects of the organization and the tangible capital involved with the push buttons. The Ford meetings to inform their employees are obvious evidence of investment in H-O capital, which is specific to the new organization and presumably to the new tangible capital. Investment in O-H capital, acquiring information about how particular employees perform with their changed responsibilities, may also have occurred. If so, the latter would be specific to the employees involved, the new organization and the tangible capital.

WHO INVESTS IN ORGANIZATIONAL CAPITAL?

One other issue deserves mention; namely, who is it that does the investing in organizational capital? Unfortunately, not much in the way of a definitive answer can be given. One could, of course, analyze the investment incentives to owners, managers and nonmanagerial workers under various assumptions. However, a complete analysis is beyond the scope of this chapter. Nevertheless, a few things should be said. First, firms (and thus, owners and certain managers) can expect significant increases in income when organizational functioning improves. Presumably in the General Motors and Ford examples above, and in countless other similar cases, the companies are investing in the expectation of these returns. In those cases where the attributes necessary for improved functioning are vested in the employees as opposed to the organization, it is likely that some of the return will accrue to the employees at the expense of the firm. The indefiniteness in the breakdown of the return between the employees and the firm is expected in situations where negotiation will determine the outcome and where uncertainty regarding the source of productivity improvements and opportunism on the part of the bargainers exist. Second, managers, as opposed to owners and nonmanagerial employees, may claim a large portion of the return to organizational capital to the extent that creating this capital is an entrepreneurial contribution and maintaining its functioning requires scarce talents. Perhaps this is one important explanation for the very high compensation that some top management people receive. Third, it should be considered that part of the return to the organization may be "psychic income." Employees in some cases may forge better and more productive relationships with other employees simply because these relationships are more satisfying. Moreover, employees who are strongly identified with the firm may initiate changes in their own attitudes to conform to organization needs (an H-O capital investment) whether or not they expect financial rewards. In sum, this abbreviated analysis suggests that organizational investment may be initiated on behalf of owners, managers or employees in response to a variety of expected but somewhat uncertain returns which may be financial or otherwise.

CONCLUSION

One important dimension of the role of organization in determining individual behavior can be appreciated by considering what happens to the behavior of a husband and wife when the marriage goes "bad." Neither may be able to talk or behave civilly to each other, and the family's level of function may be impaired. However "crazy" the couple's behavior toward each other is, their behavior toward people outside the immediate family may be perfectly "normal." What this suggests is that the marriage relationship has an existence separate from individual attributes and other relationships and determines the behavior of the couple toward each other but not in other contexts. Although the relationships in a work organization are not as intense, they similarly determine their members' behavior, and thus, exert a powerful influence on productivity independent of the attributes of workers, tangible capital or other factors.

Of course, as the review of organizational behavior in chapter 2 indicated, a dynamic corporation functions well not only in a psychological sense but because its structure and socialization processes are well suited to achieve its goals. Economic theory has in general been poorly equipped to understand the sources of the productivity of the dynamic corporation. With the possible exception of some aspects of socialization, human capital theory does not acknowledge how organizational features determine productivity. This chapter has attempted to show how the organizational capital concept remedies this defect and how organizational capital relates to the human capital concept. It also demonstrates one important way that economists can improve their theory, that is, by drawing on the behavioral insights of other disciplines.

4

Organizational Capital and Economic Growth

Naturally, as businesses add to their productive capacities through organizational change, the economy's productive capacity grows as well. Thus, organizational capital formation enables economic growth. In economists' language, the production possibility frontier shifts out as the stock of organizational capital increases. This chapter develops a theoretical view of the organizational aspects of the economic growth process and provides an empirical illustration of the process with respect to one type of organizational change, management consultant–aided change.

ORGANIZATIONAL CAPITAL FORMATION AND ENTREPRENEURIAL BEHAVIOR

The organizing activity which produces organizational capital is both innovative and imitative in nature. It is innovative in the sense of "carrying out new combinations" (see, for example, Joseph Schumpeter 1961, 75). Schumpeter (1961, 133) specifically mentions that entrepreneurial behavior includes "innovations in business organization." Organizing activity is imitative insofar as it requires entreprenerial behavior to get combinations already adopted by a first firm adopted by others.[1]

With respect to entrepreneurial organizing behavior, the distinction between programmed and unprogrammed activity is very helpful. According to James March and Herbert Simon, programmed activity is involved when "an environmental stimulus may evoke immediately from the organization a highly complex and organized set of responses" (March and Simon 1958, 141). Unprogrammed activity is directed toward the creation of new programs; this means organizational change rather than the "steady state." Thus, it is unprogrammed activity which is by nature entrepreneurial organizing, and it is the entrepreneur who is the source or initiator of new program proposals (March and Simon 1958, 178–188). Chester Barnard considers organizing the activities and interactions of individuals in an enterprise to secure their cooperation to be a very important, nonroutine function of executives.[2] He finds that "the process of interaction must be discovered or invented, just as a physical operation must be discovered or invented" (Barnard 1940, 60). Moreover, Barnard states that:

technological invention is necessary to the accomplishment of many ends economically which can be accomplished if economy is not required, by other means. On the other hand, some ends which can only be accomplished by a given technological process cannot be economically accomplished without inventions and innovations in organizational technique. (Barnard 1940, 238)

ORGANIZATIONAL CAPITAL FORMATION AND TECHNOLOGICAL CHANGE

The conception of the technological change process held by Theodore W. Schultz is most helpful for understanding the relationship between capital formation of all kinds and economic growth. According to Schultz, technical change means the process by which the technical attributes of resources (land, labor, and so on) are changed, and such changes are considered to form capital. In other words, technical change occurs as a result of investments which use up resources and alter the properties of other resources so that their productive capacities are greater than before. In Schultz's view, changes in a very heterogeneous stock of capital provide the explanation for most of economic growth (Schultz 1971, chapter 2).[3] In Schultz's words,

a technique is no more or less than a unit of capital . . . a set of techniques representing a technology is a capital structure, and . . . technical change is an alteration of a capital structure. (Schultz 1971, 20)

In sum, unprogrammed changes in organization are innovative or imitative in nature; they add to the stock of organizational capital, contribute to the technological change process and enable economic growth.

MEASURING TECHNOLOGICAL CHANGE DUE TO ORGANIZATIONAL INVESTMENT

During the last twenty-five years there have been numerous attempts to measure aspects of the technological change process. Economists have generally used the concept of the aggregate production function although there are many who consider it to have only dubious validity.[4] The aggregate production function is used below to indicate the relationships among various inputs whose growth contributes to the growth of output and to suggest how an increase in productivity caused by organizational change might be measured.

Consider first the kind of production function used by Solow (1957):

$$Q = A f(K, L)   \tag{4.1}$$

where Q represents output and K and L represent capital and labor inputs in "physical" units for given periods of time. For any state of technology, an increase in output can be obtained by increasing the inputs: this is movement along a production function which is assumed to be linear and homogeneous. If neutral technological change occurs, this is represented by a shift of the production or a change in the value of A. If equation 4.1 is totally differentiated with respect to time and divided by Q, the growth form of the equation is obtained. Thus,

$$\dot{Q}/Q = \dot{A}/A + (\partial Q/\partial K)\, \dot{K}/Q + (\partial Q/\partial L)\, \dot{L}/Q   \tag{4.2}$$

in which dots indicate time derivatives. Substituting w_k for $(\partial Q/\partial K)\, K/Q$ and w_1 for $(\partial Q/\partial L)\, L/Q$ gives

$$\dot{Q}/Q = \dot{A}/A + w_k\, \dot{K}/K + w_1\, \dot{L}/L.   \tag{4.3}$$

In equation 4.3 the weights (w_k and w_1) of the input growth rates are the respective factor shares assuming that factors are paid their marginal products, $\partial Q/\partial K$ and $\partial Q/\partial L$. Moreover, $\dot{A}/A$ is the rate of shift of the production function or the rate of technological change.

An important modification of the above is the notion that a portion of technological change may occur via the embodiment of new techniques in the inputs. With respect to capital, Solow (1960) suggested that each year's additions to the capital stock should incorporate the latest technical knowledge. If the capital stock data used in the production function is adjusted to reflect annual increases in productivity deriving from the embodiment of new knowledge, it is possible to estimate this part of the annual growth in productivity, the rate of embodiment (E). It follows that the rate of technological change is composed of two parts, the rate of embodiment and the rate of disembodied technological change (D); in symbols,

$$\dot{A}/A = E + D   \tag{4.4}$$

The rate of disembodiment has sometimes been referred to as the "residual" or the measure of ignorance regarding other identified or unidentified contributors to technological change. Among these other factors generally considered to be included in D are managerial and organizational changes.[5]

Schultz's view of technological change suggests a modification or extension of the aggregate production function approach above to the measurement of technological change. If capital formation is the essence of how productivity takes place, this implies a production function that is different than equation 4.1 and that implies

$$Q = f(L, K_1, K_2, K_3, \ldots)$$ (4.5)

where $K_i = K_1, K_2, K_3 \ldots$ indicates the heterogeneous nature of the total stock of capital.[6] In Zvi Griliches' words:

Changes in output are attributable to changes in quantities and qualities of inputs, and to economies of scale, . . . the production itself remaining constant (at least over substantial stretches of time). . . . Such an approach does not, of course, remove technical change from the explanation of growth; it aspires, rather, to transform what is currently a catch-all residual variable into movements along a more general production function and into identifiable changes in the qualities of inputs. (Griliches, 1963, 332)

Equation 4.5 explicitly recognizes improvements in the quality of inputs as types of capital and allows for the identification of new types of capital. Further, it suggests that "the concept of 'embodiment' of technical change should be extended to all inputs rather than just to capital or just to labor" (Griliches 1963, 346). Through the use of this approach and the removal of other errors in the measurement of inputs it is expected that the growth of inputs will explain all or most of the changes in output.[7]

The main argument of this article, of course, is that one of the K_i's in the aggregate production function should be organizational capital (O). Thus, increases in both the quantity and quality of organizational capital will cause output to grow. Changes in the quality of the stock of O occur either when existing organizations or systems of management are changed to incorporate new organizational knowledge or new organizations embodying new knowledge are created. Schultz asserts that "new information is of two basic parts: 1) that which is transformed into new skills, which, when acquired, are forms of human capital, and 2) that which is transformed into new materials, which when achieved, are new forms of nonhuman capital" (Schultz 1971, 9). The implication of the present analysis is that new information has at least one more part; which is transformed into new systems, procedures, patterns of activities, relationships, and so on, which are new forms of organizational capital (a type of human capital).

It may be helpful to be more explicit about the nature of the heterogeneous capital stock, K_i:

$$(K_1, K_2, K_3, \ldots) = (K, H, O, \ldots)$$ (4.6)

where K is the nonhuman or tangible capital stock; H is the stock of pure human capital, previously represented as H-H; and O, again, is the stock of organizational capital, previously represented as H-O, O-H, or O-O, its three types.[8] The growth form of equation 4.5 after incorporating equation 4.6 is

$$\dot{Q}/Q = w_l\,(\dot{L}/L) + w_k\,(\dot{K}/K) + w_h\,(\dot{H}/H) + w_o\,(\dot{O}/O) + \ldots (4.7)$$

where w_h and w_o are $\partial Q/\partial H\,(H/Q)$ and $\partial Q/\partial O\,(O/Q)$, respectively, and if these factors are paid their marginal products, w_h and w_o are the respective factor shares.[9]

Equation 4.7 is more useful than equation 4.5 because it emphasizes the growth of the capital inputs rather than the magnitude of the stocks of capital.[10] In other words,

the totality of the existing stock of capital is not an essential component in determining economic growth, because the meaning of economic growth is some rate of increase in the number of income streams in terms of dollars per year. The additions to the existing stock are what matter. In an economy in which the existing "factors of production" are fully employed, additional income streams — that is, economic growth — are some function of the classes and amounts of investment. (Schultz 1971, 6).

One reason why equation 4.7 is preferable to a growth equation with a large D factor is that the alternative types of investment that make possible economic growth along with, hopefully, their rates of return are clearly arrayed. Obviously, this is helpful to policymakers.

Edward Denison has quantified the contribution of a number of important inputs to the rate of growth of output in the United States (see, for example, Denison 1962). There are, however, a number of important capital inputs, human and nonhuman, which he doesn't quantify. As a result, the changes in the capital and labor inputs he accounts for leave unexplained a very sizeable portion of the rate of economic growth, that is, the residual. It would be interesting to see how much of the residual portion of the growth rate would be explained using methods similar to the ones Denison used if it were possible to obtain measurements not only of changes in the nonhuman tangible capital stock resulting from its improvements (that is, from new vintages) but also of changes in the organizational capital stock. To illustrate what is involved, the section on management consultant contributions provides an estimate of the economic growth contribution made by management consultants as a result of their work in client firms.

MEASURING ORGANIZATIONAL CAPITAL FORMATION

In order to measure the annual contribution of organizational capital formation to economic growth (G_O) in the way suggested above, it is necessary to measure the annual growth of the stock of organizational capital ($\triangle$O).[11] In one sense, measuring the annual investment in O is no different from measuring the annual investment in tangible capital. That is, the measure is simply the real annual cost of these capital goods, in other words, the dollar cost adjusted for price change. The measurement of O, however, is likely to present some special problems of which a few are touched on here.

From society's standpoint, all costs involve the using up of resources and thus are opportunity costs in the sense that society foregoes what these resources would have produced in their next best use. The job of measurement, however, makes it necessary to view cost from the standpoint of the firm since measurement requires collecting information from the firm's accounts. Here it is convenient to classify costs as either outlays or opportunity costs. The outlays are the direct expenditures made by firms to facilitate their unprogrammed organizational change. The opportunity costs, on the other hand, are equal to the value of output not produced because members of the firm are instead devoting their efforts to the innovative work of creating new programs. March and Simon refer to the costs of discovering, developing and implementing possible programs of action as the "costs of innovation." The problem for measurement is that "it is seldom possible to make accurate estimates of the costs of innovation, and even in situations where it is possible, such estimates are seldom made" (1958, 173). This, of course, does not mean that it is not possible to make "reasonable" estimates of these costs; it merely means that it won't be easy.

Measuring $\triangle$ O on the basis of the cost of the organizational change should be clearly distinguished from finding the value of $\triangle$ O. A firm's organizational investment has value to the extent that it is expected to make an identifiable contribution to the future earnings of the firm. Based on an estimate of the profits attributable to the organization along with the probability of their realization, one could calculate the present or capitalized value of this investment using an appropriate rate of discount. The mechanics of the present value calculation are no different in this case than in a more typical instance. Presumably, rational managers will invest in organizational change when its net present value exceeds its cost.

AN ESTIMATE OF THE MANAGEMENT CONSULTANT CONTRIBUTION TO ECONOMIC GROWTH

In this section, an estimate is made of the management consultant contribution to the annual rate of growth in the United States using essentially the same approach as Edward F. Denison (1962, 1974). In estimating the contribution of different sources of economic growth, Denison does not take into account the contributions made by management consultants (or managers for that matter) which increased the productivity of the tangible factors employed in businesses. It is not that Denison denies the importance of intangible factors; he simply does not attempt to measure them. Their contributions are included in the "advance of knowledge" portion of the residual, and Denison conjectures that "advances in management knowledge may easily contribute as much or more to measured growth as advances in technological knowledge [per se]" (1967, 280). A study by John Johnston provides support for the view that management consultants make an important contribution to economic growth; he finds management consulting work in Great Britain contributed "about one-quarter of the annual productivity increase achieved in recent years" (Johnston 1963, 249). The essence of the statistical task for the United States involves utilizing estimates of management consultant–related capital formation in conjunction with Denison's methodology to arrive at an estimate of the consultants' contribution to the annual average percent increase in total product over a certain number of years.

Denison's Calculations

The essentials of Denison's methodology can be summed up using an equation which is similar to equation 4.3 above. This equation states that the annual average percentage increase in total product (G) is equal to the annual average percentage change in each factor (P) weighted by the average fractional share of these factors in the total national income (w) plus the residual annual average percentage increase in total product (R) for some specified period of time. If the number of factors are limited to land (N), labor (L), and capital (K) following Denison, the equation is

$$w_N P_N + w_L P_L + w_K P_K + R = G \qquad (4.8)$$

or

$$G_N + G_L + G_K + R = G \qquad (4.9)$$

where G_N, G_L, and G_K are, respectively, the percentage point contributions to the growth rate of land, labor and capital. The use of this equation can be illustrated for the 1929–1969 period (Denison, 1974, 127). For this period, G equals 3.33. Other data are as follows: $G_N = 0$, $G_L = 1.31$, $G_K = .50$, R = 1.52. Labor and capital respectively, explain 1.31 and .50 percentage points or 39 and 15 percent of the growth rate. The residual accounts for 1.52 percentage points or 46 percent of the growth rate, of which .92 percentage points or 28 percent of the growth rate is attributed to the advance of knowledge.

The Estimation Method

How much of the advance of knowledge can be explained by counting the capital input resulting from management consultant efforts? In order to evaluate this, the Denison equation needs some modification as follows:

$$w_N P_N + w_L P_L + w_K P_K + w_{Kmc} P_{Kmc} + R = G. \qquad (4.10)$$

In this equation, w_{Kmc} stands for the average fractional share of the capital contributed by management consultant efforts in the total annual national income, and P_{Kmc} stands for the annual average percentage increase in this kind of capital for a specified period of time. Thus, $w_{Kmc} P_{Kmc}$ is the number of percentage points of the growth rate explained by the growth in the management consultant-related capital input. The addition of $w_{Kmc} P_{Kmc}$ to the Denison equation effectively reduces the size of R. w_K is also smaller since it is reduced by a fraction equal to w_{Kmc}. However, w_{Kmc} is very small compared to w_K; therefore, the effect of adding $w_{Kmc} P_{Kmc}$ on $w_K P_K$ is ignored here.[12]

The lack of certain types of data presents an obstacle to making estimates of P_{Kmc} and w_{Kmc}; therefore, additional assumptions are necessary. One important obstacle is the lack of knowledge of the stock of management consultant–related capital (Kmc). It is possible, however, to estimate the annual consultant–related capital formation in privately owned firms (TKFP). This will be demonstrated in the next section. Since the average capital growth rate, P_{Kmc}, is equal to the average of TKFP/Kmc over a specified period of time, knowledge of the denominator for the different years is obviously necessary. To overcome this difficulty, P_{Kmc} is assumed to be equal to the average growth rate of the amount of this capital formation ($\overline{\Delta TKFP/TKFP}$). In equation form, this assumption states that:

$$P_{Kmc} = \overline{TKFP}/\bar{K}mc = \overline{\Delta TKFP/TKFP}. \qquad (4.11)$$

The bar above the symbols indicates that these are annual averages. It is important to note that if the depreciation of this capital is negligible and the growth of this capital formation ($\overline{\Delta TKFP/TKFP}$) is constant, it can be shown that P_{Kmc} is, in fact, equal to $\overline{\Delta TKFP/TKFP}$. Although these two conditions are not likely to be entirely fulfilled, the assumption is reasonable for the purposes of this crude estimate.

w_{Kmc} is equal to the average income earned by this capital input divided by the average national income. The average of this capital income ($\bar{E}mc$) can be obtained by multiplying the amount of $\bar{K}mc$ by the average rate of return (before taxes) on this capital ($\bar{r}$). The amount of $\bar{K}mc$ can be obtained from equation 4.11 given a knowledge of $\overline{TKFP}$ for this period. That is:

$$\bar{K}mc = \overline{TKFP}/P_{Kmc}. \qquad (4.12)$$

The rate of return on this kind of capital is unknown, but given the usual mobility of financial resources, it is likely that the $\bar{r}$ on this capital would tend to equal the rate of return on other types of capital with a similar degree of risk. Assuming for the moment that this rate of return ($\bar{r}$) is known, then

$$\bar{E}mc = \bar{r}\,\bar{K}mc \tag{4.13}$$

and

$$w_{Kmc} = \bar{E}mc/\overline{NI} \tag{4.14}$$

where $\overline{NI}$ is the annual average of the national income. Using equations 4.12, 4.13 and 4.14, it can be shown that the number of percentage points in the growth of product contributed by management consultant-related capital formation over a period of time is:

$$
\begin{aligned}
G_{Kmc} = w_{Kmc}\,P_{Kmc} &= (\bar{r}\,\bar{K}mc/\overline{NI})\,P_{Kmc} \\
&= (\,(\bar{r}\,\overline{TKF^p}/P_{Kmc})/\overline{NI})\,P_{Kmc}
\end{aligned}
$$

or

$$G_{Kmc} = \bar{r}\,\overline{TKF^p}/\overline{NI}. \tag{4.15}$$

Thus, equation 4.15 shows that the use of the assumption to estimate P_{Kmc} obviates the use of estimates for $\bar{K}mc$ and P_{Kmc} in calculating G_{Kmc}.

The Capital Formation Estimate

To obtain an estimate of $\overline{TKF^p}$ for 1929–1969, TKF^p for 1970 was estimated, and TKF^p values for earlier years were obtained by assuming that the ratio of management consultants' capital forming activity to total activity remained equal to the 1970 proportion. The human capital resulting from consultants' efforts is of two types, organizational capital, and human capital vested in particular individuals (often managers). The data do not permit separate estimates of these two types of human capital formation. The estimate of TKF^p for 1970 is based on data generated from interviews conducted in 32 management consulting firms during the first three months of 1971. The interviewees were senior officers in consultant firms located largely in the New York area and selected using a variety of sampling techniques including stratified sampling. Because large firms were disproportionately included in the sample, the selected firms accounted for 20.6 percent of the estimated $1 billion of total gross billings of U.S. management consulting firms in 1970.[13]

Essentially, TKF^P (1970) is an estimate of the total cost, direct and indirect, of the human capital forming efforts of firms utilizing management consultants. The direct costs are the outlays on consultants, and the indirect costs reflect the foregone output when client personnel work along with consultants. The interviewees' responses to questions concerning both the magnitude of their capital forming type activities relative to all activities and the magnitude of direct costs compared to indirect costs were utilized in the calculations. The TKF^P (1970) estimate is $1.354 billion.[14] TKF^P figures for earlier years were obtained by assuming that the proportion of total gross billings in 1970 represented by TKF^P (1970) is the ratio of capital formation to gross billings in earlier years for which billings data were available. Estimates of TKF^P for intermediate years were obtained using calculated growth rates and the assumption of annual compounding. The resulting estimate of $\overline{TKF^P}$ is $468.4 million (current dollars).[15]

The Contribution to Growth Estimate

The estimate of $\overline{NI}$, average national income for 1929–1969, is $273.6 billion (current dollars).[16] If $\bar{r}$ is assumed to be 15 percent,

$$G_{Kmc} = (15) \ (468.4 \text{ million})/273.6 \text{ billion}$$
$$= .0257 \text{ percentage points.}$$

This result means that 0.257 percentage points of the nation's growth is explained by the growth of the capital input contributed by management consultant efforts in privately owned enterprise. This is .771 percent or about three-quarters of one percent of the total growth rate. Furthermore, this capital input accounts for 2.79 percent of the residual growth in output, which Denison attributed to the advance of knowledge.

These results, of course, are contingent on the assumed value of $\bar{r}$ used in the calculation. There are two ways in which the plausibility of the assumed $\bar{r}$ value can be examined. One uses tabular sensitivity analysis, which shows how the percent of the residual growth (advance of knowledge) explained by the growth of the management consultant–related capital input would vary with alternative assumptions. This is illustrated in Table 4.1. Obviously, the results are quite sensitive to the $\bar{r}$ values.

Further insight concerning the proper $\bar{r}$ value can be obtained by examining actual rates of return for firms in the manufacturing sector during the 1929–1969 period. Manufacturing data are appropriate because a very high percentage of management consultant work is done for manufacturing firms. For illustrative purposes, the average rate of return was calculated for a sample of 14 industries within the manufacturing sector for the period 1951–1955. Net profit on tangible net worth for these manufacturing firms was 8.15 percent during 1951–1955.[17,18] Assuming that these corporations

Table 4.1
Sensitivity Analysis of Alternative Rate of Return Assumptions on Percent of Residual (Advance of Knowledge) Growth Explained by the Growth of Management Consultant-Related Capital Input 1929–1969

Values of Rate of Return (Percent)	Percent of Residual (Advance of Knowledge) Growth Explained
5	.93
10	1.86
15	2.79
20	3.72
30	5.58
40	7.44
50	9.30

paid taxes which were between 40 and 50 percent of total profits, the before-tax rate of return on tangible equity capital would be around 15 percent. In the absence of capital market imperfections one would expect the rate of return on the management consultant–related capital expenditure to tend to equality with these other investments; thus, an r̄ equal to 15 percent would seem reasonable.

There are, however, important reasons for believing that this assumed value of r̄ is very low. First, due in part to the highly innovative character of many of the management consultant–related investments, the risk and uncertainty associated with such investments would seem to be substantially greater than the typical manufacturing investment. Second, obstacles to the free flow of information would appear to be greater in relation to these than with respect to the typical investment and finally, motivational obstacles may be important. Leibenstein alluded to these latter and the rate of return:

It is quite clear that management consulting services are not only profitable to consultants but also highly profitable to many of the firms that employ them. But it is rather surprising that more of these services are not called for. Part of the answer may be that managements of firms are not motivated to hire consultants if things appear to be going "in any reasonably satisfactory rate." There are, of course, numerous personal resistances to calling for outside advice. If the motivation is strong enough, e.g., the threat of the failure of the firm, then it is likely that such resistances would be overcome. (Leibenstein 1966, 406)

For such reasons, it is likely that the actual value of r̄ is substantially higher than 15 percent. If so, the influence of management consultants on economic growth might be much greater than estimated earlier. For example, if r̄ equals 40 percent, the percent of residual growth (advance of knowledge) explained by the growth of the management consultant–related capital input is 7.44 as compared to the 2.79 estimated when r̄ equals 15 percent (see Table 4.1). Additional research relating to the rates of return on such investments would be necessary in order to narrow the range in the estimates concerning consultants' contribution to economic growth. These calculations only suggest the influence of management consultants on economic growth, but the estimates do indicate that their role in the economy is an important one. This conclusion is emphasized by the fact that the advance of knowledge residual includes all the contributions of research and development as well as advances in organization and management not related to the work of consultants.

CONCLUSION

Organizational capital formation occurs when firms use resources to add quantitatively and qualitatively to the productive capacity of their internal social and socio-technical relationships. This chapter has provided a conceptual framework for analyzing the contribution of organizational change to economic growth utilizing the organizational capital concept; it has also provided an estimate of the economic growth contribution of U.S. management consultants, who are frequently involved when firms initiate important organizational changes. Hopefully, this chapter will stimulate further inquiry into the role of organizational and management change in productivity increase. Certainly, improved understanding of the nature, magnitude and financing of investment in organizational capital is needed. In addition, we need to know much more about what types of firms make these investments, how the investment decisions are made, and how risk and uncertainty enter into the decision process. Research on these questions will facilitate better understanding of past productivity change and the potential for future growth.

5

Worker Motivation: Toward Increased X-Efficiency

Whereas chapter 4 was concerned with the "macro" economics of economic growth, this chapter is concerned with "micro-micro" economics in order to elucidate one of the key reasons why organizational change can lead to higher productivity. "Micro-micro theory is concerned with intrafirm behavior and relations or with the interaction of persons within the firm and their influence on firm behavior" (Leibenstein 1979, 478).

An important reason for studying intrafirm behavior is to gain insight concerning the conventional view that firms are maximizers in the sense of achieving performance consistent with the organization's potential or its capacity for innovation. According to Harvey Leibenstein (1976, 95), X-inefficiency, which refers to "the degree to which actual output is less than maximum output (for given inputs)," is the usual state of affairs. During the years since his first article on X-efficiency (Leibenstein 1966) appeared, Leibenstein (1979) has developed a conceptual framework for understanding why this is so. Undoubtedly, he had led the way in an important area of economics. While his model is extremely useful for explaining the existence and persistence of X-inefficiency, it is less useful for explaining the level of worker motivation and how it can be improved through organizational change. The purpose of this chapter is to develop a micro-micro model that draws on certain concepts and findings of industrial psychology on motivation in order to improve the model's ability to explain how worker motivation is related to organizational relationships that can be developed or destroyed.

LEIBENSTEIN'S MICRO-MICRO THEORY

In seeking to explain the existence of X-inefficiency and, thus, the lack of cost minimization, Leibenstein focuses on the effort expended by individual members of the firm. Directed work effort, the critical item, has four components:

1. the choice of activities composing the effort;
2. the pace at which each activity is carried out;
3. the quality of each activity; and
4. the time pattern and length of activity. (1976, 98)

The effort positions of workers, which evolve from their job interpretations, are associated with output values. What firms usually purchase, however, is labor time, not effort or output. In emphasizing that labor contracts are incomplete in this sense, Leibenstein's model differs from standard production theory which treats human and nonhuman inputs almost symmetrically. The divergence between buying labor time and buying work effort arises because, in most work situations, individuals are confronted with incomplete information as to what is expected; they must interpret their jobs, in effect choosing an effort position. Also, it may be costly, difficult or inefficient for employers to calculate the value added to output by most employees.

In Leibenstein's model, the individual's choice of an effort position involves two kinds of compromise. The first is an internal or moral compromise between "a taste for responsiveness to opportunities and constraints within certain standards of behavior [constraint concern] and a simultaneous taste for 'irresponsible' or unconstrained behavior." (Leibenstein 1979, 485) That is, "superego" and "id" personality factors determine the effort response an individual will choose in the absence of external pressure. If the demands of the organization (including pressures from peers and authorities) are influential, the effort position actually chosen will reflect a second compromise and will differ from one chosen on the basis of internal considerations. The resulting effort position is unlikely to be in the best interests of either the employee or the employer. "The lower the degree of constraint concern, the greater the extent to which the effort position will reflect self-interest, and the less it will reflect devotion to the firm's interests." (Leibenstein 1978, 30) This behavior on the part of employees, acting as agents of the firm's principals, is referred to as selective rationality; it is clearly not the maximizing behavior of the orthodox theory of the firm.

These considerations are the essence of what determines the relationship between the utility an individual receives from a job and the amount of the individual's work effort. "The utility from effort is the sum of the utility from income derived from the job and the satisfaction obtained from effort. A plausible assumption for a representative individual is that he prefers some effort to no effort, but beyond some point effort becomes less pleasur-able, and as a result, the total utility from effort declines" (Leibenstein 1975, 592). In functional form,

$$U = F(E, P, DO) \tag{5.1}$$

where U is the individual's utility from work effort, E is the amount of directed work effort, P represents the individual's personality, and DO stands for the demands of the organization with accompanying pressure. On a graph, the relationship between U and E (U is on the vertical axis of the UE curve) slopes upward first and then downward, other things being unchanged. In the absence of other constraints, a person would be expected to choose the effort position (E*) that maximizes U (U*); see figure 5.1.[1]

How will the firm behave if it is exposed to outside pressure or a "tight" environment (for example, increased competition)? There are three pos-sibilities, but the one emphasized by Leibenstein is that management will impose "pressure" for greater performance on individuals within the firm. This "may take a variety of forms, including mixes of potential punish-ments and rewards, or a set of differential awards, of either a monetary or social approval nature" (Leibenstein 1975, 584). With the increased organi-zation demands, DO, members of the firm would be expected to adopt a compromise position involving a higher expenditure of effort. Graphically, this means a rightward shift of the UE curve. Alternatively, the firm could adopt sheltering or entrepreneurial activities (Leibenstein 1979, 489–492).

While Leibenstein's model succeeds as an explanation of X-inefficiency, it says little about worker motivation per se. Scattered throughout his writ-

Figure 5.1
The Utility versus Effort Relationship

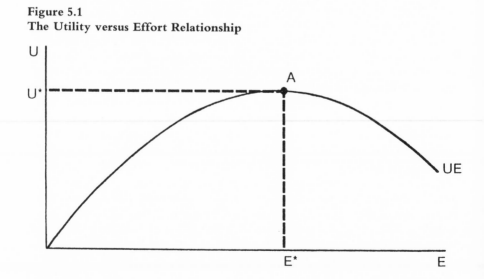

ings are a few comments relating to motivational theory, but these are not integral to his model. For example, he observes that beyond some point greater supervision involving more detailed instructions and monitoring of employees is counterproductive (Leibenstein 1979, 599–600). Similarly, he mentions the possibility that management changes can be counterproductive if they alter the "overall feeling of trust or distrust, the sense of approval or disapproval, which individuals may take into account" (Leibenstein 1976, 265). Although we learn from Leibenstein's model that increased effort generally requires more managerial pressure, it is not clear how workers can become more motivated.

AN ALTERNATIVE MODEL

Individual Work Effort

The first part of the model presented here focuses on the individual employee's choice of effort position. The main difference between this version and Leibenstein's is the inclusion of a number of new variables in the utility-effort equation to explain worker motivation. The basic relationship is

$$U = F(E, P^*, DO, WE, FG) \qquad (5.2)$$

where P^* represents a personality variable with expanded dimensions, WE represents four key dimensions of the individual's work environment, and FG represents the worker's perception that the present job will lead to opportunities for further growth. The other variables were defined previously. The four dimensions of a work environment are: 1) the match between an individual and the characteristics of both the job and the organization; 2) the existing structure and supervision of the job; 3) the existence of clear, meaningful goals for jobs and the organization; and 4) the nature and enforcement of the implicit contract between employer and employee. As in Leibenstein's model, workers have discretion to interpret their jobs and are expected to choose the effort position that maximizes their utility from work effort. In the present model, however, the workers who are well matched with the job and organization, satisfy their higher-level needs through work effort, possess considerable drive, work in a high-quality environment, and expect the job to lead to future growth opportunities will derive more satisfaction or utility from their work efforts than workers who do not, and will be more motivated, thereby choosing greater effort. The important variables and their relationships are explained below.

The choice of variables for our utility-effort relation was dictated largely by motivation theory, especially need-satisfaction theory.[2] According to Frederick Herzberg (1968, 55), a motivated employee is one who wants to work, does not require externally imposed stimulation, and is energized and goal-directed. Although motivation in this sense is intrinsic, research suggests that the desire to perform jobs well is not natural. The essence of need-satisfaction theory is that people have basic, stable needs, and that they will become motivated when those needs and the job situation correspond. In other words, when performing the job well is experienced as satisfying, the result will be high and continuing motivation.

In Herzberg's view, motivating factors intrinsic to the job include achievement, recognition, the work itself, responsibility and growth or advancement. These yield job satisfaction and motivation. On a separate continuum are hygiene or maintenance factors such as company policy and administration, supervision, interpersonal relationships, working conditions, salary, status and security. In the absence of any of these factors, job dissatisfaction (which could interfere with motivation) will be present. A lack of job dissatisfaction, however, does not imply motivation, since that derives only from the presence of the motivating factors. Merely providing things such as more pay or cleaner working conditions will not provide additional motivation.

The personality variable, P^*, in equation 5.2 includes two dimensions in addition to Leibenstein's id and superego (constraint concern) factors. The first is drive, which refers to the amount of directed energy a person has, regardless of situation. The second is maturity or psychic health. According to Abraham Maslow (1970a, 38–39), the satisfied or healthy individual is motivated to the greatest extent by self-actualization. The magnitude of the personality factor determines the degree to which a person may be motivated by characteristics of the job and job situation.

There is considerable evidence that individuals differ markedly not only in the strength of basic needs but also in preferences for different types of work, working conditions, interpersonal relationships, and so forth. Certain jobs and organizations provide a work environment that enables certain people to be motivated, but not others. The first component of the work environment mentioned earlier was the match between the individual and the job or organization. Maslow envisions the ideal match as follows:

Each task would "call for" just that one person in the world most uniquely suited to deal it, like a key and a lock, and that one person would than feel the call most strongly and would reverberate to it, be tuned to its wave length, and so be responsible to its call (1965, 10)

A second component of the work environment is the structure and supervision of the job. Industrial psychologists generally agree that the key dimensions of job design and aspects of leadership style cited below enhance higher need satisfaction and motivation. Edward Lawler (1973, 158–160) lists four core dimensions of job design: variety, autonomy, task identity, and feedback. According to Lawler, motivation is fostered when job activities are varied, workers have control over how work is done, workers are responsible for a natural "unit" of work, and workers are able to obtain useful information on the degree of success of their efforts. Jobs that facilitate interpersonal interaction and enable workers to acquire valued skills and knowledge are also likely to be motivating. Similarly, it is believed that leaders who foster participation in decision making and are considerate are most successful in motivating workers. Leader recognition of worker efforts is also an important motivating factor.

A third component of the work environment are meaningful goals, both for the organization and for particular jobs or tasks. Organizational goals enable the worker to identify with the firm and its efforts, making sense of work life and making otherwise onerous tasks worthwhile (Maslow 1965, 29, 39–41).[3] Job goals, when sufficiently specific and challenging, ensure that the ends rather than the means are the main concern and provide role clarity for the worker (Umstat 1977).

Implicit contracts are the fourth component of the work environment. Employer-employee relationships are increasingly being governed by the principle of fair play, whereby long-run considerations, perhaps involving long-run as opposed to short-run profit maximization, become paramount. Arthur Okun (1975 and 1980) calls such personnel policy commitments by firms "implicit contracts." These relate not only to wages and their rate of increase but also to many aspects of working conditions such as job design, supervision, workload and its variability, and career advancement. Implicit contracts are superior to explicit formal contracts because the latter are more rigid and involve the extra expenses of negotiation, formulation, and enforcement. When a firm's policies are guided by fairness in line with the variety of implicit contracts it has made with employees, it can reasonably expect that the occasional short-run sacrifices required for adhering to these commitments will be reciprocated by employee loyalty, as reflected in a lower turnover even in times of favorable labor markets. Clearly, when firms make and enforce appropriate implicit contracts, they will contribute to employee security and an atmosphere of mutual trust. The implicit contract notion will be further developed and utilized in chapter 7.

As noted earlier, the variable FG in equation 5.2 represents future growth. If workers perceive their present job as leading to opportunities for growth and learning rather than as a dead end, self-esteem will be higher. Higher self-esteem, in turn, should increase job satisfaction and motivation. The future growth factor should, strictly speaking, be considered separately from the promise of promotion and raises contingent on performance. Such external rewards are encompassed by the DO or pressure variable; they may be effective in bringing about the desired performance, but they are not motivators in the intrinsic sense.

According to our model, the equilibrium effort position, E^*, chosen by a worker will be the one associated with maximum total utility from work effort, U* (recall figure 5.1). In other words, we should expect workers to expend effort up to the effort point, E*, at which the marginal utility of work effort, MU, equals zero. For management to increase E*, its actions must shift the UE curve or alter its shape so that MU is greater than zero at the original E*. These factors are not considered in Leibenstein's model. For example, in our model, management might redesign jobs to add responsibility and autonomy. This would tend to shift the workers' UE curves rightward and in time lead to a higher E*.

Certain management actions might shift the UE curve vertically; these involve increases or decreases in the pure hygiene factors. With greater salary or fringe benefits, for example, workers might be more satisfied with their organization, but might not be more motivated to work. As a considerable amount of research suggests, these workers are likely to exhibit improved "membership behavior" as reflected in reduced turnover and absenteeism (Lawler 1977). This is not the same as increased motivation, but it may enhance productivity.

If the firm's environment constricts and the pressure on workers or DO increases, both Leibenstein's and the present model agree that the UE curve will shift rightward and perhaps upward. In the present model, however,

Figure 5.2
The Utility versus Effort Relationship

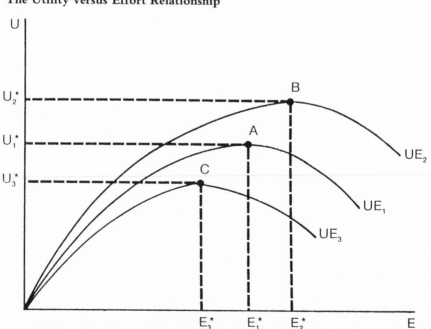

the new E* may not be a long-run equilibrium. This is because a sustained increase in DO, especially if it violates the employer-employee implicit contract, is likely to lead to a decrease in the quality of the work environment (with a decline in factors such as mutual trust, valid communication and worker autonomy). The latter, in turn, would be expected to cause a leftward (and probably downward) shift in the UE curve. If the leftward shift in UE is greater than the initial rightward shift, the long-run result of the increased pressure is less productivity, a result directly counter to the predictions of the Leibenstein model.

The sequence of events described above is represented in figure 5.2 by the movement from A to B and then to C. First, effort increases to E_2^* in response to greater pressure, but this is only a short-run equilibrium. As the quality of the work environment decreases with sustained pressure, the UE curve shifts leftward from UE_2 to UE_3, and the long-run equilibrium effort at E_3^* is lower even than the initial effort equilibrium at E_1^*.

Rensis Likert's research has led him to conclude that the value of the organization's human assets may decrease when management increases the pressure on workers.

As was demonstrated in the . . . experiment with clerical workers, putting pressure to increase production on a well-established organization engaged in work for which performance standards can be set yields substantial and immediate increases in productivity. This increase is obtained, however, at a cost to the human assets of the organization. . . . The cost was clear; hostilities increased, there was greater reliance upon authority, loyalties declined, motivation to produce decreased while motivation to restrict production increased, and turnover increased. In other words, the quality of the human organization deteriorated as a functioning social system devoted to achieving the institution's objectives. (Likert 1961, 71)

On the other hand, the value of these human assets will increase if management takes actions to improve the work environment. In the last twenty or thirty years, numerous organizational development strategies have been proposed and tried (see, for example, Huse 1975). Since, regardless of approach, improvement in the work environment may involve not only the benefits of future profitability arising from higher E* levels but also substantial costs, undertaking such a project involves an investment in organizational capital. That is, innovative efforts to improve the functioning of the organization can be considered a kind of human capital formation that shifts the production possibility frontier outward. Increasingly, corporations are viewing these organizational investments as alternatives to the more conventional capacity-increasing investments.

The present model suggests that firms often face a trade-off. Increasing internal pressure will probably increase productivity in the short run, but at the cost of long-run productivity. Organizational development efforts, alternatively, may increase long-run productivity, but the short-run costs and risks may be substantial. It should be noted that the latter endeavors represent a type of entrepreneurial response to environmental tightness not considered by Leibenstein.

Organizational Effectiveness

For an organization to be effective, it is necessary but not sufficient for employees to be motivated and make substantial work efforts. Unless the overall functioning of the organization enables these efforts to be coordinated, channeled toward the goals of the organization, and responsive to a changing environment, effectiveness will not be possible. The following equation expresses the essence of this concept in functional form.

$$OE = f\left(\sum_{i=1}^{n} E_i, OS, OF \right) \tag{5.3}$$

where OE is organizational effectiveness, $\sum_{i=1}^{n} E_i$ represents the summation of the individual efforts, E_i, of all employees, n. OS stands for the formal organization structure and OF represents a variety of the human aspects of the overall organization functioning.[4] Leibenstein's model, on the other hand, does not appear to recognize that organizational effectiveness requires more than high individual efforts.

Formal organization structure refers to the designed pattern of interactions linking individuals, groups, physical capital, technology and tasks; that is, it refers to a sociotechnical system. The basic purpose of this structure is to assist with the reliable completion of tasks and goal achievement, especially when activities are routine and repetitive. It is important that an organization's formal structure be appropriate to its situation; otherwise, resources may be squandered on unnecessary activities, necessary coordination may not occur, or energies may be insufficiently channeled into the most important endeavors. As indicated in chapter 2, developing the appropriate organization structure involves considerations such as the degree of centralization, the span of control, how special problems are dealt with and how resources are allocated.

The human aspects of the organization's functioning, beyond what happens in individual work environments, are also important in determining organizational effectiveness. According to Likert, "effective organizations have an extraordinary capacity to handle conflict" (1961, 117). They also would be characterized by their ability to adapt and respond to new demands, that is, by their overall psychological health. These characteristics are strongly influenced by top management.

When organizations incur substantial costs by making planned changes in their formal organization structures and functioning with the intent of increasing organizational effectiveness and productivity, they are investing in organizational capital.

SOME IMPLICATIONS

If, as Leibenstein has indicated, X-inefficiency is the usual state of affairs, and if the gap between potential and actual productivity is substantial, then there are many opportunities for organizational and managerial changes to increase productivity for firms and, thereby, the economy. The literature on organizational change suggests some reasons why such profitable opportunities have not been fully exploited. For example, in his historical analysis of the change of U.S. industrial firms to the multidivisional form of organization, Alfred Chandler (1962, 15 and 323) indicates that delays in introducing this needed innovation occurred because administrators were too enmeshed in day-to-day tactical activities to appreciate longer range needs and because they lacked the necessary perception because of deficiencies in their training. They also may have resisted because the "reorganization threatened their own personal position, their power, and most important of all, their psychological security." Another possible obstacle to organizational change is financial; that is, the capital assets created may not be considered a desirable form of collateral by prospective lenders. Finally, organizations are inclined to keep their important organizational innovations secret, making it difficult for would-be imitators to follow suit (Mills 1975, 124).

Resources are often underallocated to organizational change even when firms are investing up to the point at which the private rates of return equal opportunity costs if certain types of organizational change give rise to positive externalities. Benefit spillovers from businesses to the rest of society would exist if, for example, the creation of satisfying and motivating work environments enhanced the psychological health of workers. As Maslow indicates, this enhancement of psychological health would ultimately be reflected in improvements in many areas of life. Since private firms cannot be expected to take these social benefits into account in their investment decision making, suboptimal organizational investment should be expected.

From the standpoint of government policy making, there are two main arguments for government actions leading to increased organizational investment: first, to overcome organizational, proprietary and financial obstacles to investment and, second, to deal with societal spillovers not considered by private decision makers. If government is to play an important role in these areas, researchers must further identify the nature and importance of these obstacles and spillovers.

CONCLUSIONS

While Leibenstein's model is valuable as an explanation of X–inefficiency, it needs revision to explain worker motivation. It would be unfortunate if Leibenstein's model was interpreted as being essentially the same as what Douglas McGregor calls Theory X. According to McGregor, "Theory X leads naturally to an emphasis on the tactics of control—to procedures and techniques for telling people what to do, for determining whether they are doing it, and for administering rewards and punishments (1960, 132). Theory Y, the alternative, as well as the newer Theory Z, are based on a broader conception of human needs and how the ability to satisfy them on the job can be a powerful motivating force.

Theory Y . . . leads to a preoccupation with the *nature of relationships,* with the creation of an environment which will encourage commitment to organizational objectives and which will provide opportunities for the maximum exercise of initiate, ingenuity, and self-direction in achieving them. (McGregor 1960, 132)

Increasingly, businesses are finding that their survival depends on the adoption of Theory Y and even Theory Z type management as they look for ways to improve their organizations. The importance of the micro–micro economic model developed in this chapter lies in the fact that these organizational behavior considerations are explicitly part of the model.

6

Productivity Through Intrafirm Cooperation

INTRODUCTION

In the United States and other Western countries there is the growing recognition that a lack of cooperation among employees and groups within firms has contributed in recent years to below-potential output and low productivity growth. The necessary cooperation, however, has received little theoretical attention from economists. Thus, there is a need for better conceptions of cooperation, better understanding of its relationship to productivity, and greater appreciation of how it can be enhanced.

This chapter begins by explaining the nature of interemployee cooperation, describing what motivates cooperative behavior, and analyzing how it is related to productivity. The prisoner's dilemma model is used as a point of departure to explain why there is a tendency for cooperation to break down. While the pure prisoner's dilemma is useful in indicating how individual maximizing behavior can lead to suboptimal outcomes, it is limited in its ability to realistically explain interemployee behavior within firms. Based on an analysis of the shortcomings of the prisoner's dilemma model, a more realistic conception of employee decision making with respect to other employees is developed.

It is this more realistic view that allows us to understand how certain kinds of investment in organizational change have the potential to bring about greater cooperation, which leads to higher productivity and worker well-being.

THE MEANING OF COOPERATION

Cooperation is a complex term with a number of related meanings. The focus here is on cooperation within an organization. First, cooperation invariably means working with others toward a common end. The need for cooperation arises when organizations have tasks either too large for individual accomplishment or with elements requiring different specialized abilities. Individuals are said to cooperate if they work toward their common end without coercion or overt conflict. This definition of cooperation is also consistent with workers who merely perform dependably in prespecified roles, and lack discretion. Thus, this definition is closer to coordination and doesn't go far enough for our purposes.

Second, cooperation means a process that involves discretionary effort. Workers cooperate with their organization when they expend more effort than the minimum required. Moreover, they cooperate when they refrain from malingering, lowering organizational morale or otherwise obstructing accomplishment. However, this definition still doesn't go far enough.

In the third definition, cooperation is not only a discretionary effort but involves helpful behavior among the members of an organization. The need for such cooperation derives from the uncertainty, complexity and interdependence which frequently accompany a division of labor. Consider what is ordinarily the first step in doing a task, the division of the task into subtasks and their assignment to individual workers who may be evaluated according to their achievement. Problems may occur to the extent that it is difficult to anticipate the quantity and quality of labor required for each of the subtasks. The difficulty is a manifestation of bounded rationality on the part of those in charge of the division of labor. However, if spontaneous cooperative behavior prevails, there is no problem as some employees are willing to do helping work for which a good part of the credit may accrue to those they help.

In some cases, a subtask may require two or more workers' joint efforts to accomplish the mission. Since it may be difficult or impossible to evaluate the separate contributions of, say, two workers, there is an incentive for one worker to work less hard than the other. Cooperation in this situation has elements of both the second and third definition, as it means putting forth more than the minimum effort, and thereby helping a team member.

The three meanings of cooperation form a hierarchy of types of work behavior which is similar to that employed by Jay Galbraith (1977, 249–253). The hierarchy implies that if cooperation in the third sense is occurring, cooperation in the second and first senses is also occurring. In the following discussion, unless otherwise specified, the term cooperation is used in the third sense.

The Motivation for Cooperation: Benefits to Individuals

There may be a number of possible motivations for cooperative behavior. In "social exchange" or "cooperative egoism," one party helps the other because the former anticipates the need for future help and thus expects or hopes for reciprocation (Wintrobe 1981, 202). This cooperative pattern implies mutual positive externalities between the parties to the transaction. Party A's helpful actions lead to benefits for party B; A does not realize any of these benefits, but is likely to realize some later if B helps him.[1] In cooperative egoism, the motive is self-interest and the helper is not concerned with the welfare of the other party. In an organization where rewards generally go to individuals based on their performance on assigned subtasks, the cooperative patterns which develop are likely to be of the self-interest type. Self-interest is also the motive when cooperative behavior is evaluated by those in a position to bestow benefits or invoke penalties. Presumably, organization members will have greater incentive to cooperate when the organization's personnel procedures recognize and reward cooperative behavior.

There are four other motives for cooperative behavior in which self-interest plays a smaller or subordinate role. The first is "goods altruism." "In altruistic behavior . . . the donor's welfare does depend directly on the consumption level of the recipient" (Wintrobe 1981, 202; see also Becker 1976, 818); party A gains according to the magnitude of benefits received by B. The second motive is "participation altruism" in which A derives benefits from the process of helping B rather than in proportion to the benefits B receives; A in this case "has a taste for participation in social acts" (Margolis 1982, 21–22). The third motivation derives from the benefits A expects to receive when he perceives his cooperative efforts as being instrumental in advancing the common organizational purpose[2] of A and B. In this case, A cares about and derives benefits from the achievement of the shared goals. The benefits from the accomplishment of these purposes are like a public good in the sense that others in the organization who share the goals will realize them, regardless of their efforts. If A is also an altruist, he will derive further benefit from the knowledge that others (including, but not limited to B) are benefiting from the achievement of the shared goals which he helped bring about. A fourth motivation for cooperation is an individual's desire to gain acceptance by his work group, assuming that the norms of the work group are in accord with the overall organizational goals. It may, of course, be difficult to determine the mixture of cooperative motivations operatng in any given situation. Nevertheless, this analysis of motives will be helpful to the extent that it suggests the organizational incentives to which cooperation is likely to respond.

The Costs of Noncooperation: Lowered Productivity

Why is cooperation important? Consider the organization without cooperation: productivity is lower either because output is less or because more resources are used. Lowered output occurs when tasks cannot be completed due to low cooperation. Also possible is negative cooperation or sabotage.

Here A's intention is to harm B in order to gain by comparison; the result is destroyed output and perhaps a persisting mutual pattern of destructive behavior. Of course, management may intervene in these situations to correct the effects of "spontaneous" noncooperation. If so, the accomplishment of these managerial actions means more managerial resources and higher costs. Specifically, managers may counter noncooperation by doing more complete task planning, which results in less unanticipated work, and by creating new divisions of labor to accomplish work not previously anticipated.[3] Whether lower output or higher resource use results, the costs of noncooperation within the organization may be high.

Cooperation among workers can thus substitute for managerial planning and information processing at a higher level. In this sense, efforts by management to facilitate cooperation may be viewed as an organizational strategy to lower the amount of managerial information processing required (see Galbraith 1977, 49–55, for alternative strategies). Also note that establishing cooperative behavior with bosses, peers, subordinates, outsiders, and others is an important way in which managers accomplish their purposes. According to John Kotter, "effective general managers allocate significant time and effort when they first take their jobs to developing a network of cooperative relationships among those people they feel are needed to satisfy their emerging agendas" (1982, 161).

Blake and Mouton (1978, 140) indicate that the costs of noncooperation (or poor teamwork) may be higher than suggested by the analysis above. They indicate that poor teamwork is typically associated with faltering communication and poor morale. These in turn are generally accompanied by situations in which 1) the possibilities for synergy among workers are not realized, 2) duplications of effort are not eliminated and 3) outmoded practices are relied on excessively. In good teamwork, cooperation may involve both mutual simultaneous helping and joint efforts in pursuit of shared goals.

Thus, in a variety of ways, cooperative work outcomes are clearly more productive than noncooperative ones. There are also reasons to believe that cooperation is directly related to worker well-being. This will be analyzed in chapter 8.

THE PRISONER'S DILEMMA MODEL OF COOPERATION

The Pure Prisoner's Dilemma

A useful starting point is the prisoner's dilemma (PD) game, which has been used to analyze intrafirm cooperation (notably, Leibenstein 1976 (chapter 9), 1980, 1982a, and 1982b). Let us consider a modified version of the Leibenstein analysis. In the "pure" PD game, each member of the

Figure 6.1
Prisoner's Dilemma Payoff Table

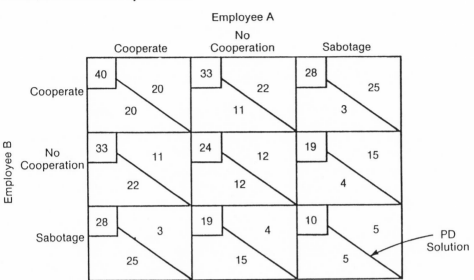

organization is presented with discrete choices on how to relate to other employees. In particular, employee A can decide to cooperate with employee B, not cooperate with him, or sabotage his efforts; employee B has the same choices.[4] The payoff table in figure 6.1 illustrates a typical PD pattern of utility outcomes or rewards to each employee given the choice of the other employee.[5] The sum of the outcomes (shown in the top left corners) is the total product (or utility) of the firm (assuming no one else claims part of their joint product). Clearly, mutual cooperation is an optimal outcome for the firm as the output is highest in this case. However, each employee can, given the choice of the other employee, gain at the expense of the other by moving from cooperation to sabotage. Thus, from the viewpoint of the "rational" or self-interested maximizing egoist, choosing sabotage is the only feasible strategy, and the PD solution (bottom right corner) is the expected result of the game. This is obviously a suboptimal result (see, for instance, Rapoport and Chammah 1965, 28–29).

In the interlevel version of the PD game (a special case of the above), the superior participant is the firm, as represented by its principals (normally either the managers or the owners), and the subordinate participant is an employee. Sabotage is not an option in this version, although it conceivably could be for subordinates. The superior, if cooperating, is offering a generous mix of organizational incentives (financial and nonfinancial), and, if not cooperating, is threatening and penalizing. The subordinate, if cooperating, is exerting more than the minimum effort. If not cooperating, the employee's effort is the minimum needed to avoid penalties, and the employee may occasionally obstruct progress from the superior's point of view. While joint cooperation is the optimum collective result, the superior who distrusts his subordinates and believes they will respond only to threats and not to positive incentives will gain by choosing the noncooperative option. Similarly, subordinates who distrust their superiors can gain through non-cooperative behavior. The expected result, again, is the suboptimal PD solution.

To illustrate the real dilemma involved for the PD participants, suppose a labor economics research project is to be undertaken by a large research organization. A labor economist and econometrician, each with equal status in the organization, are assigned to the project. The labor economist is given the subtask of writing the conceptual and descriptive part of the report, and the econometrician is assigned the empirical part. The dilemma for the labor economist and econometrician, as in all PD games, is whether to compete or cooperate with each other. The need for cooperation does arise since completing their respective parts of the research will inevitably require some mutual help. Also, some joint effort to insure that the two parts of the research fit together will inevitably be necessary. Since the researchers' future rewards will be based on how well they do on their respective subtasks, competition for relative status could lead to non-cooperation or sabotage. Thus, as Rapoport and Chammah indicate, "the choice in PD . . . [is] between competing and cooperating, between conflict and conflict resolution, between trust and suspicion, between loyalty and betrayal" (1965, 56). Besides this external conflict, there may well be internal conflict if "each is torn between a tendency to cooperate, so as to promote the common interests, and a tendency to compete, so as to enhance his own interests" (Rapoport and Chammah 1965, 9).

Toward a More Realistic Analysis

Shortcomings of the Pure PD Model. While the above is suggestive of the rich variety of outcomes from the PD model, it clearly has important short-comings. First, the PD analysis only allows employees three discrete behavior choices, whereas in reality such decisions are likely to be continuous rather than discrete. This aspect of the PD analysis could be modified by increasing the number of discrete choices as suggested by Leibenstein (1982a, 14). Second, the pure PD analysis assumes that the game can be played repeatedly without changes in employee relationships or options. The pure PD analysis lacks a time dimension: what happens is independent of past actions, understandings or expected future actions of the employees. This seems unrealistic.

A Revised PD Model. The payoff table (figure 6.1) can be used again to indicate why alternatives to the PD solution may prevail when employees consider more than one time period. The table still provides the payoffs for a given period or short run, and there is still a reward for opportunistic behavior. But now suppose that as the game is repeated members of the organization remember past payoffs and can anticipate future ones. In that case, employee A may not opportunisitically opt for the short-run gain at the expense of B (for example, A choosing sabotage, S, whereas B had chosen cooperation, C,), because A may believe that B will remember this and choose S the next period, resulting in the joint sabotage solution. In such a case, the payoff over two (or more) periods would be clearly inferior to that for continuing joint cooperation. If A does succumb to the tempta- tion to choose S or simply noncooperative, NC, behavior, B will surely respond in kind the next period. Therefore, in this model, the persisting solutions are any of the ones on the diagonal (joint C, NC or S), and there is a tendency for cooperative solutions to degenerate to less cooperative solu- tions.[6] As illustrated in figure 6.2, employees may gain by short-run hori- zontal or vertical movements from the starting point, SP, to points D, E, F or G, but the net effect of all such movements over two or more periods will be disadvantageous movements in the southeast direction to points H or J. Thus, the retaliation threat tends to maintain the cooperative outcome.

The following illustrates the two-period model. Until now employees A

Figure 6.2
Prisoner's Dilemma Payoff Table

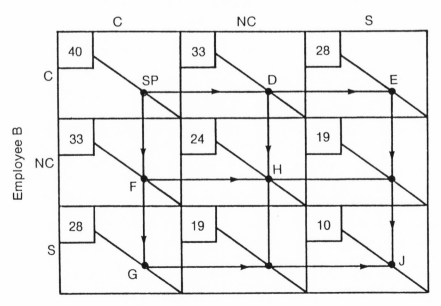

(the labor economist) and B (the econometrician) have been cooperating and sharing the 40 unit payoff. Now A recognizes that he could achieve a short-run gain of five (a payoff of 25) in the current period by sabotaging B (by purposely providing misleading labor economics advice so that B's part of the report will suffer) while continuing to receive help from B. However, before impulsively initiating sabotage, A begins to think about the two-period consequences of such an action. A anticipates that in the second period B, who remembers the first period, will retaliate and sabotage him as well by providing incorrect econometric advice, thus leaving A with a mere five, an equal share of the PD solution payoff. In two periods, A will receive payoffs of 25 and 5, a total of 30, which is clearly inferior to the two-period cooperative payoff of 40 (20 plus 20). Thus, "rational" employees confronting fellow employees who are expected to cooperate initially and remember the first-period result should cooperate, even without any cooperative convictions or values, as long as they take into account more than one period's consequences. If one of the researchers should yield to the short-run temptation to gain through sabotage, the second-period result will undoubtedly be the PD solution. Realizing the inferiority of this result, however, the employees may attempt to improve on that situation and may eventually move back toward cooperation.

The scenario sketched above is roughly consistent with the findings from experiments with the prisoner's dilemma game using student subjects. According to Rapoport and Chammah, "interaction effects [between the two players of the game] . . . are very strong . . . [and] the sessions tend to become either predominantly cooperative or predominantly uncooperative" (1965, 65), suggesting some kind of "tacit collusion." Further analysis by Rapoport and Chammah (1965, 201) indicates that the subjects typically "learn" to adjust their behavior to the realities and choose the cooperative outcome more than the other ones: "first the subjects learn not to trust each other; then they learn to trust each other."[7]

In the revised PD model, the players (or employees) are still very much competitors, even opportunists in the sense that they will not hesitate to gain at the expense of one another by disguising or misrepresenting their intentions.[8] The difference between the pure and revised PD model is that in the revision the players tend to learn that short-run opportunism doesn't pay.

Conventions and the PD Model

Consider another reason why we rarely observe the PD solution. Leibenstein argues that "an alternative way of finding a solution to prisoner's dilemma problems is for an individual to behave in a not necessarily maximizing fashion: that is, to use conventions or convention-like elements such as ethics" (Leibenstein 1982b, 94). Conventions are routines with an interpersonal component which are generally determined and supported by peer group pressures. Generally, people do not evaluate whether to adopt conventions but merely respond to stimuli by behaving in a conventional manner (pp. 92–94). Thus, according to Leibenstein, "latent prisoner's dilemma possibilities are held in abeyance by conventions, institutions, and laws, involving trust, enforcement of contracts, etc." For example, "A convention of honesty in contractual relations eliminates adversarial behavior in which both sides attempt to cheat the other. Similarly, an effective low-cost system of laws which enforces contracts may minimize the inducement to use other types of adversarial behavior" (p. 96). In Leibenstein's view, the conventional outcomes are typically midway between the optimal joint cooperation and the opportunistic PD solution outcomes.

BEYOND THE PD MODEL

Relationships and Realistic Decision Making

While Leibenstein's use of conventions undoubtedly makes the analysis more realistic, there are still significant dimensions of individual behavior in decision making which are lacking. This is because employee/players who either opportunistically maximize or follow conventions are totally programmed, that is, their behavioral responses to environmental stimuli are entirely predictable.[9] Such players are not individual decision makers who communicate subtly, weigh moral dilemmas, identify with occupational and work groups, attempt to improve their relationships with others, consciously work out strategies relating past, present and future, or have complex personal histories. As Abraham Zaleznik (1985) points out, factors such as these make the PD-type games most interesting and life-like, but preclude the possibility of determining a priori the final outcome or the optimal strategy. Utilizing these factors doesn't eliminate the dilemma; however, complex, pre-play communication and agreements are likely to determine the outcome. No doubt, some part of this communication and the resulting agreements will be guided by conventions or by simple opportunism, but a very significant part will be determined by the history of interaction of the two individuals and by their personal histories. In other words, the relationship of any two employees transcends convention and need not be opportunistic.[10]

The Organization and Cooperative Relationships

Further realism can be added when we consider that the organization has a direct stake in maintaining and developing cooperative employee relationships and that the organization can influence the cooperative outcome through its effect on important organizational variables. To avoid the PD problem created by the existence of joint production (or teamwork) activities, there must be a "cooperative contract" (FitzRoy and Mueller 1984, 28, 38). Similarly, Schelling recognizes that the PD problem "calls for some effort at social organization, some way to collectivize the choice or to strike an enforceable bargain or otherwise to restructure incentives so that people will do the opposite of what they naturally would have done" (1978, 225). In my view the essential problem is not how to motivate people to do the opposite of what they "naturally" would have done, but to motivate them to do the opposite of what they would do in an opportunistic relationship. Recall that an opportunistic relationship is not only adversarial but also involves mistrust since opponents will not hesitate to be deceitful in order to gain at the other's expense. If this analysis of the PD problem is applied to a family situation, it makes sense to advocate family therapy to overcome the lack of trust and to develop improved behaviors as Maital and Maital (1983, 12) suggest. Relationships in a firm are different no doubt, but there are similarities as well. As FitzRoy and Mueller (1984, 38) point out, following Williamson (1975, 49–56, 67–72), the essential nature of the firm is that the relationships among organization members are governed by implicit psychological contracts (Tomer 1985). Such contracts are unwritten, nonbinding understandings concerning the mutual treatments of the organization and its members. This suggests that if cooperative behavior is desired, the essence of the organization's task is to manage its implicit psychological contract with employees so that strong, reliable encouragements to cooperative behavior are provided and opportunistic tendencies are attenuated.

Organizational Features Which Promote Cooperation

What motivates cooperation? How does this relate to the implicit psychological contract? Consider a few of the answers suggested either by the organizational behavior literature or by the implications of our earlier analysis of cooperation. First, organizations should promote the acceptance of superordinate organizational goals integrated with societal goals. Organization members who identify with these goals should be motivated to efforts (including cooperation) believed to be instrumental in achieving such goals (Galbraith 1977, chapter 20). Second, if cooperating involves performing tasks to which an individual is closely identified, this behavior should be motivating (chapter 20). Such would be the case if the econometrician in our previous example derives satisfaction from providing good econometric advice. Third, organizations should develop considerate supervisors and encourage collective decision making and employee participation in order to foster strong work-group norms consistent with organization goals (Galbraith 1977, chapter 19). Fourth, organizations should foster employees' latent altruistic tendencies. This might be done by emphasizing service to others and harmonious relationships (Axelrod 1984, 134–135).

Fifth, financial and other extrinsic incentives could be used to reward employees' cooperative behavior, effectively changing their payoffs. Sixth, the organization should seek to remind employees that retaliation in the short or long run is likely to be the consequence of uncooperative efforts. Robert Axelrod's (1984) research leads him to the view that cooperation is much more likely to prevail when people practice reciprocity and penalize each others' uncooperative behavior. These future possible penalties will be much more likely to deter uncooperative behavior if the interactions among individuals (for whom cooperation is important) are made more durable, frequent, and concentrated (Axelrod 1984, 126–132, 136–139). Seventh, organizations should recognize that noncooperative behavior will be accentuated when organizations measure employee contributions narrowly or promote too much competition among employees for organization rewards. Last, since specialized career paths may make communication difficult and inhibit cooperation, organizations should reduce specialization in employee career paths.

Thus, organizations recognizing the value of cooperation may invest in improvements in their implicit psychological contract with workers as well as in certain incentives, thereby leading to more cooperative work relationships. While it is unlikely that bettering these organizational attributes will totally determine interemployee behavior, and thereby overcome negative aspects of personal histories and past employee relationships, such organizational improvements should encourage employees to adopt strategies involving cooperative behavior. A related question is whether it takes some kind of "shock," as Leibenstein (1982b, 92) suggests, to get firms to initiate very significant organizational change.

Amartya Sen's (1977) discussion of "commitment" provides another important insight to the solution of the PD problem. Cooperation seems most likely where the organization and its members make mutual moral commitments, commitments that transcend self-interested analysis of the consequences for each other. According to Sen, one who acts out of commitment is making a choice to adhere to a moral principle even if it has adverse implications for one's material well-being. For example, many Japanese companies commit themselves to retaining their permanent employees even during severe downturns in demand, and it is not unusual for Japanese employees to sacrifice their self-interests for the collective good of the company. It makes sense that employees acting out of common organizational "commitments" would cooperate much more and that these people (and other organizations) would (at least over the long run) be better off despite their lack of classical rational behavior. It is doubtful that such a conclusion could be reached strictly along the lines of utility maximization, but the PD analysis helps us to see its plausibility.

In general, cooperative effort will be encouraged when organizational factors attenuate opportunism, foster trust, encourage open communication, and promote the acceptance of common purposes and values. Of course, organizational leaders may be discouraged from making choices which would encourage cooperative effort if these choices are seen as inconsistent with prevailing ideology or government policies. For a discussion of government policies related to organizational change, see chapter 9.

CONCLUSION

The main point is that although the PD analysis, like much of economic theory, helps us understand some core insights, it is overly abstract and omits certain of the "softer" dimensions of behavior that sociologists, psychologists and psychoanalysts have tended to study. As this analysis indicates, these softer dimensions are critical and must be integrated with economic theory if one wants to understand and encourage cooperation.

Recall the two researchers in our example, the labor economist and the econometrician. The likelihood of joint cooperation between the two, and thus the chances of their completing a high-quality research report without excessive cost, would be greatly improved by organizational activities such as the following:

1. help both researchers identify with the purpose of the research and understand how it will aid policy makers in making decisions about the labor market,

2. insure that both researchers are well-trained in their respective fields and value quality work,

3. insure that the supervisor of this research behaves in a considerate and facilitative manner with respect to the researchers,

4. foster the economists' altruism and desire to contribute to larger purposes,

5. reward the researchers financially for their cooperative behavior, and

6. remind both that the consequences of sabotage (that is, retaliatory behavior) are often severe.

Of course, arranging for these organizational encouragements to cooperation has a cost, but it may be necessary if the desired level of cooperation, and thus, productivity is to be achieved (see Galbraith 1977, 365).

This analysis has implications for the decline of productivity growth in the United States in the 1970s. My speculation is that an important part of the explanation is that cooperation decreased significantly during that time. Cooperative behavior in the United States decreased in my view due to societal shocks (for example, the Vietnam War, the Watergate scandal, and the cultural revolutions of the young, minorities and women) which undermined the dominant philosophies and values guiding the nation's direction. This, in turn, led first to the quasi revolutionary behavior of the late 1960s and the early 1970s, and then to more self-serving, opportunistic behavior.

The latter was manifested in increases in law suits, crime rates, distrust of major institutions and professional groups, and the fragmented pursuit of special interests and entitlements without regard for national interest. These all suggest decreased cooperation in the United States during the 1970s. Decreased cooperation within the firm may have been just a part of a national decrease.

Given the individualistic cultural traditions of the United States, is it possible for U.S. firms to become significantly more cooperative in their orientation? I don't see why not. As Curl's (1980) documentation of many of these experiments attests, the impulse of the collective or cooperative endeavor has been an important part of our national heritage over a long period of U.S. history. True, many of these activities have been regarded as isolated and rebellious. What has been missing in the United States is a broad, pragmatic appreciation of why cooperation is necessary to achieve potential productivity. Perhaps the competitive success of Japanese corporations and, to a lesser extent, the examples of successful cooperatives like Mondragon in Spain will be the shock or incentive which will catalyze a greater appreciation of the role of cooperation. It is to the example of Japanese management that we turn in the next chapter.

7

Working Smarter the Japanese Way: The X-Efficiency of Japanese Management

INTRODUCTION

"The amount of money that they [American automobile industry] are spending doesn't bother me—capital investment alone will not make a difference. . . . When Detroit changes its management system, we'll see more powerful American competitors."
Executive Vice President of Honda as quoted in Grayson (1982)

A number of recent organizational behavior studies (for example, Ouchi 1981, and Pascale and Athos 1981) agree that the important differences between Japanese management and American management explain in large part why, since the 1950s, many Japanese industries have been able to achieve rates of growth in productivity much higher than the United States. These studies suggest that a critical dimension of Japanese management is the employer-employee relationship which motivates organization members to work "smarter" than their counterparts in the United States. In other words, Japanese firms are simply more X-efficient (their productivity is closer to potential) than U.S. firms. Why is this so? The purpose of this article is to adapt economic theory (notably X-efficiency theory and transaction cost economics)[1] to explain why one would expect organizations managed Japanese style to be more effective in achieving labor productivity closer to potential and growth in productivity.[2]

It is very clear that over the last several decades the growth of Japanese productivity has been much higher than that of the United States and significantly higher than even the fastest growing developed economies. For example, during 1960–1981, Japan's growth in labor productivity in the manufacturing sector averaged 9.2 percent compared to 2.6 percent for the United States.[3] For all industries during 1960–1976, the growth in Japan's labor productivity was 7.5 percent compared to 1.7 percent for the United States.[4] A number of empirical studies have focused on the sources of Japanese economic growth in comparison to those of the United States. However, these "aggregate explanations" of economic growth leave much to be desired and are usually vague about the role of management. Edward Denison and William Chung, for example, indicate their belief that "management is a key element in efficiency" (1976, 83), but they are unable to quantify this factor; as a result, changes in managerial performance are reflected largely in their residual, the portion of economic growth unexplained by the measured input changes. Noteworthy is Denison and Chung's (1976, p. 82) observation that Japan has been able not only to adapt new knowledge rapidly but has seemed to catch up to "best practice" whereas the gap between best and typical practice is not closing in other countries.[5] Could the nature of Japanese management be the key ingredient that enables Japanese firms to achieve high knowledge utilization?[6]

To facilitate the analysis, this discussion focuses on the essence of the Japanese management ideal removed from the cultural context of Japan. This ideal is called simply "J management" while American or Western style management is referred to as "A management." The essential characteristics of J management are very similar to what William Ouchi calls Theory Z management[7,8]; they are as follows:

1. Lifetime employment ideal is effective in practice.

2. Strong corporate culture and philosophy (or superordinate goals) provide for implicit control of employees who internalize these values in contrast to A management's emphasis on explicit control mechanisms.[9]

3. Community or family relations characterize relations among employees, and wholistic rather than pure economic relations predominate.

4. Decision making and responsibility taking are collective in nature; the decision-making process emphasizes consensus formation.

5. Careers are characterized by slow evaluation and promotion and by nonspecialization.

The operations of Japanese firms reflect the J management ideal to quite different extents. It is in the largest Japanese firms that these characteristics are most clear-cut and distinctive. Therefore, to put the analysis in the proper perspective, it is important to discuss a number of the key features of the Japanese industrial setting.

Japanese companies tend to be narrowly specialized, engaging in one line of business or a few closely related ones (Clark 1979, 49). Customarily, they are thought of as being arranged in a hierarchy according to well-established criteria. Companies achieve their status in this "society of industry" according to "the business they are in, their size and market share, their affiliations with bigger companies and banks, the level of wages they pay, their methods of recruitment, their customers and suppliers, and their shareholders" (Clark 1979, 95). Shareholding in Japan, unlike many Western countries, is largely an expression of the relationship between institutions holding shares in each other rather than an expression of individual financial interest. Thus, firms are able to subordinate the profit goal to the goals of service to society and of gaining higher status in the society of industry (pp. 95–97, 136–137). Small companies supplying the largest firms are often the ones on the lower rungs of the hierarchy; these suppliers are generally less financially secure, more dependent on and more dominated by their larger brethren. While this company "dualism" in Japan is widely cited, it is not uncommon for small companies to grow and, in the transformation process, take on the characteristics of the higher status group, including higher productivity (pp. 94–95).

The dualism above is very much reflected in inter- and intrafirm differences in employer-employee relations and the workings of the labor market. A "lifetime" of employment in a work community is clearly a widespread ideal, and companies which are substantial enough to make their promises of lifetime employment credible do practice it (Clark 1979, 79, 174–179). The best companies recruit labor from the best universities by offering an attractive "package" of financial and nonfinancial compensation over a lifetime. This keeps turnover low. Thus in Japan, the secondary labor market, relating to movements of labor between firms, is secondary both in the sense of its quantitative importance and in the sense that this labor is utilized more by lower status firms (Clark 1979, chapter 5). The best companies generally have more formal pay and promotion standards, and non-merit factors such as age, seniority and family size are more important criteria in these decisions than for lower ranking firms (pp. 45–46, 112–125). It should be noted that even many of the best companies have substantial groups of workers (such as temporary workers and women) who do not share fully in the financial and intangible benefits of company membership (p. 234). Also notable is the fact that unions in Japanese companies are enterprise unions, not unions organized for an entire industry or nation, and, although they look after employee interests, they are remarkably loyal to their companies (pp. 45–46).

The important question is: Are the Japanese firms which are managed in the J style economically successful in spite of or because of these characteristics? Some observers have maintained that these attributes are leftovers from a feudal past and bound to change as modernization progresses (see, for example, Marsh and Mannari 1976). Others feel they are the key to superior performance. My thesis is that the essential features of J management allow greater X-efficiency than A management.

X-Efficiency and Productivity

To put the following analysis in perspective, it is important to be clear about the relationship between X-efficiency (XE) and productivity. XE theory takes X-inefficiency (or productivity less than potential) to be the usual state of affairs. X-inefficiency implies that costs are above minimum and that changes in the XE factors could lower costs. The XE factors may be external to the firm (for example, the state of competition), or internal to the organization. The latter reflects the firm's investment in organizational capital (Tomer 1981a), namely, the extent to which it has made explicit efforts to achieve lasting improvements in its organization.

The labor productivity of a firm at one point in time can be considered to be a function of 1) its tangible capital, 2) its "hard" (nonmanagerial) technology, 3) the attributes of its laborers (human capital), and 4) its XE factors. The XE factors are also a chief determinant of productivity growth over time. X-inefficiency, in a dynamic context, means less innovation than possible. Less innovation, in turn, means less improvement in both the XE and non-X-efficiency (capital, technology, labor) factors than possible. The analysis below seeks to show how particular XE factors which are internal to the organization and associated with J management permit labor productivity that is either closer to potential or faster growing than A management does.

Plan of Chapter

This chapter has two main sections. The section which follows begins by extending the notion of implicit contract (a nonbinding understanding between employer and employee) to one of implicit psychological contract. Firms may be placed along a spectrum of implicit psychological contracts according to the nature of their management; J-managed firms are found on the far right of the spectrum. Perspectives from Oliver Williamson's transaction cost economics, especially the concepts of opportunism and bounded rationality, are useful in explaining why organizations located on the right of the spectrum should have lower costs.

The point of departure for the concluding section is Harvey Leibenstein's X-efficiency analysis. His effort determination analysis is modified and extended to compare J and A organizations with respect to worker motivation. The central question is: why is it rational for J workers to exert higher effort than their counterparts in A organizations?

IMPLICIT PSYCHOLOGICAL CONTRACTS, TRANSACTION COSTS, AND COOPERATION

The Implicit Psychological Contract

The essence of the relationship between the employee and his organization is described by the implicit psychological contract (IPC) which evolves between them. The IPC concept, on the one hand, is an extension of the notion of employer-employee implicit contracts developed by Arthur Okun (for example, 1981) and others. Such implicit contracts involve non-binding understandings relating to compensation, work conditions and the nature of work to be done. While more flexible than explicit contracts, implicit contracts have the power to command at least a minimum acceptable level of fulfillment; otherwise one of the parties to the contract will be considered to be in default and the continued existence of the relationship will be questioned by the other (dissatisfied) party. In the usage of both Okun and Leibenstein (for example, Leibenstein 1976, 146), implicit contracts relate largely to tangible economic concerns such as wages, hours, work breaks, job safety and other conditions. The IPC, on the other hand, is much the same as Chris Argyris's (1960) "psychological work contract," Harry Levinson's "psychological or unwritten contract" or John Gabarro's (1979) "interpersonal contract" (see also Thomas 1978). That is, the IPC "relates to a set of mutual expectations concerning performance, roles, trust and influence," and it specifies "what each should contribute to a relationship and what each should get out of it" (Gabarro 1979, 10).

It is useful to think of a spectrum of implicit psychological contracts (see figure 7.1). On the far left of the spectrum, the relationship between employer and employee is limited and of short-term duration; therefore the implicit contract is negligible since the critical elements of the relationship are considered by the explicit contract specifying the worker's contribution and compensation. In the middle of the spectrum are the intermediate or indefinite-term relationships, where, according to Okun, the "invisible handshake" (1981, 84–85), involves rules and conventions for fair play that curb distrust. On the spectrum's far right, the relationship is for a lifetime of work. In return for an implicit guarantee of lifetime security and community, the organization demands an almost total commitment from the employee—not only a technical or professional contribution but an emotional and even spiritual one.

Another important variable defining the IPC spectrum is the nature of the principal-agent relationship. On the left side of the spectrum, it is very clear that the employee is an agent of the organization's principals; the employee is expected to try and achieve what the principals decide is consistent with their goals. Moving rightward past the middle of the spectrum, the principal-agent aspect of the relationship begins to fade until, on the far right,

Figure 7.1
Implicit Psychological Contract Spectrum

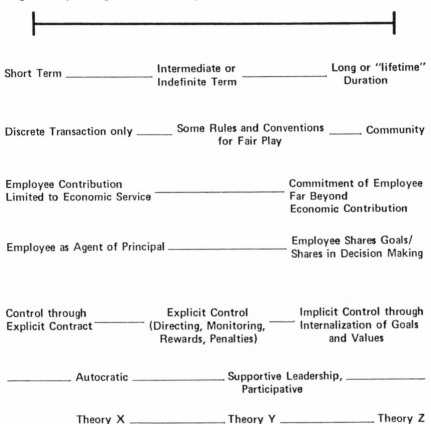

Short Term _____ Intermediate or _____ Long or "lifetime"
                          Indefinite Term   Duration

Discrete Transaction only _____ Some Rules and Conventions _____ Community
                                  for Fair Play

Employee Contribution _____ Commitment of Employee
Limited to Economic Service   Far Beyond
                                            Economic Contribution

Employee as Agent of Principal _____ Employee Shares Goals/
                                               Shares in Decision Making

Control through _____ Explicit Control _____ Implicit Control through
Explicit Contract   (Directing, Monitoring, Internalization of Goals
                        Rewards, Penalties)   and Values

_____ Autocratic _____ Supportive Leadership, _____
                                         Participative

Theory X _____ Theory Y _____ Theory Z

the employee can no longer be considered an agent of the organization; at this point, he or she is part of the community, shares its goals, and participates in its decision making.[10]

The predominate method of organizational control is another variable defining the IPC spectrum. On the far left, the explicit contract provides all or most of the control. Explicit control, which involves directing, monitoring and rewarding or penalizing behavior, begins on the left side and fades a little to the right of center. On the right, where employees share the organization's superordinate goals and values, control by the implicit mechanism of shared goals predominates. The movement from the left end of the explicit control range to the far right can be characterized as moving from Theory X (autocratic) through Theory Y (supportive leadership, participation) to Theory Z (see Maslow 1971, 274–277). Typically, A management is near the center.[11]

Why is lifetime employment, perhaps, the key ingredient in J management? My analysis suggests that when a firm decides to offer lifetime employment, it has a great incentive to develop an IPC which includes most of the other characteristics associated with the spectrum's extreme right. After all, how can an employee or an employer make a narrow economic-legal contract with a lifetime duration? The firm, for example, would be unable to predict a lifetime's worth of demand for particular products, much less demand for particular labor skills. A worker, on the other hand, will not generally be able to predict the evolution of his work preferences and abilities far in advance. Thus, when lifetime employment is involved, the understanding must be in the form of broad, enduring principles which guide and inspire the relationship. Not surprisingly, these lifetime relationships are generally characterized by trust and flexibility.

The IPC Hypothesis

My hypothesis is that companies whose IPCs are more rightward on the spectrum will be able to achieve lower costs than other companies, other things being equal.[12] As Oliver Williamson's transaction cost economics suggests, two key reasons are opportunism and bounded rationality. Opportunism is not simply self-interest seeking, but self-interest seeking with guile. An example occurs when a party engaged in bargaining makes false and misleading statements in order to gain at the expense of others (Williamson 1979, 234, 241–242). Bounded rationality refers to the distinct limits of human mental ability when it comes to performing complex calculations or planning for an uncertain future.

To appreciate how opportunism and bounded rationality are related to the IPC hypothesis, it is necessary to consider the essence of the transaction cost economics perspective. In the views of Williamson and of Ronald Coase (1937), it only makes sense to organize an extra transaction or activity within the firm when the costs associated with carrying out the transaction through market exchange or organizing in another firm are equal or higher. The market alternative will be higher cost than internal organization (or hierarchy) when the costs of making mutually satisfactory explicit contracts (or transaction costs) are relatively high. The latter are likely to stem from the need to consider many complex contingencies and the necessity to renegotiate contracts due to unanticipated events. The more one suspects the other part of opportunism, the more one is likely to devote additional resources to contract making. This is especially true when uncertain future events create the opportunity for one party to gain at the expense of the other. In Williamson's view, hierarchy will be utilized to the extent that the internal relationships (or implicit contracts) among parties in the firm act to attenuate opportunism (substituting a greater element of trust) and make relationships flexible enough so that complete anticipation of complex contingencies and periodic renegotiation are not necessary. Williamson has utilized this perspective in studying product markets; in what follows I have utilized certain of its features in analyzing labor markets, and more specifically, the relationship between employer and employee.

One reason why firms with rightward IPCs are hypothesized to have lower costs is that they are likely to experience lower labor market transaction costs, that is, the costs associated with contracting for labor. This is because rightward IPCs (characterized by shared values, community and trust) act to attenuate opportunism. As a result, there is less need for contracts protecting against the distrusted party, for contractual provisions dealing with complex anticipated contingencies,[13] and for renegotiation arising from unanticipated events. Moreover, the long-term mutual commitments involved in rightward IPCs mean fewer resources are required for firing, hiring and training employees with the termination or start of individual labor contracts. Since less resources are required for these activities, labor market transaction costs will be lower. It should be noted, however, that the organizational change required to develop more rightward IPCs may require significant resources. These and other types of organizational changes have frequently been the occasion for large expenditures on management consulting services. Those expenditures along with the output incurred when the firm's employees direct their efforts to organizational change (the opportunity costs) comprise the total organizational investment cost. (See Tomer, 1981a for an empirical analysis.) Like any investment it will be justified if the decrease in future costs is large enough relative to the magnitude of this investment in organizational capital considering the risks involved.

The implicit psychological contract concept may also be applied to the relationships among employees in a firm as Levinson et al. (1963, 37) have done. Here the IPC refers to the mutual expectations among individual employees and among groups of employees, that is, to the psychological quality of these relationships. We would expect that these IPCs would be influenced or conditioned by the IPC between employer and employees; nevertheless, employees do exercise significant discretion with respect to the relationships they develop with others in the organization. Again, it is useful to think of a spectrum of these IPCs. On the right side, the IPCs are characterized by interdependence, communication and cooperation. On the left, the employee's formal relation to the firm (his specialization, the technology used, and explicit contract) dominates his work relationship with others. Thus, there is a relative lack of interaction, communication and cooperation with others on work-related matters and relatively more independence. Clearly J firms are to the right of A firms on this spectrum, although how much further may be a matter for debate.

This brings us to the second reason why firms with rightward IPCs are likely to experience lower costs. Rightward IPCs (employer-employee) provide a more favorable environment for rightward IPCs among employees, and the latter involves more cooperation and higher productivity (lower costs of noncooperation). This was analyzed in chapter 6.

THE DETERMINANTS OF EFFORT

The superiority of J management lies not only in its reduction of labor market transaction costs and noncooperation costs relative to A management. This section argues that Z management is also associated with higher worker motivation. The starting point is Harvey Leibenstein's X-efficiency analysis which focuses on the directed work effort choices of workers. Increased worker effort may mean working with higher quality output or better coordination, or even working more innovatively, responsibly and cooperatively. The effort level chosen, according to Leibenstein (1976), reflects a compromise between personal desires and the demands of the organization. Increased pressure involving a variety of organizational rewards and punishments generally leads the worker to select a higher effort level.[14] From this standpoint, there is little reason to believe that workers in J organizations will be more X-efficient and choose higher effort than their counterparts in A organizations. Applying XE theory straightforwardly leads, if anything, to the conclusion that A organizations will be more X-efficient than J organizations since the former will generally make more explicit demands on workers. One should bear in mind, however, that XE theory was originally developed for application to A organizations, where a clear principal-agent distinction between employer and employees is involved. To properly compare J and A companies, XE theory requires some modification.

First, consider the essential features of Leibenstein's utility-effort relation. An employee's current utility from work effort, U, is a function of the effort level chosen, E, the demands of the organization, DO, and the individual's personality, P. The relationship between U and E for a worker can be depicted graphically as curve U^1 in figure 7.2 below. This worker will choose effort level, E_1^*, in order to achieve maximum utility, U_1^*.

If the organization makes increased demands on the worker, the UE relation or curve shifts to U^2 (rightward and possibly upward). Now the optimal effort point is E_2^* as the worker accommodates to increased demands and raises his satisfaction level above what it would have been at E_1^*.

The analysis of Alchian and Demsetz (1972) is parallel in a number of ways to that of Leibenstein. They argue that the "contractual structure" of the classical capitalist firm makes it more efficient in production than decentralized contractual relations (or markets) when team production yields an output higher than could laborers working separately. The key problem

Figure 7.2
The Utility versus Effort Relationship

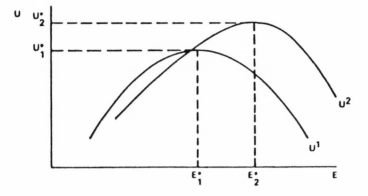

in team production is that it is next to impossible to measure each laborer's marginal product and reward each accordingly. Thus, it is necessary to monitor the behavior of each laborer to find clues regarding their productivity. Monitoring, however, is not a costless activity, and workers will generally find that an organization's incentives lead them to shirk (and substitute on-the-job leisure for work effort) more than society considers optimal. The contractual structure of the classical capitalist firm is much the same as the concept of A management. Thus, when the capitalist-managers (in the manner of Alchian and Demsetz) step up their monitoring to lower shirking in response to a decline in their residual claim on the firm's income, this is essentially the same as when Leibenstein's principals put more pressure (increased organizational demands) on worker-agents and, thus, expect greater effort. Alchian and Demsetz have not applied their analysis to J style organizational relations, and it does not follow logically that J management would lower shirking, i.e., raise effort, motivate workers, etc.

In chapter 5, we considered a useful modification of Leibenstein's UE relationship in which a work environment (WE) variable (including dimensions such as the nature of the implicit contract between employees and the company) is an important addition. With this revision, U is a function of E, P, DO and WE. Improvements in the work environment (for example, allowing more worker autonomy, improved training and personal growth opportunities and more recognition of worker efforts) are expected to shift the UE curve rightward resulting in higher effort choice; prolonged pressure, on the other hand, may have a destructive effect on the work environment and lead to lower effort (Likert 1961, 71). Insofar as J organizations have work environments reflecting more rightward IPCs than those of A organizations, and insofar as J managers are facilitators less likely to use "pressure" tactics, this revised XE theory suggests why higher effort will be chosen and why higher worker motivation is likely in J companies. However, further progress seems possible.

Suppose workers' effort choices depend on the flow of current and future utility expected from current work effort, that is, $U_t(E_0)$ for t = 0,1,...,m, where E_0 is current period effort.[15] Future utility expectations of workers are based on past and present organizational experience as well as subjective considerations. Let us assume that workers weight or discount the stream of $U_t(E_0)$, i.e., they base their E choice on the present value of $U_t(E_0)$, $U'(E_0)$, which we denote as U'. Thus,

$$U' = \sum_{t=0}^{m} \frac{U_t(E_0)}{(1 + k)^t}. \tag{7.1}$$

k is the appropriate rate of discount and m is the worker's utility time horizon which is assumed to be closely correlated with the worker's expected tenure in the organization.[16] I do not maintain that workers actually do the quantitative calculation suggested by equation 7.1, but it is my belief that they take into account expected future satisfactions such as promotion, pay increases and pride in accomplishment, and that U is weighted less further in the future. In other words, workers seem to act as though they make the calculation.[17]

Assuming workers' desire to maximize U', workers' E decisions will be similar to corporate investment decisions. Suppose workers' decisions are focused on discrete increments of E, say ΔE equal to one. Workers would be expected to accept ΔE when $\Delta U'$ (the resulting change in U') is positive, much like they might accept an investment if the net present value were positive.

$$\Delta U' = \sum_{t=0}^{m} \frac{\Delta U_t}{(1 + k)^t} \qquad \text{for } \Delta E = 1. \tag{7.2}$$

While this may seem farfetched, it nevertheless provides a useful framework for understanding the superiority of J management.

The essence of the argument is that J workers, as compared to A workers, have reason to expect higher increments in current and future utility from extra current effort, are likely to discount future utility at a lower rate, and are likely to direct more of their efforts toward organization goals. In other words, workers in J organizations are believed to find that the extra satisfactions afforded by working more responsibly, cooperatively and innovatively, with more attention to quality and organizational goals, etc., substantial and certain enough to motivate them to adopt higher effort positions.

The main reasons for expecting higher effort outcomes in J organizations are outlined below. First, $\Delta U'$ is more likely to be positive for J organizations when considering a given ΔE because the J time horizon (m_J) is generally longer than A's (m_A) owing to lifetime employment. That is, for given ΔE

$$\Delta U'_J = \sum_{t=0}^{m_J} \frac{\Delta U_t}{(1 + k)^t} > \sum_{t=0}^{m_A} \frac{\Delta U_t}{(1 + k)^t} = \Delta U'_A \qquad (7.3)$$

since $m_J > m_A$, assuming for the moment no differences in ΔU_t or k between J and A organizations.

Higher increments in current and future utility from extra effort (ΔU_t) in J organizations might be expected for the following reasons: First, the wholistic orientation of the J work environment allows workers, by virtue of their efforts, to satisfy their higher needs, (especially self-actualization) and experience high self-esteem. Second, the superordinate goals of J companies may enable worker efforts to be more satisfying as a result of the inspiration and meaning the goals provide. Third, if (as expected) relationships among workers in J organizations are based more on trust, workers can expect more future satisfaction from current cooperative efforts as other workers reciprocate their efforts.

J workers might use a lower discount rate because they associate lower personal risk with their efforts, i.e., they perceive the distribution of expected future utility outcomes to be narrower. There are two reasons for this. One is the existence of a definite and lasting corporate philosophy; this provides insurance that future work accomplishments deriving from current and future efforts will not suffer an unexpected decline in value from the organization's standpoint. Second, "automatic" pay increases and advancement, especially in the early work years, insure that in the event of failure resulting from one's efforts, the personal consequences will not be catastrophic. Third, performance evaluations emphasize the long-term and make effective use of nonquantifiable information. Thus, to the extent that rewards follow performance, there will be a more certain connection between performance and reward over the long-term, largely eliminating one of the factors that may contribute to the spread of future utility outcomes.

There are two other possible reasons for a lower discount rate in J organizations. The first is that J workers may have a lower rate of utility time preference due to their superior capacity to delay gratification. The evidence from the psychological studies summarized by Maital and Maital (1977, 188–193) is quite suggestive here. From these studies, it is clear that lack of trust and social maladjustment are positively related to an individual's rate of time preference. To the extent that organizational relationships in J companies are relatively more conducive to the development of trust and positive social adjustment, this should lead to lower rates of time preference among J workers.[18,19]

The other argument for a lower k is that J workers may be less averse to risks due to the greater prevalence of group decision making in J organizations. This phenomenon is known as the risky shift; it "states that groups influence individual decision making toward positions of higher risk a significantly greater number of times than not, and under almost any conditions" (Byrd 1974, 46). When individuals working in groups are willing to accept decisions involving higher risk for their organizations, and presumably for themselves, without greater expected rewards, this implies lower risk aversion, and thus a lower discount rate.

Why do workers in J organizations have an incentive to direct more of their efforts toward organizational goals? For one thing, workers with lifetime employment do not need to devote their energies to "resume and professional credential maintaining" activities. Second, both automatic and collective aspects of compensation serve to inhibit the most harmful aspects of competition between workers, and thus, reduce the energy devoted to competitive activity not in the organization's best interest. Third, the facilitative management style in combination with the superordinate goals may encourage workers to envision themselves making larger contributions to the organization than they could if specific work goals were defined by managers.

Are there reasons to believe that J organizations will reduce the costs of shirking by reducing both the amount that occurs and the costs of monitoring it? The analyses above that explain why J workers will exert more effort than A workers are also arguments (though not cast in the Alchian and Demsetz (1972) framework) explaining why J workers may shirk less. Robert Crawford (1983) considers the question of shirking cost explicitly, and others have developed related insights. First, Alchian and Demsetz (1972, 790–791) have pointed out, almost as an aside, that "if one could enhance a common interest in nonshirking in the guise of team loyalty or team spirit, the team would be more efficient." The development of team spirit and loyalty through "cultural socialization" is, thus, one way that Japanese companies have attempted to keep shirking to a minimum (Crawford 1983, 10). Second, the common practice in Japanese companies of paying large bonuses "proportional to the productivity of the whole team" provides the worker an incentive to behave as a cooperative team member, discouraging shirking within the team (p. 7). Cable and FitzRoy (1980a, 104) add that participation in managerial functions makes workers more aware of the reliable connection between their efforts (nonshirking) and their profit share (or bonus).

Costs of monitoring are also likely to be lower in J organizations. First, these costs will be low to the extent that employers refrain from opportunistic actions and foster mutual trust, which discourages employee deception related to job performance outcomes (Crawford 1983, 9). Such distortion of "information flows to obtain personal benefit is a pervasive phenomenon . . . [causing] increased costs of monitoring" (Cable and FitzRoy 1980a, 102). Second, slow evaluation processes in the context of lifetime employment also discourage deception since successful deception is unlikely over long periods (Crawford 1983, 9). Third, the open space of the typical Japanese office where everyone can notice everyone else contributes to low monitoring costs, especially for monitoring by peers (p. 9). Finally, peer monitoring is more likely to occur in the presence of team loyalty and bonuses of a profit sharing nature (Cable and FitzRoy 1980a, 103; Crawford 1983, 7).[20]

In addition to higher motivation, one might expect improved membership behavior such as lower absenteeism and turnover in J organizations. Assume for the moment that the nature of a J firm's IPC makes it possible for workers to experience greater current and future utility at given levels of current effort than A workers, but does not provide additional U' with extra effort. This is the situation depicted in figure 7.3; E^* is the same for the J and the A organization even though $U'_J{}^*$ exceeds $U'_A{}^*$. Since the E^* level is the same for both, J management has no motivation/effort advantage, but the J worker will receive relatively larger satisfactions by going to work each day and staying with the company rather than by engaging in nonwork activities or moving to another company.[21] According to this argument, the J worker with a good excuse for missing work is less likely to use it. Since absenteeism and turnover impose real costs on corporations, improved membership behavior may represent a significant productivity improvement. My view is that the satisfactions from working in a J organization lead to higher worker effort and improved membership behavior, that is, curve U'_J is above and to the right of U'_A.

There is also reason to believe that organizational inertia will be lower in J organizations, or more generally, lower for organizations further to the

Figure 7.3
The Present Value of Utility versus Effort Relationship

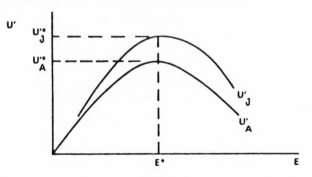

right on the IPC spectrum. The idea of inert areas refers to situations where individuals or groups could reach higher utility levels by adjusting their effort levels but are not motivated to do so (Leibenstein 1976, 111–114). Thus, individuals in inert areas are within a range where they are insensitive to external changes that would affect their utility. Leibenstein offers a variety of reasons for inert areas including fears of newness, disappointment, disapproval and conflict with others. Inert areas are important and, according to Leibenstein, seemingly inevitable. My view is that inert areas are not inevitable but instead are to a great extent a product of worker psychological and economic insecurity. Therefore, when a company succeeds in reducing worker insecurity (such as would be expected when IPCs move rightward) organizational inertia should be reduced. Reduction in inert areas implies that worker responsiveness to the organization's demands will be increased. Thus, we would expect J workers to be quicker to adjust the quantity and quality of their effort to changing organizational requirements, thereby increasing organizational effectiveness.

CONCLUSION

Japan's superior productivity growth over the last two to three decades is beyond question. How much of this growth derives from superior management? Indeed, what is it about Japanese management that is superior and how does this translate into higher productivity? My analysis, which builds on the analytical frameworks of Oliver Williamson and Harvey Leibenstein, has attempted to supply a number of important arguments directed toward these questions. In particular, J management, the essence of the Japanese management ideal, reduces labor market transaction costs, reduces the costs of noncooperation, increases worker effort, improves membership behavior and reduces inert areas more than typical U.S. management.

These benefits of J management derive from the nature of employer-employee relationships; in particular, J relations are characterized by high cohesiveness. On the one hand, the J organizational incentives are more effective than the A organizational incentives at leading self-interested employees to adopt behavior which is generally more favorable to the long-term best interests of their organizations. On the other hand, participants in J organizations share much in the way of common purposes and, ultimately, morality. In this way they keep self-interest seeking in check in such a way that disintegrative conflict and other dysfunctional organizational behavior is discouraged (see Macneil 1980, especially 95–97).

Of course, further study remains to be done. For example, one direction for future research would be to explore the extent to which J management provides incentives for rational decision making and conflict resolution. Another direction would involve empirical analysis of the hypotheses in this book. Edgar Schein (1981) has raised some important questions regarding the transferability of the Japanese management style to U.S. businesses, asking whether the basic cultural premises in the United States may be too different from their Japanese counterparts for the successful utilization of J management and what kinds of organization stand to benefit most from this Japanese style. Jay Barney (1985) has suggested that J management may only be efficient for a certain class of transactions between organizations and their workers where employees have made highly transaction-specific investments, and may not be efficient where employees skills are more general and could be used equally well in other firms or types of transactions. Clearly, these issues deserve further investigation.

Barney (1985) has also noted the strategic implications of the thesis developed here. He points out that while corporate strategies require the acquisition of resources, the high prices of these resources in competitive markets practically eliminate the possibility for firms to use them to earn supernormal returns. A more feasible strategy for achieving supernormal returns which may be open to firms is for firms to better exploit the resources already under their control. Thus, a corporate strategy founded on developing J management may very well be a more reliable path to supernormal returns than strategies based on developing market imperfections or an optimal portfolio of assets. Paradoxically, the emphasis of J management is on people, not on profit.

It is important to note that the characteristics of J-style implicit psychological contracts result not only in high X-efficiency but also create humane work places. If, as it appears, J employees have a greater opportunity for self-actualization and realization of their full potential, one can say that J firms are more α-efficient (McNally 1981, 148) than A firms, and perhaps suggest that an economy dominated by J organizations would be more α-efficient. From the standpoint of psychological health alone, it seems that society would be better off having more J firms or encouraging organizational investment in moving IPCs rightward.[22]

Will J management become important to the U.S.? Due to recent publicity regarding the virtues of Japanese management and due to increased competition from many of those same Japanese companies, many U.S. firms are learning more about Japanese management and adopting its features. My impression of these changes thus far is that most of this imitation relates to particular features or techniques, for example, quality circles, and not to the whole of J management.[23] In other words, the organizational changes involved represent only small movements along the IPC spectrum. It will be interesting to see whether bigger moves will occur.[24] Another noteworthy trend is that more and more Japanese firms are setting up shop in the United States, and are apparently having considerable success with a version of Japanese management adapted to U.S. realities.[25] Finally, "excellent" U.S. companies generally have at least some of the J management characteristics, especially the implicit control through a strong corporate culture.[26]

8

Worker Participation: Paths to Higher Productivity and Well-being

INTRODUCTION

Around the world, many different paths to increased worker participation are being trod. Not only do enterprises differ in the specific organizational changes they make, but their organizational ideals and models differ. These differences are reflected in a variety of studies related to worker participation. Despite these differences, everyone seems to agree on the main reasons for introducing greater worker participation: increased productivity and increased worker well-being. Disagreements arise when we begin to think about how increased worker participation is induced by changes in particular organizational features and why these should improve productivity and well-being. The purpose of this chapter is to develop a theoretical framework for examining the relative merits of these different approaches to worker participation. This involves developing a synthesis of several overlapping literatures. On the one hand there are the economic literatures on worker participation and self-management, X-efficiency, and property rights. On the other hand, there is a wide-ranging literature on organizational behavior which discusses industrial human relations, notably industrial democracy. A key concept utilized to integrate these literatures is that of organizational capital. The view here is that firms making organizational changes to increase worker participation are investing a kind of intangible human capital, i.e., organizational capital, thus enabling future benefits in the form of higher productivity and worker well-being. In this way the process of increasing worker participation is inherent in the process of economic growth.

THE MEANING OF WORKER PARTICIPATION

According to the dictionary, "participate" means to take part or to join or share with others. Here, we are interested in the broadest possible sense of worker participation in an enterprise. Full worker participation thus occurs when a worker is able to experience his full potential at work. To be more specific, five general aspects of worker participation are identified: 1) influence over what goes on at the workplace, 2) influence with respect to major decisions, 3) feeling part of the organization, 4) the ability to make a real contribution through exercising discretion and taking responsibility, and 5) the experience of cooperative work relationships. It should be noted that the term "worker participation" is more commonly used in a more narrow sense to denote worker participation in roles usually reserved for management. The first two elements of worker participation are strongly linked to this definition insofar as workers participate explicitly in the decision-making roles of management, but worker influence can also occur in indirect ways. The third aspect relates to worker identification with the organization and what it stands for. Participation in the sense of the fourth aspect exists when workers feel they can make a significant contribution, and not merely follow prespecified directions. The fifth relates to mutually helpful and committed relationships among peers as well as among workers and their superiors; it implies a lack of opportunistic behavior as workers decline to get ahead at each others' expense. This definition of worker participation does not directly imply any particular organizational feature. The relationship between participation and a variety of organizational features is considered below.

ORGANIZATIONAL FORMS ASSOCIATED WITH WORKER PARTICIPATION

There is no unique way to classify the different organizational forms associated with worker participation. Fusfeld's (1983, 772–774) spectrum of four institutional forms emphasizes the social division of labor among workers, manager and owners. First is "the pure capitalistic firm [in which] authority is exercised exclusively by the owners. The second institutional form is the capitalistic firm in a system of collective bargaining" where workers periodically attempt to reach agreements with managers or owners to resolve certain of their conflicts (pp. 772–773). The third form, the participatory firm, involves a shift in the structure of power to workers as workers take over some of the managerial functions at the workplace level and take on a number of functions of owner or management at the peak of the organization. Organizational changes consistent with the former include "quality circles," job enrichment and other quality of work life programs; those consistent with the latter include employee stock ownership plans and worker representation on boards of directors such as "codetermination." The fourth institutional form is the labor-managed or self-managed firm. In it the ownership of assets is separated from the management function; laborers exercise managerial control at all levels and have the right to the firm's economic profit.

G. David Garson's (1977, 1–24) four models of self management cover much of the same ground as Fusfeld's classification except that he emphasizes the identities of the parties controlling the organization and the control mechanism, which may be control through a market mechanism or through the right to vote for members of the board of directors. In addition to workers, managers and owners, Garson considers consumer control through markets and governmental control through regulation. In his interest-group model he considers the possibility of organizational control by external interest groups, perhaps through representation on boards of directors.

Jaroslav Vanek's (1975, 13–16) classification of organizational forms is the most comprehensive. His first order distinction concerns control; firms are self-managed if they are dominated by members who work in the organization and capital controlled (or dehumanized) if they are dominated by those who own capital. Vanek describes different types of self-managed firms according to the ownership of capital. For example, two of his categories are labor management[1] and producer cooperatives in which the worker members own the capital collectively or individually.[2] Capital-controlled enterprises may have any of eight different types of ownership, including "cooperative" forms such as ownership by consumers and suppliers. They are "participatory" if workers are allowed to participate in some management or ownership functions. Based on both economic efficiency and human considerations, Vanek strongly advocates the labor-managed form as the ideal. In it "all control, management and income [economic profit] . . . should always remain in the hands of those who work in a given enterprise" (Vanek 1975, 34). Also, the owners of capital who finance the firm, whether they are members of or external to the firm, are entitled to an adequate rate of return reflecting the scarcity of capital (p. 34).[3]

David Ellerman (1984) classifies firms according to their legal structure. He focuses on three rights: voting rights, the right to the firm's economic profit, and the right to the firm's net book value. He also considers who exercises these rights and whether they are personal (nontransferable) rights or property rights. In the conventional capitalist firm all these rights are property rights and are owned by the shareholders. In a producer or worker cooperative (such as Mondragon), voting and economic profit rights are the personal rights of worker-owners whereas the net book value rights are considered property rights with restricted transferability. In Ellerman's view, the legal structure of the worker cooperative is superior not only to the capitalist corporation but to employee-owned corporations, traditional worker cooperatives and Yugoslav-type self-managed firms as well.

The spectrum of organizational forms utilized by Michael Jensen and William Mechling (1979, 491–492) is based on "the degree to which the residual claims on the firm can be capitalized and sold by the claimants." In their view, the private or capitalist firm ranks highest on this spectrum of property rights and accordingly is more efficient than the professional partnership, the cooperative firm, the pure-rental firm, the Yugoslav firm or the Soviet firm.

The common element running through the above classification is that the organization's form (that is, the formal division of labor, the dominant pattern of influence, the legal structure, or the property rights in ownership) is the key to attaining the desired participation.

IDEAL ORGANIZATIONAL BEHAVIOR

In contrast to the above view is the idea that changing the organization's culture will increase desired types of worker participation. This view, associated with the practice of organization development (OD), derives primarily from the theories and concepts of behavioral theorists such as Douglass McGregor, Frederick Herzberg, Chris Argyris, Rensis Likert, Robert Blake with Jane S. Mouton, and Abraham Maslow (Lee 1976, 257). To facilitate this exposition, the focus here will be on Blake and Mouton's approach, which is known as Grid OD and which epitomizes OD by integrating the insights of most of the behavioral theorists.

The basis for Grid OD is the theory that business excellence is unlikely to be achieved through sound corporate logic and valid business techniques so long as "conflict is not faced, . . . creativity is stifled, or where dedication and commitment are low, and under circumstances where people do not have a sound approach to critique and learning. The critical ingredient—motivated people—is missing" (Blake and Mouton 1969, 75). Accordingly, Blake and Mouton advocate systematically changing the thinking and behavior of organization managers so that management will be characterized by high concern for production (getting results) and high concern for people. This is termed the 9,9 leadership style. The 9,9 style "is a goal-centered, team approach that seeks to gain optimum results through participation, involvement, commitment, and conflict solving of everyone who can contribute" (Blake and Mouton 1985, 13). The 9,9 management orientation is based on principles (1985, 100–103) which include the following:

1. High motivation follows when workers gain personal satisfaction from making significant contributions to organizations to which they are committed.

2. Organization members can make maximum contributions only when free and open communication occurs and when information pertinent to their interests and responsibilities is available.

3. Conflicts can be resolved through cooperative effort using a problem-solving approach in which mutual trust and respect are preserved.

4. Maximum contribution depends on initiative and is only possible through widespread delegation of power and authority.

5. Shared participation in problem solving and decision making stimulates active involvement in productivity and creative thinking.

In Blake and Mouton's (1969, 88–91) view, it is not participation per se that leads to high motivation and commitment; only participation of a 9,9 character will do. If participation is contrived or doesn't make sense, it will not help; in some situations, vicarious or mental participation may be all that is needed. Participation by members in a 9,9 organization culture, the objective of Grid OD, works because it involves managing people's emotions in such a way as to foster logical thinking, it creates a climate of approval essential for drawing forth creativity, and it encourages members to accept broad organization objectives, which foster not only commitment and identification, but somewhat paradoxically, creativity and innovation (1969, chapter 6). In sum,

the manager's job is to perfect a team culture that 1) promotes and sustains efficient performance of highest quality and quantity, 2) fosters and utilizes creativity, 3) stimulates enthusiasm for effort, experimentation, innovation and change, 4) takes learning advantage from problem-solving situations, and 5) looks for and finds new approaches. (1985, ix).

TOWARD AN INTEGRATION

Perhaps the contrast between the two worker participation approaches has been drawn too sharply. Nevertheless, there is a great deal of difference between the two, as one emphasizes organizational form and the other ideal organizational behavior. Will the desired participative behavior follow when appropriate organizational forms are introduced, or are the institutional forms secondary to the psychological quality of people interactions? Two authors have recently taken an integrated approach to worker participation, giving cultural and structural factors a more or less equal emphasis.

For example, Paul Bernstein (1980) has identified six organizational components which must be present to avoid the decay of workplace democratization. The components are:

1. Participation in decision making, whether direct or by elected representation.

2. Frequent feedback of economic results to all employees (in the form of money, not just information).

3. Full sharing with employees of management-level information and, to an increasing extent, management-level expertise.

4. Guaranteed individual rights (corresponding, it turns out, to the basic political liberties).

5. An independent board of appeals in case of disputes.

6. A particular set of attitudes and values (participatory or democratic consciousness). (p. 9)

While some of Bernstein's components, notably the first, second and fifth, emphasize organizational form, the sixth component, and to a lesser extent the third, emphasize ideal organizational behavior. The final component is concerned with managerial effectiveness style, the quality of human relations (especially informal relationships, the work environment, cooperation, humanization, self-expression and self-realization), and the sense of community and internalization of its norms (Bernstein 1980, chapter 9). Thus, Bernstein explicitly links the sixth component to the views of Argyris, Maslow, and McGregor, among others. For each of the six components, Bernstein indicates how a particular organization would be rated. An organization with the highest possible rating on all six components would be "fully democratized" (p. 29). Ratings above a certain threshold level would be required for an organization to classify as having a democratized workplace. It should also be noted that Bernstein (pp. 118–119) considers equalization of worker status and pay differentials to be important organizational attributes.

Richard Walton (1985b) goes a step further toward integrating organizational form and behavioral views of worker participation and defining the workplace participation ideal. The ideal is the "commitment strategy," which contrasts dramatically with the traditional "control strategy." The control strategy follows largely from the ideas of Frederick Taylor and emphasizes small fixed jobs, low motivation and skill expectations, labor as a variable cost, managerial control necessitating a substantial hierarchy with top-down communication, and adversarial relations with unionized workers. On the other hand, in the commitment strategy

jobs are designed to be broader than before, to combine planning and implementation, and to include efforts to upgrade operations, not just maintain them. Individual responsibilities are expected to change as conditions change, and teams, not individuals, often are the organizational units accountable for performance. With management hierarchies relatively flat and differences in status minimized, control and lateral coordination depend on shared goals, and expertise rather than formal position determines influence. (Walton 1985b, 79)

Also, this strategy is characterized by high performance expectations, assurances of employment security, joint problem solving with managers as advisors and facilitators, lessened adversarial relations, and the "belief that eliciting employee commitment will lead to enhanced performance" (p. 80). Walton (p. 81) uses a table to illustrate a spectrum of work force strategies from control to commitment strategy along sixteen dimensions with seven major categories. The major categories are: 1) job design principles; 2) performance expectations; 3) management organization: structure, systems, and style; 4) compensation policies; 5) employment assurances; 6) employee voice policies; and 7) labor-management relations. Clearly, Walton (p. 80) believes there are large economic and human benefits from moving a business from a control to a "comprehensive commitment strategy," but he acknowledges that there are costs. "To achieve these gains, managers have . . . to invest extra effort, develop new skills and relationships, cope with higher levels of ambiguity and uncertainty, and experience the pain and discomfort associated with changing habits and attitudes" (p. 80). Without using the term, Walton recognizes the essence of investments in organizational capital.

A UNIFIED WORKER PARTICIPATION FRAMEWORK

The comparison of different types of worker participation with respect to their likely effects on the organization's productivity and worker well-being requires a unified framework which utilizes insights regarding both organizational form and behavior and builds on the dimensions of Tomer's (1985) implicit psychological contract spectrum as well as the organizational dimensions in the frameworks of Bernstein (1980) and Walton (1985b). Table 8.1 displays the essential elements of this unified worker participation framework. It shows the 12 dimensions of the individual-organization relationship which affect the quality and quantity of worker participation. A knowledge of the characteristics of a particular firm's organization and management would enable one to locate this firm along each of the twelve left-to-right spectrums. From the location, one can get a real sense of how productive and "human" the firm's organization is by comparison to the ultimate participative ideal, Theory Z. In some respects the Theory Z or Z management concept resembles the Japanese management ideal.[4] Theory Z is the ultimate participative ideal in the sense that the organization's features are optimally motivating and need satisfying (see Maslow 1971, 270–286). Moreover, it corresponds closely to Bernstein's (1980) "fully democratized" state and to Walton's (1985b) "comprehensive commitment strategy." The participative dozen are intended to be the necessary and sufficient dimensions along which a firm's organization must develop over time to attain the ultimate participatory ideal. Alternatively, to maintain the Z management state, an organization must maintain the Z characteristics in all 12 organizational dimensions.

The Theory Z ideal combines the 9,9 culture and behavior dynamics with organizational forms that tend to guarantee the continuation of the optimum participation. It seems unlikely that either an ideal organizational structure or an ideal culture alone would suffice to provide the optimum participation in the long run. Both are needed to complement each other, enabling the other to be effective. As Rosabeth Moss Kanter and Barry Stein (Zwerdling 1980, p. x) observe, "participation requires more than the mere opening of decision making channels; it also involves practice, patience, knowledge and information, all of which take time to acquire." A Z organization will, by definition, have a relatively flat hierarchy because responsibility, along with the information necessary to exercise it, is pushed to the lowest possible level in the organization. This means less need for control and coordination by middle managers. Z workers are not only highly motivated but as much as possible are self-managed and self-controlled in line with the organization's objectives. As indicated by comparing columns 2 and 3 of table 8.1, Z management is very different from A or traditional U.S. management, which basically resembles Walton's control strategy. In A management, the emphasis is on controlling the behavior of workers who generally occupy narrowly specialized jobs; control and coordination, thus, require a steep hierarchy and involve large status and income differentials. Workers in A management are agents for the principals (external owners and top management) from whom they receive directives and with whom they may deal adversarially.

To further illustrate the unified framework, the characteristics of "ideal Japanese management" and an "ideal producer cooperative" are listed in columns four and five of table 8.1. Many observers agree that the Mondragon producer cooperatives in the Basque region of Spain come close to the ideal producer cooperative (see Vanek 1975, 26; Jones 1980, 142–143 and 148–150; and Thomas and Logan 1982). As indicated in table 8.1, the two ideals have much in common with each other and with Theory Z. They both fall far to the right side of the spectrum along most of the twelve dimensions. Thus, it is not surprising that Japanese management and the Mondragon cooperatives are increasingly being looked to as organizational models which are both highly productive and human.

This strongly supports the worker participation hypothesis: companies whose management and organization are further to the right on the 12 individual-organization dimensions of the spectrum will have higher productivity and worker well-being than other companies, other things being equal. The following indicates how the hypothesis applies to two of the dimensions. Along dimension one (duration of association and employment security) a firm which provides workers the assurance of "lifetime employment" will simultaneously add to worker well-being via the high degree of economic security and add to X-efficiency since it encourages workers to develop a long-term perspective (low rate of time preference) and high commitment to the firm. Along dimension two (basis of association or attachment to the organization) a firm in which workers attachment is based

Table 8.1
Unified Worker Participation Framework

	Five Elements of Participation	Dimensions of Individual-Organization Relationship	Organizational "A" Management or "Control Strategy"
To partici-pate: to take part; join or share with others		(1) Duration of Association and Employment Security	Employee is Variable Factor of Production, esp. hourly employees
	(1) Influence over what goes on at workplace	(2) Basis of Association or Attachment to Organization	Fixed, Defined Job Assignment
		(3) Contribution/Commit-ment Expected from Employee	Minimum stable perfor-mance on deskilled jobs, separating doing from thinking
	(2) Influence with respect to major decisions	(4) Relationship to Principal (Employer)	Agent to accomplish owner(s)' purposes [1,2]
		(5) Internal Control of Employees	Management directives top-down controls, rules
	(3) Feeling Part of the Organization	(6) Leadership Style	Authoritarian, Adversarial
		(7) Superordinate Goals, Values of Organization	Goals usually financial, if any; values reflect owner(s)
	(4) Ability to make real contribution through the exercise of discre-tion and the taking of responsibility	(8) Rights of Workers to appeal with respect to disputes & grievances	None; if union, grievance procedures
		(9) Employees' Sharing in Gains/Profits	Only external owners and/ or top management share in profits
		(10) Relationship of Organi-zation to Community/ Society	Agent with respect to spe-cific transactions
	(5) Experience of Coop-erative Work Relationships	(11) Employee Status/ Income Differentials	Status and income differen-tials emphasized
		(12) Organization's Sharing of Information with respect to firm's status and tasks	Information distributed on "need to know" basis

Notes: [1] If union, adversarial negotiation
       [2] Employee inputs allowed on narrow agenda in prescribed format

Table 8.1 (*continued*)

Behavior Models' Characteristics

"Z" Management or Fully Participative Firm	Ideal Japanese Management	Mondragon Cooperatives
"Lifetime," Secure	→	→
Member of Community	→	→
High, Varying Responsibilities; Emotional, Spiritual Commitment Expected	→	→
Established Procedures for sharing in goal determination and major decision making	Shared Goals, Consensus Decision Making[3]	Shared Goals, Worker Representatives decide on Managers, Policies
Implicit Control through Internalized Goals	→	→
Develop Teams, Supportive and Facilitative with respect to Problem Solving	→	→
Clear Goals and Strong, Humanistic Values Predominate	→	→
Guarantee of Appeal to Independent Body in disputes and grievances	?	?
Members' rights to all economic profits from firm's operations[4]	Bonuses, Collective Compensation	Members' Share in Profit Individually and Collectively
Goals Integrated with Societal Goals; Service to Society is Goal	→	→ Also Financial Contribution
Low Differentials, Advancement with Seniority and Performance	→	→
High Degree of Information Sharing	→	→

[3] De Facto ownership due to formal ownership by affiliated institutions
[4] This is separate from scarcity returns to the contributors of capital (whether they are members or external to the organization).

on membership in a worker community will contribute to worker well-being due to the sharing of goals and values, ease of communication, and opportunities for close relationships with other members; and will contribute to X-efficiency since communication and cooperation are enhanced in a work environment characterized by shared values and trust (Tomer 1985). More generally, the worker participation hypothesis can be elucidated by imagining two corporations, A and Z, with the same endowments of tangible capital goods, individual human capital, and technology. Corporation Z (with Z management) is hypothesized to have dramatically higher productivity and worker well-being as result of the very significant differences between it and corporation A (with A management) along the 12 participative dimensions. It is acknowledged, of course, that differences in technology and in tangible and intangible capital endowments will cause differences in productivity, if not worker well-being; the focus here, however, is on the very important role of the intangible organizational aspects.

WORKER PARTICIPATION AND EFFICIENCY

Allocative Efficiency

It follows directly from the worker participation hypothesis that firms closer to the Theory Z ideal will have higher X-efficiency, that is, higher productivity stemming from superior organization. X-efficiency, of course, is quite different from allocative efficiency, the traditional concern of economists (Leibenstein 1966). Because much of the economic analysis of worker participation has focused on allocative efficiency considerations, it is important to cite the more important arguments in this vein in order to differentiate them from the X-efficiency analysis. However, a full-fledged review is not necessary as others have already covered various parts of this territory (notably, Fusfeld 1983, Pryor 1983, Steinherr 1978, Meade 1972, and Stephen 1982, chapter 1).

An important aspect of allocational efficiency is the way inputs (capital and labor) are combined given the technology to produce an output. Greater allocative efficiency is possible whenever a firm can change input combinations (reallocate resources) and thereby increase absolute profit. Correspondingly, greater allocative efficiency is possible for a economy if a resource reallocation would increase society's net benefits. Given perfect competition and an absence of externalities, profit-maximizing capitalist firms help to maximize society's net benefits. Thus, it is a finding of major theoretical interest that labor-managed firms are inefficient in the short run because they don't maximize profits and because they may respond to increases in demand or price by lowering output and employment (see, for instance, Ward 1958, Domar 1966 and Vanek 1970).

These results follow because worker-managers are assumed to maximize earnings per worker by hiring or firing up to the point where the marginal revenue product of workers equals earnings per worker. Employment of more or fewer workers would lower earnings per worker. This is an inefficient short-run outcome because society's benefits (and a firm's revenues) from hiring more workers exceed the opportunity costs of labor. In the case of a rise in demand or price, the labor-managed firm's lowering of output and employment will cause the marginal revenue product of labor to be higher in this industry than in others, without any tendency to reallocate labor among industries in the short run, i.e., no tendency to eliminate the allocative inefficiency. These results are highly dependent on the following assumptions.

1. workers have only one goal, to maximize earnings per worker, with each worker receiving an equal share in the earnings,

2. labor supply is perfectly elastic,

3. the firm produces a single output and uses a single variable input, and

4. all workers are members of the firm.

The perverse or inefficient behavior of these firms will be eliminated or mitigated if certain of these assumptions do not hold. Moreover in the long run, if the entry of new labor-managed firms in response to earnings differentials is sufficient, a labor-managed economy will be just as efficient as a pure capitalist one. Thus, the equivocal conclusion is that a labor-managed firm or economy may or may not be allocatively inefficient in the short or long run.[5]

Would a Theory Z firm, or an economy of Theory Z firms, suffer from allocative inefficiency? It seems doubtful, at least not for the reasons found in the theory of the labor-managed firm. For one thing, a Theory Z firm will have multiple goals, some of which are noneconomic and integrated with societal goals (see dimensions 7 and 10 in table 8.1). Suppose the Z firm did have a single short-run, economic maximizing objective. It is likely that this objective would be essentially the same as profit maximization. This is the case in the Mondragon cooperatives where workers are paid wage rates determined with reference to market wages and also receive a claim on the surplus over labor and capital costs (Stephen 1983, 71).

Such a system would seem to avoid the drawbacks of labor-managed firms identified by the theoretical literature. It is indeed a pity that economists did not discover Mondragon much sooner since they would have found that the co-operators of Mondragon had solved the theoretical puzzles which the economists were in the process of discovering. (Stephen 1983, 71)

X-Efficiency

Will a Z firm be more X-efficient than one with less participative organizational features? In effect, will the Z firm have a higher output for a given set of inputs? Below we consider both affirmative and negative answers to this important question. The question is very important because, as Vanek has noted, the possible percentage gains in productivity from X-efficiency improvements are much greater than those related to allocative efficiency (1970, 237—253). Despite this fact, economists have devoted many more pages to analyzing allocative efficiency than to X-efficiency. Many analysts have also simply assumed that effort per unit of time (a key variable in X-efficiency theory) is fixed (Pryor 1983, 142).

Economists in the "property rights" tradition have generally argued that the pure capitalist firm is superior in both types of efficiency to organizational forms involving greater participation. Armen Alchian and Harold Demsetz's 1972 article is an influential, widely cited reference epitomizing this property rights position. They argue that due to the difficulty of detecting shirking among workers in teams, individual workers who derive utility from both work income and leisure will be led to choose more than an optimal amount of leisure. The monitors whose activities can reduce shirking to some extent must themselves be monitored, and this is best done by giving them residual income claims. It follows that the classic capitalist firm in which the manager-owners control workers and receive the rewards from the resultant savings is the most efficient type of firm. One assumption of Alchian and Demsetz (1972, 786) is that "the cost of team production is increased if the residual claim is not held entirely by the central monitor." Therefore, there would be more shirking, less effort expenditure, and more X-inefficiency under alternative arrangements involving more worker participation. The superiority of the classical capitalist firm in this view derives from its ability to exercise vertical control. Note the similarity to Walton's (1985b) control strategy.[6]

On the other hand, Jaroslav Vanek (see, for instance, 1970, 234–279) and an increasing number of other economists have argued that labor-managed firms, producer cooperatives, and firms with a variety of forms of worker participation are likely to be higher in X-efficiency than their nonparticipative counterparts. A key argument is that worker participation can contribute to better alignment of the goals of individuals and organizations and can reduce opportunism and increase trust, especially between workers and managers (Bradley and Gelb 1981, 216–217).[7] Because these workers are "working for themselves" to a greater extent, there will not only be greater self-control but also greater horizontal control, in monitoring and mutual encouragement between workers (see, for example, Bradley and Gelb 1981, 216–217 and 1982, 255; Vanek 1970, 245; Levin 1982, 46–47;

Cable and FitzRoy 1980a, 103; and Tomer 1985, chapter 7). Greater worker participation will also improve vertical control, because it reduces resistance to traditional hierarchical control by inhibiting "attitudes, informal agreements and collective understandings which serve to frustrate attempts at vertical control" (Bradley and Gelb 1981, 216–217; see also Bradley and Gelb 1982, 255, and Cable and FitzRoy 1980a, 103). These improved horizontal and vertical controls "permit reduction in the number and cost of supervisory personnel" (Fusfeld 1983, 769; see also Bradley and Gelb 1981, 216; Levin 1982, p. 46; and Tomer 1985).

Cable and FitzRoy argue that profit sharing is more X-efficient in the presence of worker participation because the latter should increase "workers awareness of a reliable connection between their individual exertions [efforts] and received profit shares, and reduce fears that managerial opportunism will deprive them of the fruits of their extra labour" (1980a, 102–104; see also Bradley and Gelb 1981, 216–217). To the extent that worker participation results in greater worker "voice" in productive arrangements participation is likely to mean better matches between workers and organizational situations resulting in greater productivity (Cable and FitzRoy 1980a, 101; Pryor 1983, 158–159). Fusfeld believes that greater participation will reduce the decision-making biases of managers otherwise consumed by the desire for status and power. But the single most important argument is that "the psychological effects of participation . . . stimulate greater effort" (Fusfeld 1983, 769; see also Vanek 1970, 234–279).

It is the latter argument that chapters 5 and 7 have developed in considerable detail by building on the economic framework of Leibenstein (1966) and utilizing insights from the organizational behavior literature. Chapter 7 explains why one would expect high worker effort in an organization with the participative features of ideal Japanese management. Furthermore, chapter 7 argues that ideal Japanese management will be characterized by lower labor market transaction costs (lower costs of making and changing contracts with workers), higher cooperation among employees, which means lower managerial costs of planning or otherwise compensating for lack of cooperation, and improved membership behavior (lower absenteeism and turnover), which lowers the costs associated with these.

Michael Conte has heavily utilized the organizational behavior literature[8] (more than the economic literature) to develop a model explaining how participative organizational features translate into high economic performance. The essence is that formal and informal organizational features (that is, worker ownership and managerial style) affect worker feelings of participation, which then affect three important attitudes that motivate workers: commitment, identification with the firm, and meaningfulness of work. These three in turn determine certain individual behaviors directly related to cost (turnover, effort, communication, tardiness, absenteeism and sickness), and these behaviors determine organizational performance (profit, worker income levels, productivity, innovation and growth) and whether the firm is able to meet its goals (Conte 1982, 213–217).

The various explanations on why participative organizational features are X-efficient demonstrate in a variety of ways why an organization with Theory Z features along all 12 participative dimensions would have the highest possible X-efficiency. Providing a detailed explanation of how each of the 12 participative dimensions are related to X-efficiency would be a tedious task. Conte's model indicates the basic logic involved through his focus on worker feelings of participation. The essence is that worker feelings of participation will be greatest in an organization with Theory Z features along all 12 participative dimensions.

X-EFFICIENCY, WELL-BEING AND ECONOMIC GROWTH

The Production Possibility Frontier

When organizational change increases potential output (perhaps due to increased worker participation), organizational capital forms. This increased endowment of intangible capital produces a shift in the production possibility frontier (PPF) enabling greater X-efficiency (Tomer 1981a, 4). Thus, if one of two comparable firms makes an investment in enhancing the participative qualities of its organization, the investing firm's potential output will be higher than the noninvesting firm, assuming a positive rate of return on the investment.[9]

The production possibility frontiers illustrated in figure 8.1 show the combined amounts of goods Y and X which it is possible for a firm to produce. The PPF labeled "true potential," Z, shows the possible output combinations for a firm that has made all the participative organizational changes necessary to become a Theory Z or fully participative firm. In theory, this firm has exhausted the production potential of organizational change given its other factor endowments and technology. The PPF labeled "actual potential" shows the possible output combinations for an ordinary firm in which there is room for X-efficiency improvement via organizational investment. If this ordinary firm is at point A it is using its existing organization to potential; however, if the firm is at a point within the frontier such as B, it is being X-inefficient in terms of the potential of its current organizational capital stock. In accord with the worker participation hypothesis, firms which move further to the right on the 12 participative dimensions will increase their production possibilities, and the actual potential frontier will move closer to the true potential (Z) frontier. In theory, otherwise equal firms could be ranked according to the percent of true potential production they achieve or their percent of true potential X-effi-

Figure 8.1
Production Possibility Frontiers

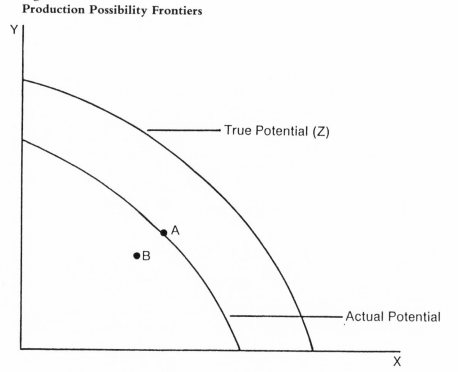

ciency, a ranking which reflects the quality and quantity of organizational capital investment.[10]

The Worker Well-being Possibility Frontier

Organizational change, particularly change in worker participation, not only affects potential output but also influences worker well-being. Worker well-being is defined in relation to Abraham Maslow's (1970b, chapter 11) hierarchy of human needs, which starts on the low end with material needs, proceeds to social needs, and culminates with self-actualization needs. To the extent that an organization's features enable a worker to satisfy these human needs, the organization contributes to his well-being. Since in developed societies most organizations do reasonably well in enabling workers to satisfy their material needs, differences among organizations in worker well-being will largely be related to how well they enable workers to satisfy their higher needs.[11] A worker's ability to satisfy his higher needs is presumed to depend on the nature of his organizational participation and on the income from his work.

When worker well-being is increased as a result of organizational change and organizational capital formation, it is fruitful to think of this as shifting the worker well-being possibility frontier (WWPF) and involving an increase in W-efficiency (the degree to which worker well-being in an organization is at its potential).[12] The WWPF plays a role similar to the PPF except that it relates not to production but to possible levels of worker well-being, given the state of the organization, the technology, and factor endowments. Any point on the frontier represents the possible levels of well-being of two workers, V and U, or two classes of workers (see figure 8.2). The WWPF labeled "true potential (Z)" in figure 8.2 shows the possible well-being combinations for a fully participative or Theory Z firm.

A Theory Z firm is one with the highest possible W-efficiency. The WWPF labeled "actual potential" shows the possible well-being combinations for a typical firm in which there is considerable room for increased worker well-being through organizational investment. The typical firm, say, at point C is using the full potential of its existing organization in terms

Figure 8.2
Worker Well-being Possibility Frontiers

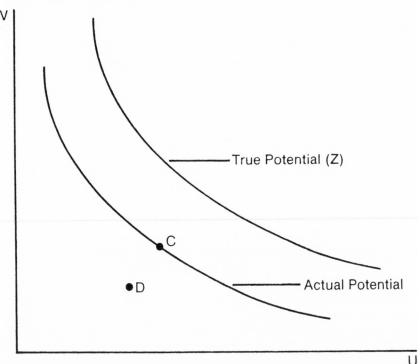

of well-being, but it is W-inefficient in the sense that there is room for organizational change to raise the well-being of all its workers.[13] A firm at point D would be W-inefficient in the sense of not fully utilizing the well-being potential of its current organizational capital stock. In line with the worker participation hypothesis, a typical firm which moves to the right on the 12 participative dimensions will increase the well-being possibilities of workers, and its actual potential frontier will move closer to its true potential frontier. Analogous to the PPF, otherwise equal firms could be ranked according to their percentage of true potential well-being, a ranking reflecting their participative organizational investments.

Why is the WWPF convex to the origin in contrast to the PPF and why doesn't it intersect the horizontal or vertical axes? Consider the organization of a typical firm as represented by the actual potential WWPF in figure 8.2. First, the frontier slopes downward because increasing the well-being of worker U means changing his organizational situation (and therefore his capacity to satisfy his needs) at the expense of worker V. There is, however, a degree of interdependence between the well-being of the two workers. This would not be the case if all the organizational features affecting worker well-being were like private goods in the zero-sum game where more for one party means less for the other. However, some aspects of the work environment are like public goods in that they are collectively consumed. If so, when worker U's position within the organization is changed to allow him greater well-being, the reduction of worker V's well-being may be less than equal to the amount of U's increase. The convexity follows from this. Moreover, regardless of how favorably the organization treats U, it is difficult to conceive of V's well-being becoming equal to zero, or vice versa. Thus, the WWPF shown doesn't intersect the axes.

The Production/Well-being Grid

Although organizational change might conceivably affect only X-efficiency or only W-efficiency, it ordinarily affects both, though not necessarily to the same degree. The production/well being grid shown in figure 8.3 provides a way to summarize our theory concerning potential production and worker well-being. The vertical axis measures actual potential production as a percent of true potential production (or the X-efficiency percentage), and the horizontal axis measures actual potential worker well-being as percent of true potential worker well-being (or the W-efficiency percentage). At the northeast corner of the grid is the Theory Z participative ideal with 100 percent of potential production and worker well-being. In this case, one hundred percent of all possible X-efficiency and W-efficiency improving organizational change have been made. The figure bears a resemblance to Blake and Mouton's (1985) Managerial Grid in that their grid's optimum, the 9,9 concern for production and people, is also

Figure 8.3
The Production/Well-being Grid

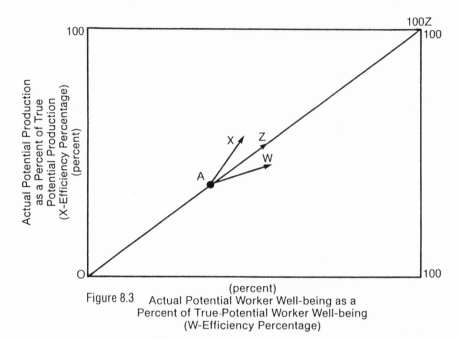

Figure 8.3   Actual Potential Worker Well-being as a
Percent of True Potential Worker Well-being
(W-Efficiency Percentage)

located at the northeast corner; furthermore, like the managerial grid, it
facilitates an understanding about the organizational gap between actual and
potential and how to close it. Suppose point A on figure 8.3 represents
typical U.S. management or Walton's control strategy. The distance from
A to Z is suggestive of the room for improvement through organizational
capital formation.

The grid can also be used to think about possible organizational transition
strategies. Is it necessary for a firm investing in organizational change to
move along the diagonal as with arrow z, or is it possible to choose off-
diagonal movement such as that indicated by arrows x or w? My suspicion
is that only movements along the diagonal have long-term viability. The
attempt to increase X-efficiency with little or no W-efficiency increase
seems likely to encounter worker resentment and eventual opposition. On
the other hand, strategies seeking to increase W-efficiency with little X-
efficiency increase may eventually falter as these organizations lose out in
product competition to firms with more X-efficient strategies. It seems that
many U.S. firms are currently pursuing X-type strategies in that they are
borrowing many of the Japanese management techniques designed to raise
output while doing too little to make their organizations genuinely participative. Could it be that some of the European strategies involving the

introduction of greater worker control are motivated more by the concern for worker well-being than by X-efficiency considerations?

The production/well-being grid is notable because it indicates an alternative line of reasoning connecting economic analysis to economic welfare. In orthodox welfare economics, increased well-being derives from increased utility experienced as a result of increases in allocative efficiency. The grid analysis above connects human well-being to X-efficiency and W-efficiency, and thus, directly to human relationships related to production and need satisfaction. It seems much more appropriate to base theories of well-being directly on how well organizations function with respect to motivation and satisfaction than to base it on the allocative ability of markets. Developing a humanistic economic welfare analysis along the lines suggested by the production/well-being grid would therefore seem a desirable task.

WORKER PARTICIPATION AND EXTERNALITIES

When workers participate in management, especially in important decision making, positive and negative externalities are much less likely to be a problem as Vanek (1970, 274–276) has recognized for labor-managed firms. This is because when "those who hold power and control also happen to be to a considerable degree those who suffer or benefit from external effects, there is strong presumption that the processes leading to the correction of the effects of externalities will be more direct and effective than they would be in other" situations (Vanek 1970, 274–275). Consider the case of the pollution of a local stream by a chemical plant. To the extent that workers live nearby and benefit from the stream and participate in decisions with an impact on the firm's pollution, the workers will be expected to consider the social disutility of the pollution as it lowers their real incomes. Although actions to correct the pollution may raise the firm's costs, these costs will be balanced against the benefit (in other words, workers' real income increases due to less pollution). The resulting decisions should be much closer to the economic optimum.

The externality analysis helps to understand a key element of worker participation: how the principal-agent relationship (the fourth of the 12 participative dimensions) varies with degrees of participation. To the extent that principals in firms lacking worker participation impose costs or benefits on agent-workers, eliminating the principal-agent relationship by introducing appropriate types of participation will reduce the inefficiency of the externality. A Theory Z or fully participative firm will by definition have eliminated all vestiges of the principal-agent relation, and thereby, all these externalities. Perhaps part of the reason why we expect workers in a Z firm to be highly motivated is that they are able to control their fate to a high degree, experience personal growth through facing these decisions, and thus realize much of their true potentials.

WORKER PARTICIPATION: THE EVIDENCE

Participation and Economic Performance[14]

There is a great deal of evidence from recent empirical studies which supports the view that increasing worker participation improves economic performance, especially productivity (Jones and Svejnar 1982, 11). As might be expected, however, these studies differ not only in their definition of participation and the economic performance variables used but in the models (or lack thereof) linking the two. The major findings from this literature do, nevertheless, shed much light on the worker participation hypothesis, even though none of the studies can be considered a test of it. The following review of these findings starts with the economic research and ends with the organizational behavior studies.

Economic Hypothesis Testing. Consider first a number of studies by economists who have attempted to test specific hypotheses concerning X-efficiency using sophisticated statistical techniques. John Cable and Felix FitzRoy (1980a, 1980b) have hypothesized that a positive relationship exists between worker participation in decision making and a firm's output (value added). They estimated their production function relationship using regression analysis on data from 42 West German firms with varying degrees of worker participation for the years 1974–1976. Data on their participation variable is a weighted average of managers' subjective evaluations of worker involvement in seven areas of decision making. The effect of participation on output is found to be positive and statistically significant (Cable and FitzRoy 1980a, 114–115, and 1980b, 168). Furthermore, "over the five years to 1976 output per man rose by more than 17 percent in high participation firms compared with only 4.2 percent in the low group," causing a reversal in the initial productivity ranking of these firms (Cable and FitzRoy 1980a, 175). They also found fairly strong support for the view that "within a participatory setting, but not elsewhere . . . profit-sharing exerts a positive effect on productivity" (Cable and FitzRoy 1980a, 118).

Jan Svejnar (1982) used a similar methodology to explore the effects on productivity of the West German Codetermination Laws. Svejnar's findings "suggest that the introduction of employee participation through the 1951 Codetermination Law and the 1952 Works Constitution Act had no significant effect on productivity. . . . The productivity effect of the 1972 Act is found to be either insignificant or mildly negative" (p. 210). The conclusions relate to worker participation in the workplace (the work councils established in the 1952 and 1972 laws) and the one-third worker representation on boards of directors in firms with 500 employees or more (1952 law), but do not relate to the equal policy decision-making powers of laborers and shareholders established in the 1951 law for iron-steel and coal mining companies. The conclusions also do not relate to the 1976 law which extended the 1951 law to all large companies. The findings are based on data from 14 industries for the period 1950–1976. Due to the limited pre-1952 and post 1972 observations, they must be considered tentative (p. 210).

Mondragon. Keith Bradley and Alan Gelb (1981 and 1982) have used data from their questionnaire survey of 1200 workers in the Mondragon cooperatives and 280 workers in two neighboring noncooperative firms to examine whether "Mondragon's commercial success can be attributed to its cooperative organization, rather than to other factors—good conventional management, access to capital, etc. By 'cooperative organization' is meant the constellation of ownership patterns, rules and community relations so distinctively part of Mondragon" (1981, 225). The many survey questions deal with such specifics as worker willingness to transfer to other firms, the perceived gulf between management and workers, worker encouragement of fellow workers, and attitudes with respect to work effort and to their financial investment in the cooperative. The responses indicate that Mondragon's cooperative organization with its high worker involvement is "its most dominant characteristic" (1982, 155). They find that "vertical control is improved by the generation and sustaining of consensus and high-trust relationships within the enterprise. Horizontal reinforcement is induced through dispersion of shareholdings and appreciation of the role of effort in the success of the enterprise" (1981, 225). Overall, the "responses indicate a more favorable industrial environment for the cooperatives [than in traditional firms], which is plausibly associated with improved X-efficiency" (1982, 156).

Henk Thomas and Chris Logan (1982, chapter 5) and Thomas (1982) take a less theoretical approach in analyzing the extent of the successful economic performance of the Mondragon cooperatives. Using three productivity ratios and four profitability ratios, they find that "productivity and profitablility are higher for cooperatives than for capitalist firms. It makes little difference whether the Mondragon group is compared with the largest 500 companies or with small- and medium-scale industries; in both comparisons the Mondragon group is more productive and more profitable" (Thomas 1982, 149). Thomas and Logan (1982, 99–106) also find that the Mondragon "growth record is superior to that of private enterprises," especially in regard to investment. While Thomas and Logan do not utilize statistical methods designed for hypothesis testing, they indicate that "the strong performance of the Mondragon cooperatives appears to be due to the fact that the system has been structured in such way as to satisfy the conditions for an efficient labor-managed sector enumerated by Horvat and Vanek" (Thomas and Logan 1982, 150).

Producer Cooperatives. Derek Jones (1980) provides a review and synthesis of the main findings of empirical research on producer cooperatives (including Mondragon) in industrialized Western economies to determine the relationship of their performance to certain of their financial and structural features. The features of interest are the intended degree of worker control (type 1 is full, equal control by workers; type 2 is majority control by workers; and type 3 involves less than majority control by workers) and Vanek's four most important rules which relate to worker control, financing, and the existence of a "shelter" organization. Jones finds that

diverse indicators of "efficiency" reveal that many producer cooperatives perform well. In general the performance of P.C.s in the third category is not as good as that of P.C.s on average in the first two categories. . . . [The] capacity for longevity varies considerably among P.C.s with the worst performers on average being those in the type three category . . . [and] for long periods . . . P.C.s can grow at least as fast as comparable capitalist firms. (p. 147)

With respect to "most measures of socio-economic performance, it is type 1 P.C.s that have performed best and type 3 . . . worst" (p. 151).[15] Also, "variation in socio-economic performance is positively related to the degree to which Vanek's fundamental rules are satisfied" (p. 151). It is noteworthy, however, that Jones is not persuaded that those rules constitute "the necessary and sufficient set of conditions for efficient P.C.s, or that the details of the rules are sufficiently rich" (pp. 151–152).

The worker-owned plywood cooperatives in the United States are notable for their long lives and economic success. Using information derived from tax-court reports, Katrina Berman (1982, 80–81) finds these cooperatives have "productivity 30–50 percent above that in non-cooperative plants, . . . [and have] in some cases . . . far higher productivity premiums." These cooperatives not only have higher output per hour but higher quality of product and economy of material use (p. 80). Berman attributes this productivity to the cooperatives' participative environment and organizational features including the solidarity deriving from equal pay and voting rights and the flexibility of job assignment (pp. 82, 83). Bellas' (1975) empirical research provides strong support for Berman's conclusions. His research utilized a participation index reflecting the plywood cooperative members' involvement in decisions, a performance variable reflecting payments to workers plus change in book value per share, and several operational variables. Bellas' "principal conclusion . . . is that the degree of participativeness explains more of the difference in performance among the cooperatives than any other variable taken alone" (Conte 1982, p. 222).

Kibbutz. Seymour Melman (1970) has analyzed the efficiency of a paired sample of 12 industrial enterprises in Israel, six under "managerial control" and six kibbutz enterprises under "cooperative control."[16] On the average, the cooperative enterprises showed higher productivity of labor and capital, higher profits, and lower administrative costs (p. 22). Melman attributes these results to institutionalized equality, democratic decision making, a community orientation, an explicit ideology and moral values, all of which induce cooperative work behavior (pp. 22–33).

Yugoslav Self-Management. Saul Estrin and William Bartlett (1982) review a number of empirical studies which have sought to identify the contribution that enterprise self-management makes to Yugoslav economic growth. While Yugoslav economic growth has been respectable by international standards, the use of production functions and "growth accounting" in these studies has not clearly isolated the effects of self-management from the fact of underdevelopment, government intervention and regulation, and market imperfections (pp. 99–102).

Employee Ownership. Employee ownership can be direct, as in the producer cooperatives, or indirect through the trust vehicle, as in the employee stock ownership plans (ESOPs). The ESOP option has attracted considerable attention recently due to the promotional efforts by Louis Kelso (1958) and others, and recent legislation providing tax breaks to corporations using them. Therefore, it is important to review the evidence of ownership per se and economic performance. The National Center for Employee Ownership (NCEO) studied 364 high-technology companies to determine whether ownership was related to growth of sales and employment. They found that those sharing ownership with most or all employees grew considerably faster than companies without employee shareholding and companies with shareholding by a minority of employees (National Center for Employee Ownership 1985, 1–18, and *Business Week* 1985, 94). In a separate study of 13 major employee-owned firms, NCEO found these firms to be superior to their conventionally owned competitors on a variety of performance measures (NCEO 1985, 22–24). Also, "in a study of 52 employee-owned companies in all industries, NCEO found that the best performers were those that made the largest stock payments to workers' ESOP accounts. These companies also had a strong 'ownership culture' and gave workers a powerful voice in decisions" (*Business Week* 1985, 94).

Two academic studies also came to similar conclusions. Richard Long (1980) used interview and questionnaire data to analyze three firms which converted to employee ownership. He found that positive attitude and performance changes varied directly according to "the degree of ownership and the extent to which traditional patterns of employee influence and participation in decision making changed subsequent to employee purchase" (Long 1980, 735). For example, a trucking firm, which had the highest extent of ownership as well as the highest employee commitment, satisfaction and motivation, made the most dramatic and favorable financial turnaround. In the second study, Michael Conte and Arnold Tannenbaum (1978) found evidence of "greater profitability among [thirty] employee owned companies than comparable sized companies in their respective industries" (p. 25). The percent of equity owned by workers was the only statistically significant variable in the equation explaining the profitability of

these companies (p. 25). Conte and Tannenbaum also reported on the responses of managers to questions asked in 98 employee-owned companies.
These managers "see employee ownership as having a positive effect on
productivity and profit, . . . [especially] where ownership is direct rather
than through a trust and where the percent of employees who participate in
the plan is relatively large" (p. 27).

Participative Management. Countless organizational behavior studies have
found positive relationships between specific worker participation features
and economic performance. For example, among the findings in the studies
assembled in Williams (1976) are:

1. The more successful Yugoslav firms in terms of net profit and employee
income are those whose managers' behavior allowed and encouraged greater work
participation, the same as in previous U.S. findings (Mozina, Jerovsek, Tannenbaum, and Likert 1976, 59–70).

2. A positive relationship was found between democratic-participative leadership
behavior and economic performance in six operating divisions of a U.S. firm
(Roberts, Miles, and Blankenship 1976, 75–90).

3. Participation in the sense of workers' feelings on their influence in decision
making was found to be positively related to individual job performance in a large
company, excluding authoritarian persons and those with weak independence needs
(Vroom 1976, 93–103).

4. The Tennessee Valley Authority's consultative program that involved workers in decisions about matters beyond the level of the workplace was found to be
positively associated with favorable worker attitudes and acceptance of work
changes introduced by management (Patchen 1976, 151–172).

John Simmons and William Mares' (1982) book provides very insightful
descriptions of employee participation in U.S. firms and its relationship to
productivity (see their Appendix 1, 285–290, for a table summarizing firm
level data on the productivity-increasing effects of the introduction of specific types of employee participation; a few research studies are also summarized in this table).

Participation and Worker Well-being

High worker well-being, by definition, means high need satisfaction. Is
participation related to worker need satisfaction? According to Paul Blumberg,

The participating worker is an involved worker, for his job becomes an extension of
himself and by his decisions he is creating his work, modifying and regulating it. As
he is more involved in his work, he becomes more committed to it, and, being more
committed, he naturally derives more satisfaction from it. . . . [Moreover,] the

traditional forms of authority in economic enterprises, in which employees are allowed little or no rights of participation, directly contradict the psychological needs of mature adults. (1975, 330)

In summarizing the empirical findings from many different studies, Blumberg concludes that

there is hardly a study in the entire literature which fails to demonstrate that satisfaction in work is enhanced . . . from a genuine increase in workers' decision-making power. Such consistency of findings, I submit, is rare in social research. (p. 324)

Other Evidence

Nonunion Companies. The 26 large, nonunion companies examined by Fred Foulkes (1980, 1981) are more creative and more participative in their approach to employee relations than most companies. The selected companies, including Black and Decker, Eli Lilly, Gillette, Grumman, Hewlett-Packard, IBM and Polaroid, are leaders in their fields. Their employee relations are generally 1) egalitarian with respect to pay and status symbols, 2) characterized by a people-oriented or humanistic philosophy, 3) evidenced by employment security, 4) pervaded with management personnel who listen, and 5) characterized by good career development programs.

It may be impossible to determine precisely by what amounts the personnel practices previously outlined actually altered the bottomline. . . . But in the view of many of those interviewed, the freedom to experiment with employee relations plans, the opportunity to deal directly with employees, and the absence of adversary relationships with employees and management result in a more profitable enterprise in the long run. (Foulkes 1981, p. 96)

Excellent Companies. Thomas Peters and Robert Waterman (1982) have analyzed the attributes of "excellent" corporations, those considered innovative and excellent by informed observers and those with long-term financial superiority. Of special interest here is that excellent companies:

1. have a strongly held basic philosophy,
2. are people-oriented in the way they treat people as adults and care for them,
3. view themselves as an extended family or community,
4. share information widely,
5. allow employees considerable autonomy, and
6. are decentralized, involving small units.

All of these attributes are reflected directly or indirectly in the 12 participative dimensions.

CONCLUSION

Increasingly, both theory and empirical findings lead to the conclusion that higher productivity and worker well-being are possible through organizational change which introduces greater worker participation. The empirical findings are particularly clear-cut on the positive relationship between participation and productivity when more than one type of participative feature is involved. Despite the consistency of these findings, a few caveats should be cited. First, there are limits to the ability and willingness of employees to participate. Some people don't respond as well to participation opportunities as others or only respond well with the benefit of appropriate types of training, socialization and experience. Moreover, developing a more participative organization is inevitably a process which takes considerable time, thought and commitment. The risk of failure is very real. More than in most kinds of innovation the personal qualities of the firm's leaders are critical to the success of organizational change.

The unified worker participation framework (table 8.1) with its 12 participative dimensions is at the heart of this chapter's attempt to integrate the diversity of theory and findings in the fields of economics and organizational behavior. The use of a very broad definition of participation and a comprehensive set of organizational features makes it possible to understand more clearly the relationship among the many types of organizational attributes and worker participation. The approach is, thus, counter to the tendency in much of the worker participation literature to use a narrow conception of participation and the organizational features giving rise to it. In the view developed here, purposeful changes in any of an organization's participative dimensions add to the stock of organizational capital, thereby making possible greater productivity and worker well-being. Theory Z management is the ultimate participative ideal, reflecting the highest possible productivity and worker well-being achievable through organizational change given the firm's other factor endowments.

This perspective leads to greater awareness of the organization-related gap between actual and potential productivity (or worker well-being) and the diversity of ways to close the gap. It shows that Japanese managers typically have done more to close the gap than U.S. managers. It helps us to see that West German codetermination is a step toward closing the gap, but not an ultimate answer. It also suggests that organizational obsolescence may be a major factor explaining why the United States has been losing its competitive advantage in international trade in many sectors. There is evidence, of course, that United States corporations are now stepping up their organizational investments with the intent of making their organizations more participative. With luck and a little help from macroeconomic policymakers, the United States should as a result begin to experience greater economic growth along with faster growth in productivity and worker well-being.

9

Developing Organizational Comparative Advantage via Industrial Policy

The cooperative relationship between business and government in Japan has frequently been cited as one reason for Japan's high economic performance since the 1950s. The oft-mentioned corollary is that the United States should emulate Japan's cooperative relationships. Before jumping to agree with either of these statements, one should answer two key questions. First, how are cooperative interorganizational relations related to productivity? Second, assuming a significant positive relationship between the two, what could government do to improve interorganizational cooperation in order to enhance a nation's economic growth? The first section of this chapter is addressed to the first question, and the second section to the follow-up.

Ideally, industrial policy involves many concerted policy measures in line with the government's long-term strategy for economic growth. In the early 1980s, industrial policy advocates by and large called for government-guided efforts to promote economic growth through restructuring activities which encouraged the emergence of new, high value-added industries and assisted in the decline of older industries. Another aspect of industrial policy, which has been less emphasized, is rationalization in which governments act to assist firms in raising productivity, perhaps by providing technological knowledge or aiding research and development efforts. The idea behind both restructuring and rationalization has been to develop a country's dynamic comparative advantage and enable it to compete better in international trade by selling more goods on the high value-added end of the spectrum. Relatively neglected in industrial policy discussions has been the type of rationalization which involves improving the management and organization of firms. Also neglected have been improvements in interorganizational relationships (the relationships between firms and governments or between firms and communities) which also affect a nation's productivity and comparative advantage. What is emphasized here are governmental measures that provide the appropriate climate and encouragement for businesses to develop patterns of behavior compatible with the nation's economic growth strategy, especially in regard to organizational considerations. In other words, how can government foster desired organizational capital formation?

FIRMS AND INTERORGANIZATIONAL RELATIONS

Interorganizational Cooperation

The Meaning and Importance of Cooperation. Interorganizational cooperation is said to occur when all three of the following are present: 1) there is an absence of coercion and overt conflict among organizations, and ideally the presence of harmony, 2) organizations refrain from obstructing the accomplishments of other organizations, and 3) organizations engage in more than a minimum amount of discretionary helpful behavior toward other organizations. The focus here is on cooperation between businesses and other organizations. Such cooperation is very important when businesses require help from outsiders to achieve their goals, that is, when they require a type of help which cannot be reliably acquired by offering financial compensation. As in the intra-organization situation, it may be very difficult for businesses to anticipate the precise kinds of help they will need. Nevertheless, if these firms and the external parties cooperate, both will be more likely to achieve their goals.

Since businesses are dependent on many outsiders who control important resources, the managers of these firms naturally try to develop cooperative relationships with them. For example, John Kotter (1982, 162) reports that general manager networks of cooperative relationships typically include individuals representing financial sources (bankers and stockholders), customers, suppliers, competitors, governments, the press and the public. What a business needs from outsiders and what it can give in return varies widely. On one occasion a firm will need information from financial institutions or a government official, while on another it may desire political support to achieve purposes requiring new legislation or a change in regulation. As Kotter suggests, the motivation behind the establishment of cooperation may be simple self-interest, with cooperation representing a kind of reciprocation or "social exchange." On the other hand, as analyzed in chapter 6, there may be many other motivations for cooperation, including altruism.

The Costs of Noncooperation. As in the intrafirm case, the costs of non-cooperation may be very high. Minimal cooperation may mean that a firm is unable to obtain crucial nonpurchasable inputs such as information it could only obtain through cooperation. This may lower the output of the firm or raise real costs if the same output requires more resources in the absence of the crucial input. Either way, productivity is lowered. Another possibility is that negative cooperation or sabotage may be initiated by opportunistic attempts by one organization to gain relative to another. Sabotage by one organization may easily evolve into a persisting mutual pattern of destructive behavior as chapter 6 indicates (see also, Axelrod 1984, 38). Regardless, the destroyed output or productive capacity involved in sabotage means lower productivity. Furthermore, the absence of "spontaneous" cooperation among organizations may in some cases be viewed as a societal problem requiring governmental attention. If the government steps in and "solves" the problem, productivity will still be lower than it would be with full cooperation because the use of government resources raises the overall cost. A number of examples illustrating the nature of the costs of noncooperation are provided later in this chapter. It should be noted that less than potential cooperation may entail some additional costs to the extent that an uncooperative social environment has a negative impact on individual well-being.

Cooperation and Externalities

Joint Cooperation: Mutual Positive Externalities. Significant insights can be gained by analyzing interorganizational cooperation with the aid of the externality concept. A firm's cooperation with another organization implies mutual positive externalities. Firm A's helpful actions toward B provide benefits to B; A does not realize these benefits (unless A is an altruist), but will realize benefits later when B has an opportunity to reciprocate. The typical payoffs for this outcome are indicated in the northwest corner of the PD game (see table 9.1) where the joint payoff is highest.

One-sided Noncooperation: Nonmutual Negative Externalities. Now suppose that firm A acts in a manner detrimental to B (say, the local community): A imposes costs on B for which B is not compensated and A is not charged. This is a nonmutual negative externality. Furthermore, since firm A is certainly not cooperating while B for the moment at least is, and since A may gain from the cost-imposing activity while B clearly loses, the outcome resembles either the southwest or northeast corner outcome of the PD game (see Table 9.2). The joint payoff is lower than in the northwest corner, but the individual payoff to A is higher.

Table 9.1

	Cooperation	Noncooperation
Cooperation	Northwest	Northeast
Noncooperation	Southwest	Southeast

There are many possible interorganizational behaviors which are consistent with this abstract analysis of nonmutual negative externalities. For example, suppose firm A uses chemicals to pollute community B's water source. Is this sabotage, a classic negative externality, or something in between these extremes? The Negative Externality Spectrum below helps to explain the range of interorganizational behaviors which could be involved.

On the right of the spectrum of interorganizational behaviors is the "classic negative externality." The pollution in this example is an unintended by-product of the production activities of firm A, which has no equal cost alternative to chemical pollution of the water. The firm may not know the magnitude of the harm caused by the pollution, perhaps because it joins with other pollution sources to cause the pollution harm. On the extreme left of the spectrum is sabotage in which firm A intentionally pollutes the water, causing a known amount of harm despite the existence of equal cost alternatives to pollution. Between the left and right extremes are six other types of interorganizational behaviors with different combinations of the

Table 9.2
Negative Externality Spectrum (Case of Water Pollution)

	Interorganizational Behavior	
Situation Attribute	Sabotage	Classic Negative Externality
Attitude or Intention with Respect to Harm Caused by Pollution	Intentional	Unintentional
Alternative to Pollution Available at Equal Cost	Yes	No
Harm Due to Pollution Known in Magnitude	Known	Unknown

situation attributes. For example, one of these is similar to the classic negative externality except that the harm is known.

What this spectrum helps us to see is that negative externalities such as pollution need not be the result of simple profit maximizing behavior (which is the essence of the classic case). Pollution may to some extent be a result of a firm's opportunistic and therefore uncooperative relationship with others. For example, a firm's pollution may be intended to harm a water-using competitor located downstream. If such opportunism is at the root of the problem, policy solutions which rely on simple profit maximizing responses to governmental incentives are not likely to work well. For success, policies need to be directed at changing the nature of the relationships between firms and others in society through the use of measures that affect the situation attributes.

Even in the classic negative externality situation, economists' conventional prescription of financial penalties to internalize externalities and eliminate the incentive to pollute needs to be rethought. This is because there are reasons why a firm might decide not to pollute (or limit its pollution) in the absence of governmentally imposed financial penalties. The decision to refrain from polluting can be considered a decision to cooperate with others, the would-be victims of pollution; such a firm is helping, and in a sense providing benefits, by not imposing costs. In gratitude, the would-be victims or others in society may be more disposed to help the firm in the future. If the firm cooperates because of this expected reciprocation, the would-be nonmutual negative externality situation is transformed into a mutual positive externality situation. Of course, other cooperative motivations such as altruism may be involved. In any case, viewing the classic negative externality case as a potentially cooperative one (with mutual positive externalities) raises important policy questions. Rather than ask what policies provide the most appropriate penalization, one may ask what policies are most likely to lead to cooperation.

When cooperation involves more than two parties, and especially when it involves a large number of beneficiaries as in the case of pollution victims, other considerations may be involved. First, neither the beneficiaries of the firm's help nor others may appreciate the nature and magnitude of the firm's efforts. In the absence of such appreciation, any reciprocation is likely to be minimal. Second, the firm may find that it is almost impossible to assess whether and how much any of its beneficiaries have reciprocated. Third, the more beneficiaries there are, the more these beneficiaries have the incentive to be free riders since they will continue to receive the benefits (assumed to have a public good character) whether or not they reciprocate. Some beneficiaries, of course, may never have any opportunity to reciprocate. If, for a variety of such reasons, firms are not able to rely on reciprocation, then the cooperative efforts they do make may be motivated more by altruism than social exchange. Nevertheless, a firm which cooperates in this way may receive valuable benefits to the extent that the company's actions contribute to an improvement in its public image. This is because people are generally more inclined to offer help to a firm with a positive image.

Joint Noncooperation: Mutual Negative Externalities. Instead of developing into joint cooperation, a nonmutual negative externality situation may degenerate into joint noncooperation or mutual negative externalities. If firm A is not cooperative and imposes costs on B (the community), B may retaliate, imposing costs on firm A. This could be done through established legal channels, through political action or through illegal means. One resulting scenario is continuing mutual destructiveness. This outcome resembles the southeast corner of the PD game, the PD solution, where the joint payoff is lowest. Of course, depending on the strategies or behavior of firm A and community B, it still may be possible to move to joint cooperation if each is forgiving and/or recognizes the futility of unending mutual retaliation (see Axelrod 1984, 38–39).

Cooperation between Business and Government. Another alternative is that community B, lacking the ability or desire to retaliate directly against A, may appeal for help to local, state or federal government. If a government decision maker determines that firm A's actions are detrimental and violate or potentially violate regulations under this agency's jurisdiction, the agency's actions will be directed at controlling the firm's behavior. In this case, the relationship between the firm and the government is the key to the outcome. Thus, it is worthwhile to analyze the subsequent moves and countermoves of firm A and the government agency from the standpoint of the PD game and the externalities involved.

According to one model, the government agency and a company subject to regulation

are in an iterated Prisoner's Dilemma with each other. The company's choices at any point are to comply voluntarily with the rules or to evade them. The agency's choices are to adopt an enforcement mode in dealing with that particular company which is either flexible or coercive. If the agency enforces with flexibility and the firm complies with the rules, then both the agency and the firm benefit from mutual cooperation. The agency benefits from the company's compliance, and the company benefits from the agency's flexibility. Both sides avoid expensive enforcement and litigation procedures. Society also gains the benefits of full compliance at low cost to the economy. But if the firm evades and the agency uses coercive enforcement, both suffer the punishing costs of the resultant legalistic relationship. (Axelrod 1984, 156)

Where there is a penchant for adversarial relationships and a tradition of hostility between business and government, the result is less likely to be a cooperative one than in societies with traditions of business-government collaboration (Johnson 1984, 243). When adversarial behavior occurs in the United States, the typical steps involved in implementing new regulations have been described as follows: "staff up with a large number of lawyers, fill the Federal Register with detailed regulations, every one the subject of prolonged consultations, public hearings, revisions and court challenges, and then flood the federal courts' already crowded dockets with complaints" (*Wall Street Journal* 1984). In Japan things are generally different. "As the Tokyo joke goes, when Japan and the U.S. both mandated emission controls on automobile exhausts, Japanese businessmen hired engineers and American businessmen hired lawyers" (Johnson 1984, 243–244). With respect to chemical wastes in the United States, there is recognition of the inadequacy of past adversarial patterns, and a major effort to achieve cooperation among businesses, government and environmental groups is being undertaken (*Wall Street Journal* 1984).

Mortgage Redlining. The case of mortgage redlining can be used to illustrate several possible scenarios, both cooperative and noncooperative, and the costs of noncooperation. Mortgage redlining is said to occur when all or most of an area's mortgage lending institutions decide to deny mortgage loans for housing in particular urban neighborhoods. These institutional decisions may be viewed as a withdrawal of cooperation with the neighborhood on the grounds that the area is judged to be "declining" with low expected profitability or high risk. The banks presumably believe that the cost of their collective cooperation with the neighborhood has become too high. In the absence of this cooperation, the likelihood of the "decline" of the neighborhood will be much greater; as a result, the value of housing as well as business and consumption activity in the area will probably fall. However, when community members begin to recognize the bankers' actions and the chain of events likely to follow, they may mobilize, as many have done, to try to prevent the banks from redlining. Such community outcries in a number of states have led to substantial community organizing efforts to confront banks concerning their lack of cooperation. Such confrontive actions include discussion, picketing, mass withdrawal of funds and lawsuits. These, in turn, have been the stimulus to the creation of new bank regulatory activities concerned with redlining, which have funded research, monitored redlining, developed policies discouraging redlining and encouraging financial investment in older urban areas, and carried out and enforced these policies.

To the extent that banks have redlined (even if in response to manifestations of real social problems), community economic and social conditions have deteriorated as a result, and community groups and governments have devoted substantial resources to discover and penalize redlining businesses, the situation involves joint noncooperation and resembles the unhappy southeast cell PD solution. Alternative cooperative scenarios can occur, however, and have occurred. In some cities, lending institutions have voluntarily commited more mortgage loan dollars to older urban areas after citizens have raised questions about their lending patterns. In the South Shore area of Chicago, a change in the top management and ownership of the South Shore Bank in 1973 led to a reversal of the bank's previous redlining policies. Since then this bank has not only been profitable but its real estate lending in the South Shore area has contributed to a turnaround of this community's decline (*New York Times,* January 30, 1986). Another antiredlining tactic attempted by a number of state governments is to enhance the financial incentives for mortgage lending in older urban areas. This approach seeks greater cooperation from lenders by increasing the financial payoff to cooperation.

Community Control: An Alternative Pattern

External Social Control and Pornography. In certain situations, neither the PD model nor the externality analysis applies, at least not without modification. This section extends the previous analysis to deal with external social control of firm behavior (Tomer 1980), situations in which firms modify their supplies of goods and services in response to social influences external to the firm. As an example consider the case of a retailer of pornographic materials who is confronted by community members other than his customers who challenge the legitimacy of his business in an attempt to drive him out of business or curtail his most obnoxious activities. If successful, this attempt at community control will lower the supply of certain types of pornography, without necessarily altering the profit incentive or obtaining the assistance of political office holders or government officials.

Let's begin with the nonmutual negative externality situation in which pornography retailer A imposes costs on certain people (B), the "victims," who "cooperate" (they don't retaliate or act to end their victimization). One class of pornography victims is made up of consumers, especially the relatively young ones, who are corrupted in the sense of acquiring unhealthy attitudes toward sex and male-female relationships. Costs are thus imposed on these consumers and, perhaps, others who interact with them. Conceivably, a mutual negative externality situation might develop if the victims seek to retaliate in some way, but this seems unlikely as the victimization process is by its nature a somewhat voluntary one. However, groups of "concerned" others acting on behalf of the victims or on behalf of a generalized perceived threat to the community have in many cases mobilized public opinion in the attempt to pressure pornography firm decision makers who, in turn, may accommodate by altering their supply of pornography.

Why would the firm's decision maker or decision makers (in the case of a coalition) accommodate to external community influences when profit may be lost? The reason is that coalition members may anticipate greater utility via acceptable social behavior than they can get from higher profits operating in a nonsocially acceptable manner. When coalition members push for policies which are expected to sacrifice some firm profit, they may expect this to involve some individual sacrifice of financial rewards. If enough coalition members exert their influence in the same direction, the firm will be expected to adopt the sought after behavior. Further, if the social realities and pressures are the same for other firms in the industry, we would expect similar trade-offs by decision makers and similar firm behavior. In many cases, it is through the actions of specific outsiders (who may or may not be organized or numerous) that influential pressures may be brought to bear. In other cases, organization members merely sense shifts in attitudes and values and respond accordingly. Nevertheless, the basic point is that a society or a community can come to have substantial control over the type and amount of business activity in its area without formal governmental action. Since external social control influences the quantity of output, it is by definition a factor influencing the position of the firm's supply curve as well as the market supply curve (Tomer 1980, 193–194).

Social Externalities. Besides the usual type of externality (sometimes known as a technological externality) involved in the pornographic situation (costs imposed on consumer victims) there is a social externality involved (Tomer 1980, 195). In the social externality, the activities of A (groups external to the organization) influence the utility level of the organization's coalition members (B) who in turn influence the policies of the firm (C). This causes changes in output which, in effect, mean increases in the firm's costs. This can be represented as:

$$U_B = U_B (q_1, q_2, \ldots q_n, X_A) \tag{9.1}$$

where U_B is the utility level of the organization's decision makers, q represents the different activities under the control of B, and X_A is the activity under the control of groups external to the organization. In addition,

$$K_C = K_C (q_1, q_2, \ldots q_m, X_B) \tag{9.2}$$

where K_C represents the magnitude of the firm's costs, q represents outputs under the control of the firm and X_B is the activity under the control of the organization's decision makers. In essence, external groups, A, influence decision makers, B, by affecting the utility they derive from decision outcomes. This social control is evident if B's decisions favor A as indicated by the firm's reduction of its supply of socially unacceptable goods. The latter implies added costs that are equal to the profit lost in reducing the firm's (C) supply. In sum, A, by controlling B, effectively controls and imposes costs on C for which A is not charged. Generally, the outsiders, A, who are successful in changing the behavior of a firm would be expected to experience utility or financial gains.

This is still a prisoner's dilemma situation, but there's a difference. The pornography PD example involved only the firms and the consumers or victims of pornography. The pornography firms had a choice of cooperating (not selling the objectionable items) or not cooperating. The consumers could have been noncooperative if, once aware of their victimization, they had retaliated against the pornography retailer; normally, however, pornography consumers choose cooperation. Thus, the typical outcome of this PD game is the southwest (or northeast) corner. The actual outcome could differ, of course, if concerned community people exerted their influence on the pornography firm's decision makers. The social externality involving the community's impact on the firm's decision makers effectively changes the utility payoffs, not the financial payoffs, to the choices of the firm's decision makers. This leads all but the most "dedicated" pornography retailers to cease sales of the most objectionable items or services.

Other Examples. There are many other situations where external social control affects the supply of goods and services. For example, there is evidence that for many years the supply of loans to gambling firms was lower than would be expected on the basis of profit and risk criteria because of the stigma associated with gambling (*Wall Street Journal* 1979). Dow Chemical, which was the target of numerous protests during the late 1960s in connection with its napalm production, finally discontinued its napalm production for the U.S. government. Dow Chemical never publicly admitted that the protests were a factor, but it is clear that Dow's management was worried about the effect of the protests on its long-term public image and its ability to recruit top quality students (Vogel 1978, 43–51 and Tomer 1980, 205). Outside pressures were also influential in Bristol-Myers's decision to cease promoting its infant formulas in hospitals, clinics and doctors' offices in poor countries (Tomer 1980, 205). Mortgage redlining is a particularly interesting example, because the external social influences have at times conflicted. On the one hand, the mortgage lender bias against certain older neighborhoods appears to be an accommodation to the "predominant housing market ideology" and social pressures to adopt policies and practices which are in conformity to those adopted by real estate brokers and appraisers, home builders, life and fire insurance companies, bank regulatory agencies and other federal agencies with a role in housing finance (Tomer, 201). On the other hand, once redlining occurs, concerned people residing in the redlined community have often pressured banks to end the bias that victimizes their neighborhoods.

Acquiring Legitimacy and Avoiding External Social Control. While business organizations require legitimacy and generally conform to prevailing social pressures, they may attempt to manage their social environment (Tomer 1980, 207). Firms do this when they attempt to change the definition of legitimacy, avoid influence of particular outsiders by manipulative means, avoid influence by reducing their dependence on those controlling important resources, and attempt to shape the demands made upon them, perhaps through the use of public relations advertising (pp. 207–208).

Government Policy. One important government activity is the regulation of illegitimate profitable business activities that are not easily influenced by "spontaneous" external social control. Highly toxic water pollution is an example. To counteract such problems, governments may facilitate desirable external social control and hinder undesirable types by providing information and education and by generally raising public awareness about the important concern (Tomer 1980, 209–212). Alternatively, governments have in instances of market failure typically used laws, regulations and enforcement to effectively change the payoffs to firms acting in illegitimate ways. The role of economists has generally been to advise policy makers on the type of regulatory incentives most likely to lead to allocative efficiency. Thus, economists qua economists have tended to focus on relatively technical considerations and have often lost sight of the larger picture which involves considerations of legitimacy, conflict resolution, cooperation and patterns of social influence.

The Ideal Firm

How would the ideal or Theory Z firm interact with other organizations? It is important to be explicit about how firms ought to behave with each other if potential productivity and well-being are to be achieved.

First, firms ought to behave in such a way as to develop cooperative relations with other organizations since the societal payoffs of productivity and well-being (as reflected in repeated PD games) will be highest. Following Axelrod (1984), this presumably means that firms should be nice (avoiding unnecessary conflict by cooperating initially and whenever the other organization does), forgiving (returning quickly to cooperation after the other has been noncooperative), retaliatory (immediately responding noncooperatively to others' noncooperative behavior, but in a way that doesn't escalate the conflict), and clear (acting in a way comprehensible to other organizations). Second, firms ought to conform or adapt readily to socially acceptable behavior patterns while at the same time participating in societal debates about what is legitimate or acceptable. Third, firms should not settle for merely cooperative, legitimate behavior, but ought to set very high goals and integrate these with societal goals so that they make the greatest possible contribution to society. Such goals, especially if clear, strong and humanistic, should not only motivate organization members but also facilitate cooperation among organizations to the extent that the high-level goals are shared.

The Theory Z behavioral ideal is one that integrates a firm's interorganizational with its intraorganizational behavior. Economists will inevitably ask what such a firm is seeking to maximize. Assuming it is possible to maximize something, the Z firm will attempt to maximize the value to society of their total capital, which includes all tangible and intangible capital. This means that Z firms are concerned with improving the productivity of their individual employees, organizational relationships, and tangible capital goods, as well as with improving the acceptance and reputation of their products and improving relationships with governments and external communities. In short, Z companies are concerned with their basic organizational health and viability over the long run (Tomer 1983, 63–64). By suggesting that Z companies will be concerned with the value of their total capital, I don't mean to imply a concern for the market value of the company's equity. Although the market value of equity should faithfully reflect the value of the firm's total capital in efficient markets where owners have the same time preference as others, the market value focus is too narrow. It suggests a concern for values in capital markets and a desire to please the equity participants via stock prices that will be relatively lacking in Z companies (p. 63). The value to society of the firm's total capital will be at a maximum if the firm has done everything possible internally and externally to increase the flow of satisfactions to society.

Japanese companies seem to have evolved types of behavior which approximates the ideal with respect to these goals. Because shareholders are principally associated companies which are not primarily interested in profits and dividends, Japanese companies are largely controlled by employees, especially management (Clark 1979, 136). Their employees acquire desired status more through their membership in the firm than through their position in the organizational hierarchy. Thus, employees of Japanese companies seek to gain higher status by actions that enable their firm to rise in the "society of industry" (Tomer 1983, 96).

The essence of the society of industry is that firms are placed in order according to simple criteria: "the business they are in, their size and market share, their affiliations with bigger companies and banks, the level of wages they pay, their methods of recruitment, their customers and suppliers, and their shareholders" (Clark 1979, 95). The attempt to rise in position influences practically every decision they make including what type of management, where to borrow money, how to recruit employees and where to buy supplies. Since the criteria used to rank Japanese firms are broad and related to service to society, striving to move up as far as possible in the society of industry implies maximizing the value of the firm's capital to society. Furthermore, evidence on Japanese companies cited by Clark (pp. 136–137) indicates that high profitability is not a very important goal, but sales and market share are; service to society is a very important objective; and a high value is placed on good human relations within and outside the organization. (See also Tomer 1983, 63.)

This is not to suggest that U.S. firms should precisely imitate Japanese behavior. However, understanding what the Japanese do and how it is related to the Theory Z ideal makes the ideal seem more attainable. Presumably, non-Japanese companies can develop alternative behavior patterns enabling them to perform closer to the ideal. The next question is: can government facilitate this development?

INDUSTRIAL POLICY AND ORGANIZATIONAL DEVELOPMENT

What are the implications of intrafirm and interorganizational behavior for a nation's industrial policy? The intent here is to establish the plausibility of an industrial policy with a significant organizational dimension and to provide a framework for thinking about how it might work. The purpose of the organizational dimension of an industrial policy (organizational policy) is to bring the behavior of the country's firms closer to the Theory Z ideal and, therefore, to achieve an organizational comparative advantage. Before exploring these organizational aspects, it is first necessary to review some of the essentials of industrial policy. The following overview focuses on key elements of the case for an industrial policy (in particular the contemporary Japanese variant) while largely ignoring the recent controversy generated by these proposals.

Industrial Policy Overview

One of the most important functions of the state is to facilitate economic development. . . . Since industrial activity is the cornerstone of national economic development, all states practice a wide variety of industrial policies, albeit under different names and in different forms. (Sadanori Yamanaka, MITI minister, April 18, 1983, as quoted in Johnson 1984, 18)

These policy differences follow from the great differences among governments in their orientation with respect to economic activity. For example, in Japan the orientation of state activity is developmental, whereas in the United States it is regulatory (Johnson 1982, 19). This is indicated in Japan by the fact that "for more than fifty years the Japanese state has given its first priority to economic development" (Johnson 1982, 305). The regulatory approach of the United States does not recognize the need for an explicit economic development policy or strategy on the national level. Industrial regulation in the United States has generally been related to short-run macroeconomic problems, in response to negative externalities, or in response to political pressures such as those for protectionism. "The private market mechanism [in the United States], operating at the micro level, is assumed to be capable of achieving the optimum allocation of resources" (Ozaki 1984, 67). On the other hand, "the central premise of an industrial policy [such as Japan's] is that the nation's welfare and interest cannot be optimized by the private market alone" (p. 48).

In a positive, explicit sense, industrial policy means the initiation and coordination of government activities to leverage upward the productivity and competitiveness of the whole economy and of particular industries in it. Above all, positive industrial policy means the infusion of goal oriented, strategic thinking into economic policy. (Johnson 1984, 8)

The conception, content and forms of an industrial policy will differ from nation to nation depending on each country's particular historical and economic circumstances (Johnson 1984, 6).

Any nation's industrial policy will be aimed at achieving a dynamic comparative advantage in the international marketplace. Unlike the classical or "static" notion of comparative advantage, in which a nation's advantage derives from geographical and natural endowment differences, the newer, "dynamic" concept of comparative advantage relates to "such elements as human creative power, foresight, a highly educated work force, organizational talent, the ability to choose, and the ability to adapt" (Johnson 1984, 8). Thus, a country might try to increase its international competitiveness by utilizing an industrial policy aimed at enhancing the qualities of its management along with improvements in labor-management relations in its globally competing enterprises (Johnson 1984, 9).

The emphasis of most industrial policy advocates has been on coordinated government actions that would accelerate and ease desired long-term industrial restructuring as a supplement to the market. These proponents argue that

while the market is efficient in allocating resources in the short run, it is not necessarily reliable in anticipating and solving long-term economic problems, especially those problems that have national (as against industry-specific) implications. (Ozaki 1984, 67–68)

Therefore, to maintain competitiveness and minimize harsh social dislocations, Magaziner and Reich (1982, 4–7, 332) recommend industrial policies that would accelerate the flow of labor and capital toward businesses with higher value added per employee and ease the adjustment away from older, low productivity industries in a way that pays attention to market signals. The essence is that the governmental long-term strategy embodied in the industrial policy would condition the strategic choices of private companies so as to make the effects of these private decisions consistent with long-term economic development goals.

Another aspect of industrial policies is rationalization. The term rationalization has often been used with respect to the structure of competition and cooperation within particular industries; nevertheless rationalization in this context refers to policies aimed at reducing costs, enhancing quality or otherwise improving productivity by "inducing a) capacity expansion, b) process innovation, or c) adoption of new technology in particular firms" (Dholakia and Wish 1983, 15). According to Johnson, the essence of such rationalization is

the attempt by the state to discover what it is individual enterprises are already doing to produce the greatest benefits at least cost, and then, in the interest of the nation as a whole, to cause all the enterprises of an industry to adopt these preferred procedures and techniques. (1982, 27)

Our concern is with rationalization policies the aim of which is to promote better intrafirm and interorganizational behavior. Johnson points out one aspect of the Japanese companies' organizational success:

Japanese workers are loyal to their enterprises, strike them rarely and only for short periods of time, and accept wage cuts to keep their products competitive (as well as to keep their jobs), not because of some cultural predisposition but because of explicit incentives that make such behavior rational. (1984, 13)

Framework for Organizational Policy

The conventional regulatory approach for dealing with illegitimate firm behavior and negative externalities involves laws, regulations and enforcement. It may very well foster interorganizational cooperation by lowering the payoffs to noncooperative behavior. Our analyses in the previous section suggest that conventional approaches are insufficient because they do not address other important causes of interorganizational noncooperation. Furthermore, conventional approaches are not at all addressed to intrafirm noncooperation.

The essence of organizational policy is to encourage organizational rationalization leading to Theory Z firm behavior. Within the firm, it means encouraging organizational developments that attenuate opportunism, encourage open communication, and promote the sharing and acceptance of common purposes and values. It also means providing an appropriate structure of extrinsic incentives to cooperation, fostering latent altruism, reminding members about the negative future consequences of noncooperation, and providing ample opportunities for worker participation. In essence, it concerns developing a favorable (or rightward) implicit psychological contract between the organization and its members. As indicated in chapter 7, Japanese companies have developed a particularly favorable implicit psychological contract, and the Japanese federal government has encouraged this development.

Both similarities and differences exist between encouraging cooperation between organizations and encouraging internal cooperation. Opportunistic behavior needs to be discouraged. Governments should not merely foster socially acceptable firm behavior but should challenge firms to adopt voluntarily humanistic goals integrated with societal goals. Firms whose members internalize these values should find it much easier to cooperate with members of other organizations with whom they share values, easier to conceive of cooperative solutions to negative externality situations, and more disagreeable to impose costs on other organizations.

Japan is notable for the pattern of cooperation that has evolved between government and business. This seems in sharp contrast to the frequently hostile and adversarial relations in the United States (Johnson 1982, 311). Japan's Ministry of International Trade and Industry has performed the difficult role of fostering and maintaining this cooperation. MITI

makes continued efforts to build a consensus between government and business on what is good for the country. The Japanese experience suggests that so long as an atmosphere of confrontation and mutual distrust prevails between the state and private business, industrial policy will be inoperative. (Ozaki 1984, 66)

For a U.S. example of successful industry policy involving government-business cooperation, see Johnson's (1984, 19–20) account of the Texas Railroad Commission and the domestic petroleum industry from the 1930s to the 1970s.

In William Ouchi's view, the essence of a good industrial policy involves a participative democratic process in which there is a balance of teamwork (or cooperation) and competition among business and other organizations. The desired role of government is "to create an atmosphere of balanced competition in which each firm strives to outdo the others, but in which all work as a team to resolve their differences directly" (1984a, 25). For this to happen, there is especially a need for "peak associations that can bring the private contenders together, sustain a dialogue between them, and do it in an atmosphere conducive to . . . [the desired] balance" (p. 163). If this and a few other organizational changes were made, Ouchi believes that the resulting social integration would enable the nation to avoid the kind of social gridlock that has contributed to low industrial productivity. In other words, investment in organizational change to create cooperative in-terorganizational relations is the key to making industrial policy work and thereby achieving higher productivity.

As we move beyond simple profit-maximizing models of firm behavior toward realistic behavioral models, it becomes easier to see that the state can condition and influence industrial behavior in many ways. For example, the analysis of external social control indicated how governments can facilitate desirable community influences on firms and dampen undesirable ones. Desirable cooperative behavior is also likely to be fostered when various federal agencies send consistent signals to companies, government policy is not subject to abrupt shifts, and government policy demands are consistent with business strategic capabilities (Leone and Bradley 1981, 93). Government policy makers need to realize that government actions not only influence business actions toward nongovernmental organizations but influence business decisions on how to behave in relation to government. Unfortunately, it is all too possible for government and business to wind up fulfilling the unhappy prophecy of the southeast cell of the prisoner's dilemma game.

CONCLUSION

Conjure up a vision of an ideal society. In this society, not only are productivity and incomes growing at relatively high rates because of the efforts of dynamic internationally competitive companies, but the air and water are pollution-free, book stores and newsstands are free of pornography, and highly motivated people enjoy their work. Obviously, the United States is not about to realize this state of affairs overnight; the behavioral patterns that contribute to the persistence of our problems undoubtedly have deep roots. Hopefully, however, this chapter has shed some light on these interorganizational behavior patterns, particularly noncooperation, which lie at the heart of many of our social problems. Solving these problems will require new kinds of leadership and new kinds of policy. Although the policy analysis here is merely suggestive, there are reasons for believing that organizational policy, a relatively neglected dimension of industrial policy, would by its very nature operate on the source of these problems because it would encourage needed investments in organizational capital. Developing the details of such policies remains a subject for future research.

10

The Organizational Challenge of the Third Wave

"America has a choice: It can adapt itself to the new realities by altering its organizations, or it can fail to adapt and thereby continue its present decline. (Reich 1983, 20–21)

There is therefore progress in human history; but it is a progress of all human potencies, both for good and evil. (Reinhold Niebuhr, *The Nature and Destiny of Man,* 1945, as quoted in Bell 1980, 32)

INTRODUCTION

Is a fundamental, irreversible social and economic restructuring occurring in the United States and other industrialized countries? Is a third wave now breaking upon the shores of our civilization? Is a postindustrial society emerging from our present industrial one? Many believe so, and a number of important writers argue convincingly that the rapid social changes and crises we have experienced in the last fifteen years are evidence. If such a sea change is occurring, it is important to inquire into the underlying nature of this change in order to make sense of current events and future possibilities. Understanding the essence of these subsurface phenomena should enable us to adapt individual decisions and governmental policies in order to make the best of the future. Unfortunately, the writers who have attempted to char-acterize the principles of the new emerging social structure frequently disagree, not unlike the seven blind men who described the shape of an elephant based on the parts they were able to touch. Of course, it is natural for these writers, like the blind men, to view things differently as their viewpoints reflect differing professional orientations. Yet there is also much in common in these characterizations of the emerging civilization. The purpose of this chapter is to review a number of visions of the future in order to anticipate some of the major sources of change with an impact on the organization of work. In effect these views constitute a challenge. In the future will we be able to create the new organizational structures and patterns that will enable us to realize our full human potential, or will we underachieve because we cannot change what were previously successful behavior patterns.

The subject of broad-based societal change involves large scale synthesis and interdisciplinary thinking, and it places a premium on intuitive perception. This is in contrast to the usual style of economists, which involves careful, logical reasoning. It is true, of course, that some of the most influential economic thinkers such as Marx, Veblen, Schumpeter and Galbraith have dealt with the structure of the economy, its changes, and interactions between it and other aspects of society, but they have tended to be the exceptions to the rule. It should be noted, however, that even the most rigorous model-building economists need to be concerned with the structure of the economy. This is because their models tend to function well only for a given economic structure, and it is necessary to revise these models in light of significant structural change. Since the concern of this book is with organization and organizational capital formation, the following review and analysis of anticipated societal change will focus largely on organization-related matters.

THE EMERGENCE OF A NEW CIVILIZATION

The Third Wave

Alvin Toffler's *The Third Wave* (1980) describes the dying old civilization and "presents a careful, comprehensive picture of the new civilization bursting into being in our midst" (p. 2). It is well-written, provocative and often convincing on the nature of these social changes. In Toffler's view, the first wave of change, the agricultural revolution, and the second wave, the rise of industrial civilization, will be followed by the third wave. Out of the current crises will come a quantum leap forward, a "revolution" involving new codes of behavior and new potentials.

Second wave civilization, according to Toffler, involved a

system with parts that interacted with each other in more or less predictable ways—and . . . the fundamental patterns of industrial life were the same in country after country, regardless of cultural heritage or political difference. (1980, 18)

The second wave system is characterized by the use of mass-produced, mechanistic technology, mechanistic thinking, and the idea of progressing through the exploitation of nature. Moreover, second wave behavior involves standardization, synchronization, centralization, specialization, maximization and concentration of energy, money and power. Third wave civilization, on the other hand, will emphasize customized, flexible production, will be more compatible with nature because of its use of renewable, less centralized energy, and will be more decentralized geographically and for communication purposes. The new technologies will be the non-mechanistic, electronic, information technologies with less need for standardization or synchronization. Third wave civilization will emphasize the creation of communities and shared meanings. The organization most representative of the second wave is the

classical industrial bureaucracy: a giant, hierarchical, permanent, top-down, mechanistic organization, well designed for making repetitive products or repetitive decisions in a comparatively stable industrial environment. . . . Third Wave organizations have flatter hierarchies. They are less top-heavy. They consist of small components linked together in temporary configurations . . . [and are] capable of assuming two or more distinct structural shapes as conditions warrant. (p. 263)

In the smaller, self-managed, decentralized third wave corporations, workers would have higher morale and be able to satisfy their needs for belonging, meaningfulness and community (pp. 369–379). Third wave workers are those "who demand that their work be socially responsible" (p. 386). Besides being efficient and responsive to workers, third wave corporations will need to set goals responsive to the biosphere, the social environment, the info-sphere, the power-sphere and the moral sphere (pp. 235–243).

Megatrends

John Naisbitt's *Megatrends* (1982) is in a sense an update on *The Third Wave* using different methods. Naisbitt's vision of the future is derived explicitly from an analysis of current trends. Like *The Third Wave,* it is a celebration of positive societal trends, a hopeful look at the potential of the United States, and it has an air of inevitability about the direction of these changes. Naisbitt tells us that if we can only anticipate clearly this newly evolving world, we will be a "quantum leap ahead of those who hold on to the past" (p. 279).

Amont the important trends cited by Naisbitt are:

1. the move from an industrial society to an information society,

2. a move to increased participatory democracy,

3. a move from hierarchies to networking,

4. a shift toward a long-term orientation in business,

5. a move to decentralization,

6. an increase in entrepreneurial behavior and self-employment, and

7. along with the move toward high technology, a counterbalancing move to "high touch" (very human) personal nontechnological responses.

In Naisbitt's (1982, pp. 211–229) view, because of the failure of hierarchy, the new management system will be based on the networking model. Thus, communications will be lateral, diagonal, bottom up, and cross-disciplinary; and the organization style will be egalitarian, entrepreneurial, participative, nurturing, empowering, nonexploitive, team-oriented and wholistic.

Post-industrial Society

No serious effort in social forecasting can afford to ignore Daniel Bell's *The Coming of Post-industrial Society*. Bell, writing in the best sociological tradition, has extrapolated important social structural changes into the future and explored their implications for the future. In post-industrial society, knowledge (especially theoretical knowledge) is the strategic resource. The five key characteristics of postindustrial society, as different from pre-industrial and industrial societies, all relate to the increasing importance of knowledge (Bell 1973, 14–34):

1. Service sector activities, especially trade, finance, transport, health, recreation, research, education, and government employ the majority of the labor force.

2. The professional and technical classes are preeminent in the occupational distribution.

3. Codified theoretical knowledge has become the all-important basis for innovation and policy formation.

4. Technological forecasting, involving an orientation to the future, is used to plan for and control technological growth.

5. Decision making increasingly uses new intellectual technologies, typically involving logical, mathematical or statistical calculation techniques often made possible by the computer.

In Bell's vision of postindustrial society, economic activities and functions are increasingly subordinate to political control using new control systems. Although Bell indicates that the move to a postindustrial society will involve many changes in relationships and structures and that the new society will emphasize interpersonal relations (it's "a game between persons" [p. 117]), he does not give explicit attention to changes in management and organization.

The Next American Frontier

In the views of Toffler and Naisbitt the recent economic and social tur-
moil is merely a necessary prelude, like labor pains, to the birth of the new
civilization. In contrast, Robert Reich's *The Next American Frontier* (1983)
develops the view that it is possible for the United States to respond to the
new realities and to develop more successful patterns of business and government behavior, but he sees a very real possibility of a failure to adapt and
a continuation of the present decline. Unlike Toffler and Naisbitt, Reich
does not make a rosy social forecast but explains past patterns, new realities,
and hard choices, and prescribes governmental policies to reverse the
decline.

At the heart of Reich's argument is his call for increased "flexible system
production," which in contrast to high-volume standardized production is
more adaptable to changing circumstances. This is because it uses more
flexible technologies, more highly skilled employees and better functioning
organizations. These organizations have flat organization structures, provide workers with employment security and treat them fairly, require a
high degree of worker participation, place a premium on teamwork and
cooperation, require the integration of traditionally separate business functions, and require a "less rigidly delineated relationship between management and labor and a new relationship with government" (Reich 1983, 129–
130, 134, 257–259, 278). In Reich's view, businesses' adjustment to flexible
system production will require assistance from government in the form of
strategic (or industrial) policies in which businesses and government collab-
orate to achieve societal development goals. One problem with Reich's
analysis is that his concept of flexible system production is not developed
extensively or precisely, even though it is clear that he finds Japanese organizational forms attractive. Because of this his vision of the possible future is
clouded.

The Second Industrial Divide

In Michael Piore and Charles Sabel's *The Second Industrial Divide* (1984),
they present the optimistic possibility that future technology and organization may be dominated by "flexible specialization" rather than by mass
production and its accompanying organization. Flexible specialization
(which is not the same as flexible system production)

is a strategy of permanent innovation . . . [that] is based on flexible—multi-use—
equipment; skilled workers; and the creation, through politics, of an industrial
community that restricts the forms of competition to those favoring innovation.
(Piore and Sabel 1984, 17).

Piore and Sabel explain that because of the technological and organizational diversity which now exist, we have a second opportunity (the "second industrial divide") to choose between flexible specialization, which is associated with craft forms of production, and mass production, which was chosen at the first industrial divide. Flexible specialization in its different forms is, in Piore and Sabel's view, superior to mass production. Their analysis is designed to explain the significance of the choice between the two. Piore and Sabel hypothesize that the previous choice and development of the mass-production paradigm does not mean that this path was natural or inevitable because of greater economic efficiency. However, once mass production was chosen by those with resources at their command, others tended to follow in developing this path (Piore and Sabel 1984, p. 15 and chapter 2). If we were to choose flexible specialization today, Piore and Sabel believe it would mean not only greater prosperity but it would also require us to develop more communitarian institutions and a "yeoman democracy" in which "the state is responsible for creating conditions conducive to a republic of small holders" concerned with serving the community (p. 305).

Some Extensions and Modifications

Despite their differences, these five authors' views of the future provide a useful point of departure for inquiring into the nature of the organizational future. Before proceeding, it is important to note a few areas in which my views diverge from or extend these authors' views with respect to the likely trajectory of society. First, I do not agree with Toffler and Naisbitt's analysis to the extent that it involves a simple technological determinism. In other words, I do not believe that the use of particular technologies leads inevitably to a certain type of society. It seems to me that other choices, such as political and organizational ones, have much to do with how technology is used and thus how it affects our lives. Second, I believe that the development and diffusion of new oganizational knowledge may be every bit as important as these processes are for technological knowledge. Further, to extend Daniel Bell's insight regarding technology, I feel that in recognition of the importance of organization, societies will increasingly plan for and control organizational growth. In this vein, recall that chapter 9 provided a few suggestions regarding governmental policies to facilitate desired organizational and interorganizational developments. Third, I believe that new technology, particularly because it may provide an opportunity to reevaluate organizational choices, will be a more important determinant of organizational change than either demographic factors or the increased global competition. Therefore, I will emphasize the latter less in what follows.

THE ORGANIZATIONAL CHALLENGE: REALIZING THE POTENTIAL OF THE EMERGING CIVILIZATION

The nature of our society's organizational future is more important than generally realized. As Alfred Chandler points out,

historically the key entrepreneurial act has been creating an organization. . . . Technological innovations are no good until you exploit them organizationally. That doesn't mean a big organization, it means understanding how to get people to work together and making very clear what the team should do and what each member of the team should do. Organizational innovation is really important in all of these. Historically, the person who really cleaned up was the one who picked up the innovation and then created a team. (Hartman 1985, 54)

Let's assume that the five authors considered in the previous section are correct, and that the present period represents a major turning point. If so, the following questions must be raised. Will business entrepreneurs initiate organizational innovations enabling us to take full advantage of the potential inherent in the emerging order? Which features of the new order are mismatched with the existing organization, and which factors will determine whether businesses successfully adapt their organizations to the new realities? What form will the new organization take, and how will its use spread among businesses? There are the key questions considered in the next two sections.[1]

The Challenge of New Technology

If you don't let people grow and develop and make more decisions, it's a waste of human life—a waste of human potential. If you don't use your knowledge and skill it's a waste of life. Using the technology to its full potential means using the man to his full potential. (Worker from Tiger Creek pulp and paper plant, quoted by Zuboff 1985, 139)

Following Walton (1985c, 200), "the new work technology referred to here includes robotics, numerical control machining, computer-aided design, computer-aided manufacture, manufacturing planning requirements, automated storage and retrieval, automated process controls, point-of-sale systems, word processing, and many applications of new information technology to the unique requirements of the telecommunications industry, such as automated test equipment and work-force scheduling." Manufacturing in particular offers a wide opportunity for the application of advanced information technology;[2] applications abound in other sectors as well.

Calvin Pava (1985, 76–93) argues that when a business adopts a new technology it tends to reexamine many aspects of its organization and management. Old patterns of behavior may not work well with the new technology, and this forces the firm to give explicit managerial attention to previously fixed organizational factors. The growing pervasiveness of new technology and consequent organizational change opportunities mean that the organizational future will be different from the present and suggest it may be better.

The challenge to business of new technology is to renovate organizations so that technical functionality can be translated into tangible benefits. Such effective utilization of the technology occurs when

the applications of the technology are designed and implemented so as to (1) yield the cost, quality and service benefits for the enterprise that are potential in the technology; and (2) minimize adverse effects on the work force and promote positive organization effects. (Walton 1985b, 201)

Unfortunately, as Walton's (1985c, 200–201) research indicates, managers have rarely been guided by such a concept of effectiveness. Thus, many of the effects (both positive and negative) arising from the applications of new technology have been accidental and unanticipated.

With respect to utilization of new technology, Shoshana Zuboff (1985, 105–106) points out that management in effect must choose between two technology strategies; they must either "automate" of "informate." If operations are automated, human effort and skill will be displaced, as when robots are used in place of workers to spray the paint on cars. If operations are informated, the information capacity of the technology is used by workers to enhance their capabilities and productivity, often allowing greater utilization of their abilities. Ideally, these choices relate to both the design and the implementation of the technology. The choice is certainly not dictated by the characteristics of computer-based technology, which is extremely flexible and easily adapted to either technological strategy. Walton's (1985c, 202) research indicates that U.S. decision making on new technology has been biased toward automation largely because only economic and technical criteria are used in these decisions to the exclusion of social or human organizational criteria. Thus, decisions to deploy new technology are being made which view the side effects as inevitable rather than as an element that could be improved by better planning and management. In order to understand better management's new technology options, it is necessary to consider both of these strategies in more detail.

The Automation Strategy. In a full-fledged automation strategy, worker efforts may be eliminated, made more routine and less skilled, and made subject to greater external control. This is the essence of Taylorism or what Walton (1985a) has called the "control strategy." The attraction to managers of automation derives from the fact that managers are rewarded on the bases of their ability to get more done, more efficiently, with fewer people. Such structural pressures reinforce an underlying but potent managerial fantasy of achieving perfect control through total automation and thus avoiding the messiness and potential conflict of human interaction. . . . Managers frequently comment on the pleasure they take in robots that do not require coffee breaks or automatic systems that perform continually without demands for overtime pay. (Zuboff 1985, 130–131)

In Harley Shaiken's (1984, 45) view, managerial desires to reduce direct labor and to increase control are pervasive managerial purposes.

The problem with the automation or control strategy is that it can produce many adverse social and organizational effects (see Walton 1985c, 203–204, for a list) and that workers generally try to either ameliorate these adverse effects or to retaliate. "Whether worker reactions were spontaneous or deliberate, protective or aggressive, these reactions undermined the technical and economic performance of the new work technology" (Walton 1985c, 201). When management assumes that employees are apathetic and antagonistic toward work, and when management's adoption of technology replaces labor, deskills and routinizes work, and monitors workers, employee apathy and antagonism will be generated and reinforced resulting in lower economic performance (Walton 1985c, 207–208).[3] As Zuboff (1985, 133–134) points out, the automation strategy widens the gulf between managers and workers and leads to a more sharply hierarchical organization in which there are few opportunities for advancement from the lowest levels. Shaiken has highlighted a few other problems of the control strategy in the context of the decision to adopt numerically controlled metal cutting machines.

Seeking to isolate the machinist from any real input in this highly integrated system cuts the entire operation off from vital shop floor feedback. For another, when machines are designed to require few skills, few skills may be available when they are needed. And, a further cost is the destruction of creative and meaningful work, an ironic development given the capacity of computers and microelectronics to enrich work. (1984, 68)

The Informating Strategy. When work is informated using computer-based technology, precise information about the nature of the work process must be obtained and converted into data that is stored in the computer and available for display. Based on worker understanding of the production process and their observation of continually changing data, workers control the work process, solve problems regarding it, and propose innovations. A good example of this is Zuboff's (1985) account of the adoption by three pulp and paper firms of new microprocessor-based instrumentation that allows laborers to interact remotely with these firms' continuous production processes. Using this new technology and their newly acquired intellective skills (involving cause and effect understanding of the work process) workers utilize their capacity to a much greater degree than formerly in guiding production operations.

One benefit of informating technology is that the fundamental distinction between workers as physical doers and managers as knowledge workers breaks down, making possible an increase in social integration. Accordingly, "the differences between organizational levels are now defined more by comprehensiveness and range of responsibilities than by differences in everyday work experience" (Zuboff 1985, 135). Secondly, the greater information and knowledge at the disposal of the workers allows them to think critically and creatively about the work process and to take responsible action based on their perceptions (p. 132). This greater, more meaningful participation generally leads to greater worker commitment and effort, and thus improved economic performance (Walton 1985c, 201). Indeed, higher motivation is more of a necessity for information or knowledge workers because it is more difficult to detect shirking on knowledge tasks than on physical tasks. It follows that less employee apathy and antagonism is generated when using an informating technology strategy compared to an automating one. Moreover, Walton (1985c, 210–215) believes that if managers and workers jointly consider the design and use of proposed new technology before its adoption, the technology will be more likely to be used effectively because it will satisfy both economic and social/organizational criteria.[4]

The informating option, of course, is not without costs or disadvantages. Typically, a greater investment in training and organizational change is required than for automating. This is especially true because information workers require intellective skills and the kind of organizational environment conducive to higher motivation and commitment (Zuboff 1985, 137–138). It should also be noted that workers whose jobs are transformed by the new technology will inevitably experience feelings of loss associated with the obsolescence of their old skills and the lack of physical contact with the production process (pp. 110–115). A very significant problem that arises with the informating option is the threat it poses to managers, especially middle managers, who may resist the change. This is because workers take on roles formerly associated with management, and managers are no longer in a clearly dominant position (p. 136). Thus, as Peter Drucker (1986b) observes, managers "have to be redirected; they have to acquire new vision, new values and new skills."

From this comparison of the automation and informatization alternatives, it is clear that "informatization . . . renders inadequate the Tayloristic [automation/control] approach to work organization. . . . Creativity, and collaboration, and innovation [must] replace control as guiding managerial objectives" (Zuboff 1985, 138). Through the use of informating technology and an implementation process characterized by mutuality between workers and managers, it is possible to minimize the adverse consequences for the work force and to realize the technology's economic performance potential.

The Challenge of the Baby Boomers

There are two related demographic trends that pose a challenge for work organization. First, the relatively high birth rate during the 1946–1964 period has meant high rates of labor force entry by young people for the past 15 to 20 years and high competition for lower-level positions. Second, whether they were born in the "baby boom" period or since then, today's young workers and labor force entrants have a different set of expectations from their predecessors. This generation recognizes and anticipates the shift into knowledge work and out of manual work. It expects white collar, knowledge jobs, not blue collar positions (Drucker 1982, 93).[5]

The question this raises is how organizations can change to take maximum advantage of these trends. With respect to the second trend, the organizational implication is fairly clear. It requires businesses to gear technology and organizations to the use of knowledge workers rather than manual workers. It requires shifting work from operating machines to programming machines and processes, and to operating informating types of technology (see Drucker 1982, 94–95). Otherwise, the mismatch between worker expectations and their organization settings will cause low economic performance.

One problem already being experienced by the baby boom generation is frustration caused by slow advancement through the management ranks because many are competing for promotion to relatively few higher positions. The answer is "to restructure jobs on the assumption that even a capable and hard-working person may have to spend many years on or near the entrance level. Early assignments will have to be made more demanding and more challenging" (Drucker 1982, 170). In addition, Drucker indicates the need for changed incentives, appraisals, manager development, and counseling of young workers (p. 170). It should be noted that the organizational implications of these two demographic trends are consistent with the organizational implications for new technology. In other words, the organization form most compatible with an informating technology strategy is also the form that would enable a company to realize the potential contribution of its young workers given their attributes and numbers.

The Challenge of Global Competition

Much of the current impetus to U.S. technological and organizational change derives, of course, from the fact that U.S. firms have experienced an increase in competition from foreign imports, particularly those from Japan among the advanced industrial countries and from newly industrializing

countries (NICs) such as Taiwan and Korea.[6] In the case of Japanese companies, the competitive threat is posed by their use of advanced technology
along with a management style (like Toyota's), "which emphasizes thor-
ough training and participative management, lean layers of middle management, and decision making pushed as close as possible to the assembly line"
(*Business Week* 1986a). In the case of NICs, the threat is posed by a combination of low wages and these countries' increasing mastery of mass-production techniques, often in relatively mature industries. Thus, in the U.S.
mature industries using older technology are losing out to the NICs, while
newer and more progressive industries are experiencing competitive pressure more from Japan.

If U.S. companies are to survive in sectors where competition is strong,
they must learn to do at least as well as Japan and use a similar approach to
technology and management. This is the essence of what Abernathy, Clark
and Kantrow (1983) have learned by studying recent developments in the
auto industry.

To give workers inadequate training in the technologies with which they must deal,
to treat them as mindless drones suitable only for dull, repetitive tasks, or to ignore
the vast contribution they can make when integrated into a coherent manufacturing
system is to throw away through sheer carelessness or, worse, unthinking prejudice
a uniquely valuable corporate resource. There may have been a time when a sweat-
shop mentality, whatever its social noxiousness, proved useful in the market. That
time has long since disappeared. . . . The future does not belong to firms that try to
make up for poor work-force management or sloppy plants with cutting-edge
technology. Nor does it belong to firms that do not bother with new advances in
technology because their factories are well run by present standards. The future
belongs only to those firms—and managers—who eagerly seize opportunities on
both fronts. (Abernathy, Clark, and Kantrow 1983, 125)

PATHS TO THE ORGANIZATIONAL FUTURE

Because some of the desirable characteristics of Japanese management
were explored in the section above and in chapter 7, it seems unnecessary to
examine Japanese management further. Rather, let's take a look at a slightly
different management model for the future.

The Atomized Organization

Deal and Kennedy (1982) believe that a decentralized structure that they
call the atomized organization would be best suited to deal with the challenges of the future. This organization would consist of

1) Small, task-focused work units (ten to twenty persons maximum),
2) Each with economic and managerial control over its own destiny,

3) Interconnected with larger entities through benign computer and communications links,
4) And bonded into larger companies through strong cultural bonds. (Deal and Kennedy 1982, 182–183)

This organization is seen as a "no-boss business" where middle management rungs are replaced by mechanisms of social influence, that is, cultural ties. The small work units would provide an intimate, simple work environment where entrepreneurial behavior would be encouraged (p. 177). It would differ from Japanese management primarily in its extreme decentralization and its mechanisms for linking the small units to the whole. Deal and Kennedy believe that the atomized organization would make good use of computer technology, would be well adapted to attributes of the baby-boom work force, and would be able to respond well to a complex, rapidly changing environment (chapter 10). It should be noted that Deal and Kennedy's atomized organization is similar to Piore and Sabel's (1984) flexible specialization insofar as the latter involves loose links (often of an ethnic or cultural nature) between autonomous small units such as those among Italian or New York City garment makers or the federations among some Japanese companies (the descendants of the pre-World War II *zaibatsu*). It also resembles the emerging "hollow" or "dynamic network" corporations that are industrial companies that farm out to other companies just about every functional aspect of bringing a product to market (*Business Week* 1986c, 65–71). Hollow corporations, which are in some ways like trading companies, may be very flexible and fast-moving but lack some advantages of more integrated companies.

The Management/Leadership Obstacle

Regardless of the particular organization of the future (Japanese, atomized, Mondragon-style producer cooperatives or some other form), it is clear that new managerial and leadership behavior will be required. Since the new organization forms involve new sets of managerial roles, the authoritarian styles of the past will fail. For example, in the atomized organization, managers will be facilitators, promoters and creators of culture, balancers of competing interests, and developers of appropriate structures (Deal and Kennedy 1982, 189). Furthermore, a society populated by these new organization forms will require leadership of a new character in business and government at all levels. As Michael Maccoby (1981, 23) puts it, "the old models of leadership no longer work"; they no longer fit our changed social character. New leadership must

correspond to the most positive attributes of the new social character [and thus involve] 1) a caring, respectful, and responsible attitude; 2) flexibility about people and organizational structure; and 3) a participative approach to management, the willingness to share power. Furthermore . . . [leaders must be] concerned with self-development for themselves as well as others. (p. 221)

Maccoby points out six leaders that embody these qualities but leaves open the question whether the predominant old styles of leadership (the "company man," the "gamesman," and so on) will eventually give way to the newer developmental style. A key question here is whether new organizational forms will proliferate and develop the types of needed leadership.

Scenarios for Organizational Change

Old leadership patterns, values and thought processes are certainly an obstacle to change, but this doesn't mean that new organizational forms won't spread. If the new forms are better adapted to emerging realities, there are many ways in which these forms will become more prevalent. Let's examine a number of scenarios.

Japanese Companies. In the first scenario, Japanese management spreads as Japanese companies buy U. S. firms or establish new businesses in the United States. This scenario is fast becoming a reality as "a new wave of Japanese investment is sweeping across America" (*Business Week* 1986b, 45). The success of Japanese management at NUMMI (New United Motor Manufacturing Inc., the Toyota-General Motors joint venture in California) is illustrative of this phenomenon.

Adding little new technology, NUMMI's Japanese bosses set up a typical Toyota production system, with just-in-time delivery and a flexible assembly line run by teams of workers in charge of their own jobs. They hired back most of the former United Auto Workers members who wanted work—even their militant leaders. NUMMI makes a single auto, while GM built several models. But its 2500 employees can assemble 240,000 cars a year, roughly equal to what it took 5,000 or more people to produce under GM. There are only two grievances outstanding, and absenteeism is running under two percent. . . . In many of the most basic manufacturing sectors—from ball bearings to industrial filters to machine tools—the Japanese are buying companies and forming joint ventures. Although there are some horror stories, the newcomers often run factories better than the U.S. owners did (*Business Week* 1986b, 47)

The New Small Companies. In scenario two, small companies using progressive management and technology grow at the expense of the large, less efficient, previously dominant corporations. According to Zolton Acs (1984), this is what is happening in the U.S. steel industry, where 61 "minimills" using the best modern technology are continuing to take away market share from the 15 large integrated producers because the minimills are the lowest-cost steel producers in the country. According to Ken Iverson

("Steel Man Ken Iverson," *Inc.* 1986), chief executive officer of Nucor Corporation, which operates several minimills, Nucor "produces more than twice the steel per man-hour as workers in large steel companies" (p. 41). Much of their high productivity is attributed to good organization and management. For example, their organization structure includes only four management layers which allows for better and faster decisions and better communication (p. 44). Also, Nucor tries "very consciously to eliminate any differentiation between management and everybody else" (p. 44), and compensation at all levels is a function of company performance.

Excellent Companies Grow and Give Birth. According to Peters and Waterman (1982), the U.S. companies with superior economic performance over a substantial period of time are companies with superior management characteristics. On the average these companies have grown faster over the 20 years from 1961–1980 than other companies (pp. 22–23). These companies also have a tendency to give birth to new organizations with similar characteristics. For example, managers leaving Hewlett-Packard have established such progressive and participatively managed corporations as Intel and Tandem. (See Deal and Kennedy 1982, 8–13, for a description of Tandem's culture.)

Organizational Renewal. In scenario four, in response to competitive pressure major established U.S. corporations begin to make systematic revisions in their approaches to human resource management to move away from a philosophy of control and toward a philosophy of commitment and mutuality. According to Walton (1985a, 62–64) an increasing number of major companies are making such moves, which are now being supported and promoted by senior management. This trend is in contrast to the early 1970s. Lawrence (1985a, 351–357) reports that in the view of these senior executives this is a major and nonreversible change which is being driven forward by the forces of competition. These executives

responded that for any organization facing significant change and strong competition, the answer was that it must change or perish. [They believe that] firms experiencing the traditional adversarial split between labor and management would not survive. . . . [For example,] Proctor and Gamble executives cited the fact that ten or so plants using the new ways have consistently outperformed their more traditionally managed plants with similar products and technology by a margin of 30–40 percent in overall product costs year after year for the past ten years. (pp. 352–353)

General Motors and Ford are among the companies that have begun efforts to achieve organizational renewal in part by borrowing so-called Japanese ideas, but unfortunately the assumption that high technology and automation alone will solve their competitive problems seems deeply embedded. It may indeed be related to some of their recent problems (*Business Week* 1986a, 103–104). Thus, despite the accelerating rate of transformation, there are significant problems in achieving renewal, and as Walton admits "only a small fraction of U.S. workplaces today are managed by the . . . commitment model" (1985a, 65).

Frustrated Employees. According to the fifth scenario, employees in large corporations, frustrated with old organizational styles and their inability to participate meaningfully, quit to form companies which embody more participative forms of management. It is difficult to say precisely how important this scenario is currently. However, the rise in annual new business formations from around 200,000 in 1965 to around 600,000 in 1983 (Acs 1984, 209) and the frequency of articles in the business press reporting on instances of people quitting to start new businesses suggests its importance (see, for example, Rout 1986).

In sum, despite real obstacles there are enough plausible scenarios for the emergence of organizations better adapted to the future to make one hopeful.

CONCLUSION

The organizations best adapted to the future will be ones that make the most effective use of new technology by adopting two complementary strategies, an informating technology strategy (as opposed to an automating one) and a highly participative human resource management strategy (as opposed to a control strategy). Because Tayloristic or control strategies have predominated in the U.S. and continue to have a strong hold on the minds of industrial managers, it is not clear whether an organizational transformation will take place in the near future. All one can say is that there are a number of very plausible scenarios in which market forces could bring about a dramatic new system of human resource management.[7] Because businesses now have so much to gain, and much to lose by doing nothing, the current rates of return to investment in organizational transformation would seem to be very high. Thus, I expect to see a growing level of organizational capital formation.

In other parts of the world, similar organizational transformations can be expected because developments in new technology and global competition will affect them similarly. In my recent visit to Israel, I heard about the pressures for change on Israel's kibbutzim. The kibbutzim, which involve collective worker ownership and consumption, are now contemplating organizational changes that would facilitate their use of new technology in their industrial enterprises. While kibbutzim have from the very beginning been characterized by high worker participation and egalitarian relationships, there seems to be a need for organizational changes in order to better coordinate and motivate members' work as well as to achieve economies of scale. Obviously, the specific organizational changes that a kibbutz would need to make would be very different from those needed by a U.S.

company, but in responding to similar realities these differing changes may indicate a convergence toward similar human resource management strategies.

While market forces might bring about organizational transformation, I believe for reasons indicated below that increasingly governments in the United States and elsewhere will play a role in this transformation. First, there is a growing appreciation not only of the importance of organization but the large economic losses a nation might experience if its business enterprises are not well adapted or adapt too slowly. Second, the organizational role that government might play is very much the same as the U.S. and other governments already play with respect to technology, that is, fostering new technology and controlling its use. Third, knowledge of human relationships and how to change them has expanded greatly over the last several decades. Thus, it seems likely that governments will come to play a significant role not only in fostering the development and diffusion of organizational knowledge but also in encouraging its use by companies investing in organizational change. Through such efforts to influence organizational structure and especially culture, governments may do more to tap their society's human potential for productivity and well-being than in any other way. While in the past nations occasionally benefited from the organizational talents of a few rare entrepreneurs, nations in the future will want to ensure that more systematic efforts are made to create efficient and humane organizations.

If I am right about the organizational future, is Toffler also right about the organizational nature of the Third Wave? He is right in some ways and wrong in others. His intuition about the coming of more participative, less hierarchical organizations seems on target. In Toffler's view, however, the organizational wave of the future is inextricably linked to other elements of the third wave, a wave that will break as inevitably as an ocean wave. Also, Toffler provides little analysis to explain his beliefs about the organizational future. He could be right, but I am not as sanguine about the future.

11

Conclusion

THE IMPORTANCE OF ORGANIZATIONAL CAPITAL

The organizational capital concept is a tremendously important one. First, this concept directs our attention to aspects of human relationships that economists have generally ignored, and it enables us to understand how these relationships affect important economic outcomes. In contrast to economics, within the behaviorally oriented social sciences, it is widely recognized that human relationships shape the behavior of the people involved in them whether in businesses, government or families. It follows that the quality of organizational relationships influences worker behavior, and thereby, not only determines an organization's productive capacity but affects the well-being of its members. The term, organizational capital, simply recognizes the similarity between this capacity, which is related to how well organizations function, and other types of capacity such as those embodied in tangible inputs. With respect to increasing productivity, investment in organizational capital is very much an alternative to other investments such as those in tangible capital or worker training.

Another reason for the importance of the organizational capital concept is that it helps to integrate economics and knowledge of organizational behavior. This is true because it focuses attention on the characteristics of organizational relationships related to productivity and well-being. Also, it should be noted that integrating all types of behavioral knowledge with economics, and not only organizational behavioral knowledge, is an important activity that is increasingly being tackled by those in newly emerging disciplines such as behavioral economics.

THE NEGLECT OF ORGANIZATIONAL RELATIONSHIPS

Economists, by and large, have had little to say about either the internal operations of corporations or organizational relationships more generally; nor have they said much about how these influence productivity.[1] The heart of modern economics, after all, is concerned with behavior within markets. Accordingly, economists have tended to view businesses as responding to signals originating in the markets for products and factors of production. As cost minimizing/profit maximizing responders, businesses either choose the best available technology and organization or face extinction in the long run.[2] From this perspective, it is hard to believe the notion that many corporations have significant opportunities to improve their organizations, which could lead to substantially increased productivity and growth. If such improvement were possible, the conventional wisdom suggests, these corporations would either have quickly adopted these organizational improvements or, in the absence of change, would be losing out to competitors who did. Moreover, if these were the only two alternatives, there would be little reason for economists to be concerned with the nature of business organization or its change; organization and organizational knowledge would be simply two more inputs with a price, and business use of the conventional profit maximizing calculus would determine how much of them to use. It turns out that organizational realities give the lie to this overly simplistic view. As I have tried to indicate, there is much to be learned by focusing the analytical tools of economists on human relationships within and between organizations.

There is another reason why economists have avoided analyzing organizational matters. The analytical tools of economists are most clearly applicable when human behavior is motivated solely by materialistic concerns. Within organizations, however, motivation is complex; people are motivated to satisfy both higher and lower needs. Moreover, the highest motivation seems to be possible only when people have an opportunity to satisfy their highest (nonmaterial) needs. This obviously puts those who restrict themselves to conventional economic analysis at a disadvantage. According to Abraham Maslow (1971), "we must say harshly of the 'science' of economics that it is generally the skilled, exact, technological application of a totally false theory of human needs and values, a theory which recognizes only the existence of lower needs or material needs" (p. 310). Even if one believes Maslow's indictment is too harsh, it is clear that conventional analysis fits poorly within the organizational sphere.

ORGANIZING: THE OPPORTUNITY AND THE PAYOFF

One reason for the existence of many organizing opportunities is the significant number of factors that discourage organizing, which otherwise would have led to a better organization. First, there are substantially different paradigms or views about the characteristics of good organization and management. This is why, for example, one can speak of Japanese management as being quite different from typical U.S. management. Second, even within a particular paradigm, a firm has many organizing options because different aspects of an enterprise require organization, and no activity ever seems "totally" organized. Third, every enterprise is unique, and its organization must be tailored to its particular goals, strategies, technology, employees, resources and so on. Fourth, organizing is an important activity that requires significant time and attention on the part of skilled managers, who face many competing demands. Thus, it should not be surprising to find that there is much room for improvement in the typical corporate organization.

Despite these discouragements to organizing, much organizing activity is taking place. Perhaps because of the difficulties the payoff to organizing appears to be high. Broadly, this activity involves complementary activities: creating the desired organizational structure, creating an environment that fosters high motivation, and encouraging cooperation. Organizational structuring channels, patterns, and controls work, making for reliable completion of regularly occurring or routine tasks. Creating a high-quality work environment is, if anything, more difficult than organizational structuring because of its complex, intangible nature; it is also very necessary because without such an environment corporations cannot be expected to respond dynamically to external challenges. With increasing world competition and a growing number of corporations with organizational climates conducive to cooperative and motivated work, this aspect of organizing is becoming more crucial.

ORGANIZING LESSONS AND THE ACHIEVEMENT OF ECONOMIC POTENTIAL

To increase productivity growth, competitiveness, and standard of living in the United States requires learning the correct lessons about organization and successfully applying them throughout the economy. This means learning how increased worker participation can add to productivity. It means identifying the features of Japanese management that lead to high performance and analyzing how they can be adapted to U.S. organizations. It means learning about how the organizational structure of the Mondragon cooperatives contributes to motivation and productivity. It means reexamining past practices to select the kind of management and organization that is characterized simultaneously by high concern for people and production. It means that people-oriented participative human resource management should be at the heart of a firm's competitive strategy, and of a nation's as well. Also, it means recognizing that good management of people need not come at the expense of utilizing the best technology. Should this kind of organizational learning and application take place, and should the United States adopt rational macroeconomic policies designed to maintain full employment, the United States ought to regain the world economic leadership it presently seems to be losing. In other words, I believe that only by making the best possible investments in organizational capital throughout the economy will it be possible for the United States to reverse its current economic decline.

Consider what can be learned from the success of the Mondragon Cooperatives in the Basque region of Spain regarding industrial development. First, it should be noted that there are those who assert that Mondragon's success is primarily a product of the character and solidarity of the Basque people. However, the fact that Mondragon's enterprises have experienced substantially better economic performance than others in the Basque region indicates that the characteristics of the Basque people can not alone account for Mondragon's performance. Close observers of Mondragon are largely in agreement concerning the reasons for its success.

There are two vital elements in the success of Mondragon: one is the sophisticated management and ownership structure of the individual firms, which balances managerial effectiveness and employee participation. The second is the combination of profit-sharing for the employee-owner with the reinvestment needs of the firm. Taken separately, the ideas do not appear new, but when combined they have produced competitive and self-renewing organizations. Equally important is the management and financial support the co-ops get from the bank. It is as if a small American firm could afford financial advice from Morgan Stanley and could keep Arthur D. Little on retainer. (Simmons and Mares 1985, 141–142)

Creation of Mondragon-style organizational structures elsewhere certainly would not be an insuperable task, but the questions of leadership and dedication remain.

Whether or not a system such as Mondragon will be able to develop further and to flourish elsewhere will depend on whether or not people are available who are prepared to show similar competence, commitment and persistence as that shown by Father Arizmendi and the first cooperators of Mondragon. (Thomas and Logan 1982, 191)

Currently, there are groups such as the Industrial Cooperative Association of Massachusetts that are helping enterprises in the United States learn and apply the lessons of Mondragon. Perhaps, Mondragon-style cooperatives will flourish some day in the United States; at the moment it is too early to tell.

A similar issue arises with respect to Japanese management as its detractors have claimed that the successes of Japanese companies are related primarily to Japanese cultural characteristics. The implication is that these successes cannot be duplicated elsewhere. The accumulating evidence on both Japanese companies operating outside Japan as well as non-Japanese companies' use of Japanese management methods suggests the falsity of this view. Further, the more that is learned about Japanese management, the more it is clear that the advent of contemporary Japanese management was neither an historical accident nor determined entirely by its feudal past; rather it evolved out of a purposeful learning process. Much of the learning involved borrowing the best of U.S. management and combining it with the Japanese ethos. Today, of course, the United States is borrowing much from the Japanese and appears to be gaining from this process.

PRODUCTIVITY IMPLICATIONS

According to Hayes and Abernathy (1980, 69), the decline of U.S. productivity growth both absolutely and relative to other countries is due to a

broad managerial failure—a failure of both vision and leadership—that over time has eroded the inclination and the capacity of U.S. companies to innovate. This failure is related to adverse changes in the attitudes, preoccupations and practices of American managers. . . . By their preference for servicing existing markets rather than creating new ones and by their devotion to short-term returns and "management by the numbers," many of them have effectively forsworn long-term technological superiority as a competitive weapon. In consequence, they have abdicated their strategic responsibilities. (Hayes and Abernathy 1980, 70)

At present it is simply impossible to determine precisely how much productivity growth the United States has lost because of managerial deterioration or obsolescence (Guth 1984, 264). However, it is interesting and important to raise such questions. Suppose U.S. firms were to do everything possible to improve their internal management and organization as well as their interorganizational relationships. Might this mean not only a return to former productivity growth rates but an increase to the levels achieved by the Japanese economy in recent years? Evidence from differences in firm productivity attributable to differences in management practices and motivation indicates the possibility of substantial gains (Guth 1984, 264). Hopefully, future empirical research on the relationship between management and productivity will provide us with more insights on this matter.

Another factor contributing to the deterioration of U.S. businesses' human relationships, and presumably of productivity as well, is the new wave of hostile takeovers. In some cases the negative effects have occurred merely because the threat of takeovers has forced managements into counterproductive actions (Drucker 1986a, 12–14). For the companies acquired,

the record . . . is uniformly dismal. . . . Almost without exception the result of a hostile takeover is . . . severe damage to the true productive resource, the human organization, its spirit, its morale, its confidence in its management, and its identification with the enterprise that employs its people. (Drucker 1986a, 14)

Despite such dismal news, there are underlying trends that provide a basis for optimism. According to D. Quinn Mills and Mary Lou Balbaky (1985, 283), "human resource planning is taking root in many companies." In a minority of the companies, "human resource systems or programs fit together, complement and reinforce each other as building blocks of a larger human resource plan that is developed in relation to the overall strategic business plan of the company" (p. 265). In these companies, human resource planning involves building a culture guided by a philosophy; profitability is not the end of these efforts, but rather a desirable by-product (pp. 282–283). Further, according to the 35 senior executives who gathered in May 1984 with the Harvard Business School faculty, this "current wave of interest in high commitment HRM systems" is not a passing fad; it is a "major, nonreversible" trend that the forces of competition will drive forward (Lawrence 1985a, 352). When these companies with progressive human resource management become the rule rather than the exception, the United States will, I believe, successfully revitalize its industry and concerns about low productivity growth will have largely vanished.

BEYOND PRODUCTIVITY

According to psychologist Ernest Becker, "man is driven by an essential 'dualism'; he needs both to be a part of something and to stick out. He needs at one and the same time to be a conforming member of a winning team and to be a star in his own right" (Peters and Waterman 1982, p. xxiii). In realizing their potential, humans need, first, to find meaning and significance in being part of a larger effort and, second, to develop and use their unique talents to their potential and to be recognized for this. When organizations enable people to satisfy these needs to a high degree, their members will not only be highly motivated but will experience high well-being. Achieving one's full potential in relationships with others and with respect to one's unique abilities is the essence of becoming a mentally healthy, self-actualizing person. Correspondingly, organizations that foster these ideal individual outcomes are themselves ideal, that is, they are Theory Z organizations.

In Abraham Maslow's (1971) view, members of an organization with a

Theory Z culture may be able to achieve not only self-actualization but transcendence of everyday life, and thus experience the highest ("B") values of truth, justice, beauty, love and so on.

This higher, spiritual "animality" is so timid and weak, and so easily lost, is so easily crushed by stronger cultural forces, that it can become widely actualized *only* in a culture which approves of human nature, and therefore actively fosters its fullest growth. (Maslow 1971, 315–316)

In such a Z culture, Maslow believes that people may be able to transcend the dichotomy between "should" and "want," and thus will yearn to work selflessly for causes linked to the highest values (pp. 317–318). Developing Z organizations, and more generally a Z realm, is thus a prerequisite to attaining the highest levels of well-being, involving not only full humanity but even the experience of one's spiritual dimension. It should be noted that Maslow's humanistic views on this subject are very close to Gandhian thought. (See, for example, Diwan and Lutz 1985.)

In a Z organization, people, and not machines or systems, control their own work; this fosters individual imagination and creativity as well as their sense of the subtle (Schleuning 1986, 6). An ideal organization will also enhance the quality of people's feeling and caring natures in contrast to standardized, mechanized environments (p. 7). Moreover, developing Z organizations means creating environments where work is art, and which are characterized by intimacy and connection (pp. 7–8).

TOWARD A THEORY Z ECONOMY

What kind of socioeconomic system would best foster the development of Theory Z culture? Is Z culture most compatible with capitalism, socialism/communism or perhaps a third way? Marx and other critics of capitalism have argued that man's alienation from himself and others is inherent to production for profit in capitalistic societies. Certainly, alienation has been a persistent feature of workplaces in capitalistic societies. However, others have pointed out that socialistic or communistic societies have not been particularly successful in eliminating alienation from their workplaces. Still others believe that alienating working conditions are part and parcel of the mechanization of industrialized societies whether capitalistic or socialistic. While all these views have some truth, the successes of Japan and Mondragon have led me and a growing number of others to the view that there may be a "third way."

In my view, industrial production per se is not the source of the problem, nor is it the formal legal and social relations that constitute the definitions of capitalism and socialism/communism. The conditions that make work alienating are rooted in the quality of the interpersonal relations among workers; these are conditioned by the incentives deriving from an organization's structure and culture. Thus, enterprises in the United States or the Soviet Union are confonted with the same difficulty. To lower alienation they need to create the kind of organizational and interorganizational relationships that will bring out workers' uniquely human attributes, enabling them to achieve all that they can. Organizations that commit themselves to high purpose and enable people to take responsibility for their lives and be recognized for their unique contributions permit working people to be at their best.

Creating the kind of socioeconomic system that fosters people-oriented organizations is obviously a huge task. It requires the help both of visionary humanists and of inspired people who are willing to work hard to bring the vision into reality. It also requires learning from concrete examples of success like companies in Japan and Mondragon and certain excellent U.S. companies. For me, the possibilities for achieving a humanistic transformation of working conditions in places like the United States are very real. What is not clear is whether sufficient leadership and energies will be mobilized to turn the possibilities into realities.

Notes

CHAPTER 2

1. For a review and synthesis of more recent research on organizational life cycles, see Quinn and Cameron (1983).

2. Findings cited by Ouchi and Price (1978, 26–27) indicate that OD efforts are not reliably successful. To achieve organization effectiveness and individual psychological success, Ouchi and Price (1978, 36–44) believe that a corporation needs to develop a humanistic hierarchy characterized by clan-like functioning (cultural homogeneity deriving from a high degree of socialization) which should reduce the negative effects of hierarchy.

3. Alfred Chandler (1962) has ably examined how a number of large U.S. corporations, most notably Du Pont, General Motors, Standard Oil of New Jersey, and Sears Roebuck were among the first to choose the multidivisional form of organization because it fit their corporate strategies which were in turn shaped by market demand patterns.

CHAPTER 3

1. This differs slightly from the definition in Tomer (1981a, 1).

2. The concept of organizational capital was first developed by Tomer (1973, 267–281).

3. T. Y. Shen's (1981) article includes a useful review of organizational economic research in which elements of organization are treated as production inputs along with capital and labor. Shen emphasizes that the function of the organizational

input is to contribute to the transformation of information. Among others, Shen cites Oliver Williamson who has analyzed organizational features which are both helpful and harmful in this regard. On the one hand, the growth potential of large organizations is limited as they are likely to become afflicted by information loss (Williamson, 1967); on the other hand, the organizational structure of multidivisional firms helps by reducing information-coordination needs (Williamson, 1970).

4.   One can certainly conceive of managerial or organizational changes which would be accurately characterized as movements from within the production possibility frontier to its surface. A firm would be within its frontier if it had allowed the functioning of its organization to deteriorate through neglect. Such a firm could then improve the functioning of its organization without resort to programmatic change or the use of new organizational knowledge by merely reinstating previous practices, thereby achieving increased economic performance and reaching the frontier.

5.   It could be argued that pure human capital is specific to the employees embodying it, but this seems trivial as one cannot conceive of separating the human capital attribute from the individual. In effect, the employee along with his attributes is the flexible factor of production being made specific to the technology or the portion of it related to his job.

6.   Although he didn't go further in analyzing the organizational aspects, Gary Becker recognized that "resources are usually spent by firms in familiarizing new employees with their organization" (1962, 17).

7.   It is possible that an investment in changing the attributes of an employee could be made with the purpose of improving his ability to interact with particular other employees, with the expected result being higher productivity through better teamwork. While this is possible, I suspect it is a rare occurrence; thus H-O capital is not classified as employee-specific.

8.   Although general, education in a particular nation is still likely to be specific to the types of organization commonly existing in that country.

9.   "The collective memory of [the organization's] participants . . . is insufficient for organization purposes, first, because what is in one man's mind is not necessarily available to other members of the organization, and second, because when an individual leaves an organization, the organization loses that part of its 'memory.' Hence organizations . . . need artificial 'memories.' . . . Among the repositories which organizations may use for their information are records systems, correspondence and other files, libraries, and follow-up systems" (Simon 1957, 166–167).

10.   Prescott and Visscher's (1980) concept of organizational capital includes not only information on employees' suitability for particular tasks and their ability to work as a team with particular fellow employees, but also firm-specific human capital vested in individual employees.

11.   Again, although he didn't go further in the analysis, Becker (1962, 18) recognizes that firms' expenditures to acquire information on employees are a firm-specific investment. Moreover, "[firms] try to increase their knowledge [of new employees] in various ways—testing, rotation among departments, trial and error, etc.—for greater knowledge permits a more efficient utilization of manpower" (p. 18). Becker also includes as human capital a firm's accumulation of information as a

result of "time employed in interviewing, testing, checking references," of prospective employees (p. 18).

12. Having worked in the same Ford plant for three summers while a college student, and having recently learned much about Japanese management, I could particularly appreciate my cousin's story.

CHAPTER 4

1. Notable also are Sombart and Werner (1967) who gave early recognition to the organizing role of the "undertaker" or entrepreneur and Frank Knight who recognized that the manager/organizer often performs an enterpreneurial role in the context of uncertainty (Knight 1921, chapters 9 and 10).

2. Gordon L. Lippitt (1969, 91) refers to this organizing role of the manager as the "extrapolative planner." He states that for the initiation of an organizational change process "some one person or group has to be the stimulus at the right time, in the proper manner, and with appropriate resources" (Lippitt 1969, 270).

3. This argument is essentially the same as that made in Jorgenson and Griliches (1967, 249).

4. For a brief review of some of these arguments, see Lave (1966, 13–15).

5. See Pray (1976, 123–124) for examples of managerial and organizational changes in this category.

6. Note that, strictly speaking, it is the services of K_i which should enter the production function, not the stocks. This implies the need for a data adjustment if inputs are not fully utilized.

7. For an interesting application of this approach to the U.S. agricultural sector, see Griliches (1964). In Jorgenson and Griliches (1967), the approach is applied to the whole U.S. economy.

8. It should be noted that the intent here is to suggest the quantitative production relationships implied by the organizational capital phenomenon; it is not to be definitive as to the best specification of the production function relationships. Further investigation of these aspects is obviously warranted especially if empirical work is to be done. Putting the production function in the form indicated by equations 4.5 and 4.6 raises some difficult questions. For example, if the production function is thought to exhibit constant returns to scale, do all the K_i (assuming that changes in K_i are merely quantitative and not qualitative where new knowledge is embodied) have to double, say, in order to double output, or can some K_i increase by more than double and some by less to double output? If the latter is true, is it correct to refer to this as constant returns to scale? Moreover, if some K_i are growing faster than others, wouldn't such a change in factor proportions suggest diminishing returns either have or will set in? For two-factor production functions (given state of technology), characteristics such as returns to scale and diminishing returns have been quite thoroughly explored. For production functions with three or more inputs (especially when inputs such as H and O are included) it would appear that special considerations are involved so that conclusions derived for the two-factor case cannot be extended in a straightforward way.

9. Because H and O are included as separate factors in equation 4.7, this implies

that one can consider the marginal productivity of labor independent of that for H and/or O. While this makes some sense from a conceptual standpoint, measurement of some of these quantities may pose a difficult problem. For example, how does one measure the wage rate or marginal product of "pure" labor separately from the H or O factors? While this may be difficult, however, it doesn't seem to be an unsolvable problem.

10. Note that weighting the growth of inputs by factor shares may provide biased estimates of the contribution of each of these factors to the output growth rate if a continuous disequilibrium exists. This disequilibrium would introduce a disparity between the marginal products of some factors and the rates at which these factors are rewarded. Griliches suggests that this type of disparity has existed in the agricultural sector (see Griliches 1963, 334). It is conceivable that this could be the case for O-type inputs.

11. The discrete form of equation 4.7 is

$$\Delta Q/Q = w_l\,(\Delta L/L) + w_k\,(\Delta K/K) + w_h\,(\Delta H/H) + w_o(\Delta O/O) + \ldots \quad (A)$$

where ΔT, the change in time, equals one and

$$w_o = O\,(\Delta Q/\,\Delta O)/\,Q$$

In (A), the proportion of the annual growth in output accounted for by organizational capital formation (G_O) is

$$G_O = (O\,(\Delta Q/\,\Delta O)/\,Q)\,(\Delta O/\,O) = ((\Delta Q/\,\Delta O)/\,Q)\,\Delta O \quad (B)$$

Thus, to calculate G_O in addition to data on Q one needs $\Delta Q/\Delta O$, the marginal product of O assumed to be equal to its rate of return, and ΔO, the net addition to the stock of O. If we assume that management is successful in its important ongoing job of maintaining the quality of the organization and preventing depreciation of this capital, then ΔO is the total cost of creating new organizational capital. Note that the activity involved in maintaining the productivity of the existing organization is presumed to be a programmed one so its resource cost is not included as part of O. Conceivably, O could be subject to significant obsolescence as a result of external changes. If so, then the ΔO figure would have to be adjusted downward to reflect this.

12. This analysis is based on the assumption that the return (income) to the capital input contributed by management consultant work is part of the profit of the owners of the total amount of tangible capital, since in the main they own and have paid for this kind of capital. To the extent that management consultant-related capital is human capital (which is vested in individuals who receive a wage or salary return from it) the analysis above is not strictly correct.

13. This estimate was made by Philip Shay, Executive Director of the Association of Consulting Management Engineers.

14. For more on the estimation procedure and for the amounts of capital formation resulting from the efforts of particular firms, see Tomer (1977, 7–14; and 1973).

15. For more on the procedure used, see Tomer (1977, 17–23, and 1973).

16. National income data for 1947–1962 are published by the U.S. Department

of Commerce, Office of Business Economics, in *The National Income and Product Accounts for the United States, 1929–1965: Statistical Tables, A Supplement to the Survey of Current Business* (1966). The data for 1929–1939, 1939–1946 and 1963–1969, respectively, were found in the 1959, 1969 and 1973 *Supplements to the Survey of Current Business*.

17.   The averages are simple (unweighted) averages for a sample of 14 out of 42 industries in the manufacturing sector. The data on which the calculated figure is based comes from Roy A. Foule, *Twenty-Five Years of 14 Important Ratios* (New York: Dunn and Bradstreet, Inc., 1957).

18.   The period (1951–1955) may be fairly representative of the longer period (1929–1969) because it includes a war period (Korean War, 1951–1953), a recessionary period (1953–1954), and a peace time boom year (1955).

CHAPTER 5

1.   Left out of this summary is the concept of inert areas, which is developed in Leibenstein (1969).

2.   For a useful summary and critique of need satisfaction theory, see Salancik and Pfeffer (1977).

3.   Goals that reflect a firm's "concern for company as subsystem in total system" (for example goals that account for the impact of the firm's activities on the world's ecological balance) are considered a particularly important factor for motivating workers born after World War II. See Lawrence Foss (1973, 68).

4.   An improvement in OE is synonymous with an increase in X-efficiency (and thus productivity increase) as a result of improvements in the functioning of a firm's organization. OE only reflects changes internal to the firm, not external developments which have an impact on productivity. Equation 5.3 is intended to illustrate the determinants of OE, not to be comprehensive. One determinant of OE left out of the equation is membership behavior, which was analyzed earlier.

CHAPTER 6

1.   Another possible pattern is nonreciprocal cooperation—at least nonreciprocal among the parties involved. An example would be the mentoring relationship in which a mentor helps a junior member of the organization without the expectation of receiving help directly from the junior employee. There may, however, be the implied expectation of reciprocation to the organization as a whole. It is well known that mentoring is an established part of Japanese management. While mentoring occurs in U.S. companies, the practice appears to be less established and less encouraged.

2.   Following Galbraith (1977), the common organizational purposes of two organizational members could be their identification with the organization's overall goals or their involvement in particular types of tasks (for instance, the tasks typically done by groups such as skilled craftsmen or scientists or other professionals).

3.   A similar observation is made by Leibenstein (1982a, 9).

4.   In Leibenstein's analysis the sabotage choice doesn't exist.

5.   See Rapoport and Chammah (1965, 33–36) for an explanation of the pris-

oner's dilemma payoff pattern. For an extension of the PD analysis to the multi-person situation, see, for example, Schelling (1978, chapter 7).

6.   Luce and Raiffa have analyzed the temporal repetition of the prisoner's dilemma. They find that "in the repeated game the repeated selection of . . . [joint cooperation] is in a sort of quasi-equilibrium: it is not to the advantage of either player to initiate the chaos that results from not conforming, even though the non-conforming strategy is profitable in the short run (one trial). It is intuitively clear that this quasi-equilibrium pair is extremely unstable; any loss of 'faith' in one's opponent sets up the chain which leads to loss for both players (1957, 97–102).

7.   These findings are consistent with the beliefs of Luce and Raiffa about what will happen when the game is played many times and players are interested in the sum of the utility outcomes: "We feel that in most cases an unarticulated collusion between players will develop, much in the same way as a mature economic market often exhibits a marked degree of collusion without any communication among the participants. This arises from the knowledge that the situation will be repeated and that reprisals are possible" (1957, 101).

8.   Note that the opportunistic PD game is different from a competitive zero-sum game. The latter does not necessarily involve opportunism despite the fact that one person is trying to win and make the other lose. Opportunism is not involved as long as the players abide by the rules; to the extent they do, they cannot be accused of deceptive or illegitimate behavior.

9.   See Robert Axelrod (1984) for a discussion concerning a variety of pro-grammed strategies and how they performed against each other in a prisoner's dilemma game.

10.   See Maital and Maital (1984) for a description and analysis of a variety of games reflecting interpersonal relationships in which possibilities for both coopera-tion and conflict are present.

11.   The large Japanese companies have typically done much more to encourage cooperation than their U.S. and European counterparts. Takeuchi (1981, 14) and Hatvany and Pucik (1981, 14) both emphasize the value that Japanese managers place on developing cooperative work groups.

CHAPTER 7

1.   Transaction costs refer to the costs of carrying out transactions in markets. This includes the costs of making a satisfactory contract.

2.   Robert Hayes and William Abernathy (1980) have argued that the typical characteristics of U.S. management during the 1970s especially have made it rela-tively inefficient.

3.   Bureau of Labor Statistics, *News,* June 2, 1982.

4.   COWPS, *Report on Productivity,* July 1979, as quoted in Hayes and Aberna-thy (1980).

5.   A study by Dale Jorgenson and Mieko Nishimizu (1978, 723) finds similarly that by 1974 the gap between U.S. and Japanese technology had been closed.

6.   Insofar as Japanese management leads to lower worker resistance to labor-saving innovations, Denison and Chung (1976, 82) suggest a "yes" answer.

7.   The J management referred to in this article differs slightly from the Z

management of Ouchi (see Ouchi and Price 1978, 39). My version is intended to be the Japanese management ideal whereas his is intended to be a more general ideal (see Ouchi 1981, 58). This difference reflects our different purposes. In earlier versions of this chapter the term "Theory Z management" was used to refer to the Japanese management ideal.

8. The notion of Theory Z as the next higher level on a continuum beginning with Theory Y was first developed by Abraham Maslow (1971, 270–286). Maslow's characterization of Theory Z organization goes deeper than Ouchi's in the sense that it is less a list of specific organizational features and more of a characterization of the orientation and behavior of individuals in a hypothetical Z organizational setting. Such individuals are not only self-actualizers with high motivation and commitment to task and team but are also able to transcend the concrete reality of organizational experience.

9. In Japanese organizations, the guiding philosophy or spirit of harmony (*wa*) which derives from the Confucian cultural tradition has a very important influence. See, for example, Riggs and Seo (1979).

10. The difference in the principal–agent relationship between Japanese and U.S. management is suggested by the different attitudes of Harold Geneen, formerly chief executive officer of ITT, and Konosuke Matsushita, founder of Matsushita Electric Company. According to Pascale and Athos, "Geneen seemed to regard other people as objects to be used to achieve his purpose, while Matsushita seemed to regard them as both objects to be used and subjects to be honored in achieving his and their purposes" (1981, 83).

11. Ian Macneil (1980, 10–35) uses a similar spectrum which starts with discrete transactions and ends with the relational contract (especially the modern variety). The IPC spectrum in contrast relates to implicit contracts between employers and employees. On the left of the IPC spectrum the employment relation is very much the same as Macneil's discrete transaction. Moving righward along the spectrum we come first to relations where the social cohesiveness between employer and employee is relatively low, and thus, self-interested maximizing behavior predominates. Moving further right we finally come to relations where social solidarity is very high and where self-interest has a much more circumscribed role to play. According to one interpretation (Tomer, 1983a, 60), Ouchi (1980) views Theory Z or clan style management as one of three distinct types of relations between employers and employees rather than a spectrum of possible relationships.

12. This hypothesis is intended to apply only in "modern" societies in which economic organizations utilize systematic, rather than traditional, methods in striving for economic success.

13. Writing in the *New York Times,* John Holusha cites one type of evidence of lower labor market transaction costs in Japan. Holusha states that "labor contracts in Japan are models of brevity compared with the bulky, legalistic documents that emerge from negotiations in the United States. This freedom from encumbering detail is said by analysts to be an important source of Japan's advantage over American auto makers" (March 30, 1983).

14. In a recent communication, Leibenstein (1982c, 872–873) acknowledges that individual performance may get worse (implying lower effort) as pressure gets "too great." This, he indicates, is a departure from the assumption typically implicit in his writings.

15.   In slightly more detail, $U_t(E_0)$ represents the total expected benefits (or utility) arising from effort E_0 expended in the current period, but realized in period t. As an example, $U_t(E_0)$ might be thought of as the share of period t profits which a worker expects if his current effort is E_0. Clearly, $U_t(E_0)$ involves a complex assessment process, accounting for the relationship between E_0 (one's own current effort) and many other variables, such as other workers' current and future effort, management decisions, and so on. We make no attempt to spell out how $U_t(E_0)$ is actually calculated, but simply use it here to make several points regarding the impact of the expectations of future benefits from current effort decisions.

16.   It is quite possible that workers in their effort decisions will consider future satisfactions (from current effort) expected to be received as members of a different organization. However, since the probability of their realization is likely to be lower, these utility expectations are not considered here.

17.   This analysis is similar to psychologists' expectancy theory (see, for example, Lawler and Rhode 1976, 19–22). In contrast to the present analysis, expectancy theory emphasizes two steps; first, work efforts lead to probable performance and second, probable performance leads to probable outcomes more or less valued by workers. Workers are presumed to be rational in the sense of attempting to maximize the value of desired outcomes in effort decision making.

18.   Japanese workers may possess low rates of time preference even before they enter work organizations for reasons related to their culture, rearing and school adjustment. However, these arguments are strictly unrelated to the functioning of Z organizations.

19.   There is considerable controversy about the risky shift phenomenon, and serious questions have been raised concerning the validity of the empirical research supporting the risky shift hypothesis. See, for example, Cartwright (1979).

20.   FitzRoy and Mueller (1977, pp. 15–16) conclude that firms characterized by homogeneity, small numbers, consensus decision making, high trust, much informal communication, and cohesion will save monitoring costs and minimize shirking.

21.   Strictly speaking, the argument for reduced turnover would not apply unless workers' employment alternatives lack J organizations. In Japan, low turnover is encouraged by the diminished status and opportunities of mid-career entrants. The latter seems largely to reflect the time it takes to become part of the new organization's community and internalize its values.

22.   Tomer (1981b) has pointed out that the psychological health benefits of improved work environments are positive externalities or spillovers, and that therefore, firms taking only private incentives into account will tend to underinvest in such organizational change. It seems plausible, however, that if a substantial number of firms in a society were to move to the right on the IPC spectrum, these external societal benefits would tend to get internalized to the firm.

23.   Essentially the same point is made by Peters and Waterman (1982, 241).

24.   There are, of course, alternative strategies and courses of action which organizations may choose for increasing productivity through transformation of the IPC. The growing and voluminous literature on organizational development includes many examples.

25.   This, of course, is supportive of the contention that the virtues of J management are ones which can be transferred successfully to non-Japanese cultures. Pas-

cale and Athos (1981) acknowledge that Japanese culture provides advantages, but they do not believe that the features of U.S. culture represent an insuperable obstacle.

26. "Without exception, the dominance and coherence of culture proved to be an essential quality of the excellent companies" (Peters and Waterman 1982, 75).

CHAPTER 8

1. Strictly speaking, Vanek (1975, 15–16) distinguishes between pure labor-management in which labor-managers rent all their capital and worker-management in which the labor-managers utilize and control state-owned capital as in Yugoslavia.

2. Frederic Pryor's definition of a producer (or production) cooperative is essentially the same as Vanek's. He contrasts them with collectives, communes and organizations with "workers' participation" and "profit sharing" (1983, 135–137).

3. These are among Vanek's (1975, 33–36) 12 necessary conditions for an optimal and viable self-managed firm or economy.

4. In Tomer (1985, chapter 7) in contrast, the Theory Z concept largely reflected the characteristics of the Japanese management ideal, a use similar to that of Ouchi (1981).

5. Other allocative efficiency arguments have been made. For example, Jensen and Meckling (1979, 486–488) maintain that because labor-managed workers can't diversify their portfolios due to restrictions on transferring their claims on the firm, their holdings will have higher risk than if diversification were possible. As a result, these laborers will require higher rates of return on reinvested earnings, thereby reducing the demand for capital goods below the optimum attainable in a capitalistic system. Similarly, in the case of internally financed labor-managed firms, workers will require a rate of return on investments above their rate of time preference because the individual loses the principal of his investment (Stephen 1982, 10–11).

6. For other arguments in this vein, see Jensen and Meckling (1979) and comments by Fusfeld (1983, 772) and Levin (1982, 45–46).

7. According to Vanek (1970, 244), "the most important function of labor management is precisely to produce the conditions of a single collective mind."

8. In the organizational behavior literature on participative management, "the predominant prescriptive advice given to administrators is to be supportive, consultative, or democratic. It is widely assumed that such behavior . . . will yield high productivity and increased worker satisfaction" (Williams 1976, p. vii). Moreover, "the model of organizational behavior which predominates among the management of an organization will affect the success of that whole organization" (p. 4). There are however, many different views with respect to the most desired types of worker participation and how they are related to productivity and satisfaction. It is beyond the scope of this paper to review this literature.

9. The notion that participation affects a firm's production possibilities is explicit in the production function equation used by Cable and FitzRoy (1980a, 111–112). They don't, however, use the organizational capital concept.

10. Levin discusses the idea of ranking firms "according to their technical efficiency or total factor productivity by comparing the amounts of output that they can

produce for any given level of inputs. It is possible to rank productive organizations on a Farrell-type index where a value of 100 is given for firms that are maximally efficient or on their production frontiers, and values of less than 100 are given for less productive firms. Theoretically, then, it might be possible to rank labor-managed and conventional capitalist firms on such a scale to see which ones seem to be most productive (1982, 48).

11.   See Lutz and Lux (1979, 9–19) for an interpretation of Maslow's hierarchy of needs and a discussion of its relevance to economics. On page 171, Lutz and Lux refer to human well-being in relation to human needs and the quality of work.

12.   W-efficiency resembles Mary McNally's (1981, 148) α-efficiency. It differs in that α-efficiency relates only to self-actualization needs of people in a community rather than the whole range of human needs of workers in an organization.

13.   Strictly speaking, X-efficiency is independent of W-efficiency. Thus it is theoretically conceivable for the actual potential WWPF to shift out to the true potential frontier as a result of W-efficiency improving organizational change without any X-efficiency change.

14.   Despite the fact that much of the theoretical literature of the labor-managed firm focuses on allocative efficiency questions, little of the empirical research focuses on allocative efficiency. As Jones and Svejnar (1982, 10) point out, this is due to the difficulties involved in making inferences about allocative efficiency. Because X-efficiency is the primary focus here, the several empirical studies relating to allocative efficiency are not reviewed here.

15.   Only the Mondragon cooperatives meet the type 1 criteria.

16.   An ideal Israeli kibbutz is a labor-managed firm with collective ownership as opposed to the individual ownership of the producer cooperative. A kibbutz generally involves significant collective consumption and communal living arrangements.

CHAPTER 10

1.   George Huber's (1984) article is similar to this one in that it examines organization features believed to be most adapted to postindustrial society. His article differs in two ways. First, he believes that the most important characteristics of postindustrial society are the rapid growth of knowledge, the increasing complexity of knowledge, and increasing turbulence. The second, following from the first, is his view that decision making systems in postindustrial society will have to be designed to deal with these characteristics. Essentially, this implies better formal and informal methods of utilizing information in decision making as well as more use of advanced communication and computing technologies.

2.   See Zuboff 1985, 103–104, for a list of the most typical tasks.

3.   See Perl (1984) for an account of the use of computer monitoring to process medical claims by a major insurance company.

4.   According to Peter Drucker (1986b), "the shift to knowledge work and knowledge workers . . . creates a need to rethink and to restructure career ladders, compensation and recognition." In the traditional existing organizational structure, the manager is the "boss" and everybody else is "subordinate." Drucker suggests that "in the knowledge-based organization" knowledge workers are the "bosses" and the "manager" is in a supporting role as their planner and coordinator.

5.   James O'Toole (1981, 10–11) argues that there has been a decline in the willingness to work hard and that this is related to broader cultural change in the United States. This cultural change reflects the trauma of the Vietnam era, changes in the relationship of men and women, changes in attitudes to authority and changes in what people believe they are entitled to. In O'Toole's view, "the managerial challenge of the 1980s is to find ways to break this syndrome by creating a philosophy and organization of work that is responsive to the underlying shifts in social values and expectations" (p. 11). For documentation of the kind of cultural change referred to by O'Toole, see Yankelovich (1981a and 1981b). For a more optimistic view, see Ferguson (1980). While these changes in values have been well documented, what is debatable is the need to accommodate organizationally to value changes, some of which seem unrelated to the transition from manual to knowledge-related work. To the extent these value changes are dysfunctional for organizational productivity, it would in my view be more appropriate for organizations to shape the values of young workers rather than accommodating to them.

6.   William G. Shepherd's (1982) research indicates that one of the three main causes of the large and widely spread rise in competition during 1958–1980 in U.S. markets was rising import competition.

7.   See Lawrence 1985b, 15–34, for an historical analysis of earlier human resource management systems in American industry.

CHAPTER 11

1.   A significant recent exception to this is Eli Ginzberg and George Vojta's *Beyond Human Scale: The Large Corporation at Risk* (1985) that raises questions about the adequacy of fit between the structures of contemporary corporations and their managerial personnel.

2.   This is so basic to economists that many cannot imagine nonmaximizing behavior. See Leibenstein (1985).

References

Abernathy, William J., Kim B. Clark, and Alan M. Kantrow. 1983. *Industrial Renaissance: Producing a Competitive Future for America.* New York: Basic Books.

Acs, Zoltan J. 1984. *The Changing Structure of the U.S. Economy: Lessons from the Steel Industry.* New York: Praeger.

Alchian, Armen A., and Harold Demsetz. 1972. "Production, Information Costs, and Economic Organization." *American Economic Review,* 62 (December), 777–795.

Argyris, Chris. 1960. *Understanding Organization Behavior.* New York: John Wiley.

Argyris, Chris. 1964. *Integrating the Individual and the Organization.* New York: John Wiley.

Axelrod, Robert. 1984. *The Evolution of Cooperation.* New York: Basic Books.

Barnard, Chester I. 1940. *The Functions of the Executive.* Cambridge, Mass.: Harvard University Press.

Barney, Jay B. 1985. "Theory Z, Institutional Economics, and the Theory of Strategy." In Paul R. Kleindorfer, ed. *The Management of Productivity and Technology in Manufacturing.* New York: Plenum.

Becker, Gary S. 1962. "Investment in Human Capital: A Theoretical Analysis." *Journal of Political Economy,* 50 (October Supplement), 9–49.

Becker, Gary S. 1964. *Human Capital: A Theoretical and Empirical Analysis, with Special Reference to Education.* New York: National Bureau of Economic Research and Columbia University Press.

Becker, Gary S. 1976. "Altruism, Egoism, and Genetic Fitness." *Journal of Economic Literature,* 14 (September), 817–826.

Becker, Selwyn W., and Gerald Gordon. 1966. "An Entrepreneurial Theory of

Formal Organizations." *Administrative Science Quarterly,* 11 (December), 315–344.

Bell, Daniel. 1973. *The Coming of Post-Industrial Society: A Venture in Social Forecasting.* New York: Basic Books.

Bell, Daniel. 1980. *The Winding Passage: Essays and Sociological Journeys 1960–1980.* Cambridge, Mass.: Abt Books.

Bellas, C. J. 1975. "Industrial Democracy Through Worker Ownership: An American Experience." In Jaroslav Vanek ed. *Self-Management: Economic Liberation of Man.* Baltimore, Md.: Penguin Books.

Berman, Katrina V. 1982. "The United States of America: A Co-operative Model for Worker Management." In Frank H. Stephen, ed. *The Performance of Labor-Managed Firms.* New York: St. Martin's Press.

Bernstein, Paul. 1980. *Workplace Democratization: Its Internal Dynamics.* New Brunswick, N.J.: Transaction Books.

Blake, Robert R., Warren E. Avis, and Jane S. Mouton. 1966. *Corporate Darwinism: An Evolutionary Perspective on Organizing Work in the Dynamic Corporation.* Houston: Gulf Publishing Co.

Blake, Robert R., and Jane S. Mouton. 1969. *Building a Dynamic Corporation Through Grid Organization Development.* Reading, Mass.: Addison-Wesley.

Blake, Robert R., and Jane Srygley Mouton. 1978. *The New Managerial Grid.* Houston: Gulf Publishing Co.

Blake, Robert R., and Jane S. Mouton. 1985. *The Managerial Grid III.* Houston, Texas: Gulf Publishing Co.

Blaug, Mark. 1976. "The Empirical Status of Human Capital Theory: A Slightly Jaundiced Survey." *Journal of Economic Literature,* 14 (September), 827–855.

Blumberg, Paul. 1975. "Alienation and Participation: Conclusions." In Jaroslav Vanek, ed. 1975. *Self-Management: Economic Liberation of Man.* Baltimore, Md.: Penguin Books.

Bradley, Keith, and Alan Gelb. 1981. "Motivation and Control in the Mondragon Experiment." *British Journal of Industrial Relations,* 19 (2), 211–231.

Bradley, Keith, and Alan Gelb. 1982. "The Mondragon Cooperatives: Guidelines for a Cooperative Economy." In Derek C. Jones and Jan Svejnar, eds. *Participatory and Self-Managed Firms.* Lexington, Mass.: Lexington Books.

Bruyn, Severyn T., and Littza Nicolaou-Smokovitis. 1979. "A Theoretical Framework for Studying Worker Participation: The Psychosocial Contract." *Review of Social Economy,* 37 (April), 1–23.

Business Week. 1985. "ESOPs: Revolution or Ripoff?" (April 15), 94–108.

Business Week. 1986a. "High Tech to the Rescue." (June 16), 100–108.

Business Week. 1986b. "Japan, U.S.A." (July 14), 45–55.

Business Week. 1986c. "The Hollow Corporation." (March 3), 57–85.

Byrd, Richard E. 1974. *A Guide to Personal Risk Taking.* New York: AMACOM.

Cable, John, and Felix FitzRoy. 1980a. "Productivity, Efficiency, Incentives, and Employee Participation: Some Preliminary Results for West Germany." *Kyklos,* 33 (1), 100–121.

Cable, John, and Felix FitzRoy. 1980b. "Cooperation and Productivity: Some Evidence from West German Experience." *Economic Analysis and Worker's Management,* 14 (2), 163–180.

Cartwright, Dorwin. 1979. "Determinants of Scientific Progress: The Case of Research on the Risky Shift." In Richard T. Mowday and Richard M. Steers, eds. *Research in Organizations: Issues and Controversies*. Santa Monica, Calif.: Goodyear.

Chandler, Alfred D., Jr. 1962. *Strategy and Structure: Chapters in the History of the Industrial Enterprise*. Cambridge, Mass.: The M.I.T. Press.

Child, I. L. 1954. "Socialization." In G. Lindzey, ed. *Handbook of Social Psychology*. Volume II. Cambridge, Mass.: Addison-Wesley.

Clark, Rodney, 1979. *The Japanese Company*. New Haven: Yale University Press.

Coase, Ronald H. 1937. "The Nature of the Firm." *Economica*, New Series 4, 386–405.

Conte, Michael. 1982. "Participation and Performance in U.S. Labor-Managed Firms." In Derek C. Jones and Jan Svejnar, eds. *Participatory and Self-Managed Firms*. Lexington, Mass.: Lexington Books.

Conte, Michael, and Arnold S. Tannenbaum. 1978. "Employee-Owned Companies: Is the Difference Measurable?" *Monthly Labor Review*, 10 (July), 23–28.

Cook, James. 1982. "The Molting of America." *Forbes*, (November 22), 161–170.

Crawford, Robert G. 1983. "Organizational Structure and Productivity: The Economics of Theory Z." Paper presented at the Second U.S.-Japan Business Conference, April 5, in Tokyo.

Curl, John. 1980. *History of Work Cooperation in America*. Berkeley: Homeward Press.

Deal, Terrence E., and Allen A. Kennedy. 1982. *Corporate Cultures: The Rites and Rituals of Corporate Life*. Reading, Mass.: Addison-Wesley.

Denison, Edward F. 1962. *The Sources of Economic Growth in the United States and the Alternatives Before Us*. Supplementary Paper No. 13. New York: Committee for Economic Development.

Denison, Edward F. 1974. *Accounting for United States Economic Growth 1929–1969*. Washington, D.C.: The Brookings Institution.

Denison, Edward F., and William K. Chung. 1976. *How Japan's Economy Grew So Fast: The Sources of Postwar Expansion*. Washington, D.C.: The Brookings Institution.

Denison, Edward F., and Jean-Pierre Poullier. 1967. *Why Growth Rates Differ: Postwar Experience in Nine Western Countries*. Washington, D.C.: The Brookings Institution.

Dholakia, Nikhilesh, and John R. Wish. 1983. "Industrial Policy and International Marketing Success: A Comparison of the United States, Japan, and Western Europe." Paper presented at the Second Japan-U.S.A. Business Conference, Tokyo, April 4–6.

Diwan, Romesh, and Mark Lutz. 1985. *Essays in Gandhian Economics*. New Delhi: Gandhi Peace Foundation.

Domar, E. D. 1966. "The Soviet Collection Farm as a Producer Cooperative." *American Economic Review*, 56 (September), 734–757.

Drucker, Peter F. 1965. *The Practice of Management*. London: William Heinemann Ltd.

Drucker, Peter F. 1982. *The Changing World of the Executive*. New York: New York Times Books.

Drucker, Peter F. 1986a. "Corporate Takeovers—What Is to Be Done?" *The Public Interest*, 82 (Winter), 3–24.

Drucker, Peter F. 1986b. "Goodbye to the Old Personnel Department." *Wall Street Journal,* (May 22).

Ellerman, David P. 1984. "Theory of Legal Structure: Worker Cooperatives." *Journal of Economic Issues,* 18 (September), 861–891.

Faxen, Karl-Olof. 1978. "Disembodied Technical Progress: Does Employee Participation in Decision Making Contribute to Change and Growth?" *American Economic Review,* 68 (May), 131–134.

Ferguson, Marilyn. 1980. *The Aquarian Conspiracy: Personal and Social Transformation in the 1980s.* Los Angeles: J. P. Tarcher.

FitzRoy, Felix R., and Dennis C. Mueller. 1977. "Contract and the Economics of Organization." Paper presented at Fourth Interlaken Seminar on Analysis and Ideology, May–June.

FitzRoy, Felix R., and Dennis C. Mueller. 1984. "Cooperation and Conflict in Contractual Organizations." *Quarterly Review of Economics and Business,* 24 (Winter), 24–49.

Foss, Lawrence. 1973. "Management Strategy for the Future: Theory Z Management," *California Management Review,* 15 (Spring), 61–68.

Foulkes, Fred K. 1980. *Personnel Policies in Large Nonunion Companies.* Englewood Cliffs, N.J.: Prentice-Hall.

Foulkes, Fred K. 1981. "How Top Nonunion Companies Manage Employees." *Harvard Business Review,* 59 (September–October), 90–96.

Fusfeld, Daniel R. 1983. "Labor-Managed and Participatory Firms: A Review Article." *Journal of Economic Issues,* 17 (September), 769–789.

Gabarro, John. 1979. "Socialization at the Top—How CEOs and Subordinates Evolve Interpersonal Contracts." *Organizational Dynamics,* (Winter), 3–23.

Galbraith, Jay. 1973. *Designing Complex Organizations.* Reading, Mass.: Addison-Wesley.

Galbraith, Jay. 1977. *Organization Design.* Reading, Mass.: Addison-Wesley.

Garson, G. David. 1977. "Models of Worker Self-Management: The West European Experience." In G. D. Garson, ed. *Worker Self-Management in Industry: The West European Experience.* New York: Praeger.

Gerth, H. H., and C. Wright Mills. 1958. *From Max Weber: Essays in Sociology.* New York: Oxford University Press.

Ginzberg, Eli, and George Vojta. 1985. *Beyond Human Scale: The Large Corporation at Risk.* New York: Basic Books.

Grayson, C. Jackson. 1982. "Emphasizing Capital Investment Is a Mistake." *Wall Street Journal,* (October 11).

Griliches, Zvi. 1963. "The Sources of Measured Productivity Growth: United States Agriculture, 1940–1960." *The Journal of Political Economy,* 71 (August), 331–346.

Griliches, Zvi. 1964. "Research Expenditures, Education, and the Aggregate Agricultural Production Function." *The American Economic Review,* 54 (December), 961–974.

Guth, William D. 1984. "Productivity and Corporate Strategy." In Arthur P. Brief, ed. *Productivity Research in the Behavioral and Social Sciences.* New York: Praeger.

Hartman, Curtis. 1985. "The Spirit of Independence." *Inc.,* (July), 46–91.

Hatvany, Nina, and Vladimir Pucik. 1981. "Japanese Management Practices and Productivity." *Organizational Dynamics,* (Spring), 5–21.

Hayes, Robert H., and William J. Abernathy. 1980. "Managing Our Way to Economic Decline." *Harvard Business Review*, 58 (July–August), 67–77.

Herzberg, Frederick. 1968. "One More Time: How Do You Motivate Employees?" *Harvard Business Review*, 46 (January–February), 53–62.

Huber, George P. 1984. "The Nature and Design of Post-Industrial Organizations." *Management Science*, 30 (August), 928–951.

Huse, Edgar. 1975. *Organization Development and Change*. Boston: West.

Jensen, Michael C., and William H. Meckling. 1979. "Rights and Production Functions: An Application to Labor-managed Firms and Codetermination." *Journal of Business*, 52 (October), 469–506.

Johnson, Chalmers. 1982. *MITI and the Japanese Miracle: The Growth of Industrial Policy, 1925–1975*. Stanford: Stanford University Press.

Johnson, Chalmers, ed. 1984. *The Industrial Policy Debate*. San Francisco: Institute for Contemporary Studies.

Johnston, John. 1963. "The Productivity of Management Consultants." *Journal of the Royal Statistical Society*, 237–240.

Jones, Derek C. 1980. "Producer Cooperatives in Industrialized Western Economies." *British Journal of Industrial Relations*, 18 (July), 141–154.

Jones, Derek C., and Jan Svejnar, eds. 1982. *Participatory and Self-Managed Firms*. Lexington, Mass.: Lexington Books.

Jorgenson, Dale W., and Zvi Griliches. 1967. "The Explanation of Productivity Change." *The Review of Economic Studies*, 34 (July), 249–283.

Jorgenson, Dale W., and Mieko Nishimizu. 1978. "U.S. and Japanese Economic Growth, 1952–1974: An International Comparison." *The Economic Journal*, 88 (December), 707–726.

Kelso, L. O., and M. J. Adler. 1958. *The Capitalist Manifesto*. New York: Random House.

Knight, Frank H. 1921. *Risk, Uncertainty and Profit*. Boston, Mass.: Houghton Mifflin.

Knight, Frank H. 1967. *The Economic Organization*. New York: Augustus M. Kelley.

Kotter, John P. 1973. "The Psychological Contract: Managing the Joining-Up Process." *California Management Review*, 15 (Spring), 91–99.

Kotter, John P. 1982. "What Effective General Managers Really Do." *Harvard Business Review*, 60 (November–December), 156–167.

Kotter, John P., and Leonard A. Schlesinger. 1979. "Choosing Strategies for Change." *Harvard Business Review*, 57 (March–April), 106–114.

Kuznets, Simon. 1965. *Economic Growth and Structure: Selected Essays*. New York: Norton.

Lancaster, Hal. 1979. "Atlantic City Fever." *Wall Street Journal*, (February 1).

Lave, Lester B. 1966. *Technological Change: Its Conception and Measurement*. Englewood Cliffs, N.J.: Prentice-Hall.

Lawler, Edward, 1973. *Motivation in Work Organizations*. Monterey, Calif.: Brooks/Cole.

Lawler, Edward. 1977. "Developing a Motivating Work Climate." *Management Review*, 66 (July), 25–28.

Lawler, Edward E., and John G. Rhode. 1976. *Information and Control in Organizations*. Santa Monica, Calif.: Goodyear.

Lawrence, Paul R. 1985a. "The HRM Futures Colloquium: The Managerial Perspective." In Richard Walton and Paul R. Lawrence, eds. *HRM Trends and Challenges*. Boston, Mass.: Harvard Business School Press.

Lawrence, Paul R. 1985b. "The History of Human Resource Management in American Industry." In Richard Walton and Paul R. Lawrence, eds. *HRM Trends and Challenges*. Boston, Mass.: Harvard Business School Press.

Lee, James A. 1976. "Behavior Theory vs. Reality." In Ervin Williams, ed. *Participative Management: Concepts, Theory and Implementation*. Atlanta, Ga.: School of Business Administration, Georgia State University.

Leibenstein, Harvey. 1966. "Allocative Efficiency vs. 'X-Efficiency.'" *American Economic Review*, 56 (June), 392–415.

Leibenstein, Harvey. 1969. "Organization or Frictional Equilibria, X-Efficiency, and the Rate of Innovation." *Quarterly Journal of Economics*, 83 (November), 600–623.

Leibenstein, Harvey. 1975. "Aspects of the X-Efficiency Theory of the Firm." *Bell Journal of Economics*, 6 (Autumn), 580–606.

Leibenstein, Harvey. 1976. *Beyond Economic Man: A New Foundation for Microeconomics*. Cambridge, Mass.: Harvard University Press.

Leibenstein, Harvey. 1978. *General X-Efficiency Theory and Economic Development*. New York: Oxford University Press.

Leibenstein, Harvey. 1979. "A Branch of Economics is Missing: Micro-Micro Theory." *Journal of Economic Literature*, 17 (June), 477–502.

Leibenstein, Harvey. 1980. "X-Efficiency, Intrafirm Behavior, and Growth." In Shlomo Maital and Noah M. Meltz, eds. *Lagging Productivity Growth: Causes and Remedies*. Cambridge, Mass.: Ballinger Publishing Co.

Leibenstein, Harvey. 1982a. "The Japanese Management System: An X-Efficiency Game Theory Analysis." Harvard Institute of Economic Research. Discussion Paper No. 938, November.

Leibenstein, Harvey. 1982b. "The Prisoner's Dilemma in the Invisible Hand: An Analysis of Intrafirm Productivity." *American Economic Review*, 71 (May), 92–97.

Leibenstein, Harvey. 1982c. "Worker Motivation and X-Efficiency Theory: A Comment." *Journal of Economic Issues*, 16 (September), 872–873.

Leibenstein, Harvey. 1985. "On Relaxing the Maximization Postulate." *Journal of Behavioral Economics*, 14 (Winter), 5–20.

Leone, Robert A., and Stephen A. Bradley. 1981. "Toward an Effective Industrial Policy." *Harvard Business Review*, 59 (November–December), 91–97.

Levin, Henry. 1982. "Issues in Assessing the Comparative Productivity of Worker-Managed and Participatory Firms in Capitalist Societies." In Derek C. Jones and Jan Svejnar, eds. *Participatory and Self-Managed Firms*. Lexington, Mass.: Lexington Books.

Levinson, H., C. Price, K. Munden, H. Mandel, and C. Solley. 1963. *Men, Management and Mental Health*. Cambridge, Mass.: Harvard University Press.

Levitan, Sar A., and Diane Werneke. 1984. "Worker Participation and Productivity Changes." *Monthly Labor Review*, 107 (September), 28–33.

Likert, Rensis. 1961. *New Patterns of Management*. New York: McGraw-Hill.

Likert, Rensis. 1973. "Human Resource Accounting: Building and Assessing Productive Organizations." *Personnel*, (May–June), 8–24.

Lippitt, Gordon L. 1969. *Organization Renewal: Achieving Viability in a Changing World*. New York: Appleton-Century-Crofts.

Long, Richard J. 1980. "Job Attitudes and Organizational Performance Under Employee Ownership." *Academy of Management Review,* 23 (4), 726–737.

Luce, R. Duncan, and Howard Raiffa. 1957. *Games and Decisions: Introduction and Critical Survey.* New York: John Wiley.

Lutz, Mark A., and Kenneth Lux. 1979. *The Challenge of Humanistic Economics.* Menlo Park, Calif.: Benjamin/Cummings.

McCain, Roger A. 1982. "Empirical Implications of Worker Participation in Management." In Derek C. Jones and Jan Svejnar, eds. 1982. *Participatory and Self-Managed Firms.* Lexington, Mass.: Lexington Books.

Maccoby, Michael. 1981. *The Leader: A New Face for American Management.* New York: Simon and Schuster.

McGregor, Douglas, 1960. *The Human Side of Enterprise.* New York: McGraw-Hill.

McNally, Mary. 1981. "On X-Efficiency." *Journal of Post Keynesian Economics,* 4 (Fall), 145–148.

Macneil, Ian R. 1980. *The New Social Contract: An Inquiry into Modern Contractual Relations.* New Haven: Yale University Press.

Magaziner, Ira C., and Robert B. Reich. 1982. *Minding America's Business: The Decline and Rise of the American Economy.* New York: Harcourt Brace Jovanovich.

Maital, Shlomo, and Sharone Maital. 1977. "Time Preference, Delay of Gratification and the Intergenerational Transmission of Economic Inequality: A Behavioral Theory of Income Distribution." In Orley C. Ashenfelter and Wallace Oates, eds. *Essays in Labor Market Analysis.* New York: John Wiley and Sons.

Maital, Shlomo, and Sharone L. Maital. 1983. "The Game of Change: A Game-Theoretic System for Interpreting Dynamic Relationships in Families." Paper presented at the Fourth International Congress of Family Therapy, Tel Aviv, July 3–6.

Maital, Shlomo, and Sharone L. Maital. 1984. *Economic Games People Play.* New York: Basic Books.

"Management Discovers the Human Side of Automation." 1986. *Business Week,* (September 29), 70–79.

March, James G., and Herbert Simon. 1958. *Organizations.* New York: John Wiley and Sons.

Margolis, Howard. 1982. *Selfishness, Altruism, and Rationality.* Cambridge: Cambridge University Press.

Marsh, Robert M., and Hiroshi Mannari. 1976. *Modernization of the Japanese Factory.* Princeton: Princeton University Press.

Marshall, Alfred. 1961. *Principles of Economics.* New York: Macmillan.

Maslow, Abraham. 1965. *Eupsychian Management: A Journal.* Homewood, Ill.: Richard D. Irwin.

Maslow, Abraham. 1970a. "A Theory of Human Motivation." In Victor Vroom and Edward Deci, eds. *Management and Motivation: Selected Readings.* Baltimore, Md.: Penguin Books.

Maslow, Abraham. 1970b. *Motivation and Personality.* New York: Harper and Row.

Maslow, Abraham H. 1971. *The Farther Reaches of Human Nature.* New York: Penguin Books.

Meade, J. E. 1972. "The Theory of Labor-Managed Firms and Profit Sharing." *The Economic Journal.* 32 (March Supplement), 402–428.

Melman, Seymour. 1970. "Industrial Efficiency Under Managerial vs. Cooperative Decision-Making." *Review of Radical Political Economics,* 2 (Spring), 9–34.

Mills, D. Quinn, and Mary Lou Balbaky. 1985. "Planning for Morale and Culture." *HRM: Friends and Challenges,* 255–283.

Mills, Ted. 1975. "Human Resources—Why the New Concern." *Harvard Business Review,* 53 (March/April), 120–134.

Mozina, Stane, Janez Jerovsek, Arnold S. Tannenbaum, and Rensis Likert. 1976. "Testing a Management Style." In Ervin Williams, ed. *Participative Management: Concepts, Theory and Implementation.* Atlanta, Ga.: School of Business Administration, Georgia State University.

Nadler, David A., J. Richard Hackman, and Edward E. Lawler. 1979. *Managing Organizational Behavior.* Boston: Little, Brown and Co.

Naisbitt, John. 1982. *Megatrends: Ten New Directions Transforming Our Lives.* New York: Warner Books.

National Center for Employee Ownership. 1985. *Employee Ownership: Research Review.* Arlington, Va.: National Center for Employee Ownership.

Okun, Arthur. 1975. "Inflation: Its Mechanics and Welfare Costs." *Brookings Papers on Economic Activity,* 2, 351–90.

Okun, Arthur. 1980. "The Invisible Handshake and the Inflationary Process." *Challenge,* 22 (January/February), 5–12.

Okun, Arthur M. 1981. *Prices and Quantities: A Macroeconomic Analysis.* Washington, D.C.: The Brookings Institution.

O'Toole, James. 1981. *Making America Work: Productivity and Responsibility.* New York: Continuum.

Ouchi, William G. 1980. "Markets, Bureaucracies and Clans." *Administrative Science Quarterly,* 25 (March), 129–141.

Ouchi, William G. 1981. *Theory Z: How American Business Can Meet the Japanese Challenge.* Reading, Mass.: Addison-Wesley.

Ouchi, William G. 1984a. "M-Form: Making Decisions and Building Consensus." *Challenge* 27 (July/Aug.), 31–37.

Ouchi, William G. 1984b. *The M-Form Society: How American Teamwork Can Recapture the Competitive Edge.* Reading, Mass.: Addison-Wesley.

Ouchi, William, and Raymond L. Price. 1978. "Hierarchies, Clans and Theory Z: A New Perspective on Organization Development." *Organizational Dynamics,* (Autumn), 25–44.

Ozaki, Robert S. 1984. "How Japanese Industrial Policy Works." In Chalmers Johnson, ed. *The Industrial Policy Debate.* San Francisco: Institute for Contemporary Studies.

Pascale, Richard T., and Anthony G. Athos. 1981. *The Art of Japanese Management: Applications for American Executives.* New York: Simon and Schuster, 1981.

Patchen, Martin. 1976. "Labor-Management Consultation at TVA: Its Impact on Employees." In Ervin Williams, ed. *Participative Management: Concepts, Theory and Implementation.* Atlanta, Ga.: School of Business Administration, Georgia State University.

Pava, Calvin. 1985. "Managing New Information Technology: Design or Default?" In Richard E. Walton and Paul R. Lawrence, eds. *HRM Trends and Challenges.* Boston, Mass.: Harvard Business School Press.

Perl, Peter. 1984. "Computer Monitoring—Efficiency or Slavery?" *Times Union,* (September 9).

Peters, Thomas J., and Robert H. Waterman, Jr. 1982. *In Search of Excellence: Lessons from America's Best-Run Companies.* New York: Harper and Row.

Phillips, Stephen. 1986. "Small Bank Revives Urban Area." *New York Times,* (January 30).

Piore, Michael J., and Charles F. Sabel. 1984. *The Second Industrial Divide: Possibilities for Prosperity.* New York: Basic Books.

Porter, Lyman W., Edward E. Lawler, and J. Richard Hackman. 1975. *Behavior in Organizations.* New York: McGraw-Hill.

Pray, Thomas F. 1976. "Technical Change and Productivity in a Salt Producing Firm." Unpublished Ph.D. Dissertation, Rensselaer Polytechnic Institute.

Prescott, Edward C., and Michael Visscher. 1980. "Organizational Capital." *Journal of Political Economy,* 88 (June), 446–461.

Pryor, Frederic L. 1983. "The Economics of Production Cooperatives: A Reader's Guide." *Annals of Public and Cooperative Economy,* 54 (2), 134–172.

Quinn, Robert E., and Kim Cameron. 1983. "Organizational Life Cycles and Shifting Criteria of Effectiveness: Some Preliminary Evidence." *Management Science,* 29 (January), 33–51.

Rapoport, Anatol, and Albert M. Chammah. 1965. *Prisoner's Dilemma: A Study in Conflict and Cooperation.* Ann Arbor: The University of Michigan Press.

Reich, Robert B. 1983. *The Next American Frontier.* New York: Times Books.

Reilly, William K. 1984. "Cleaning Our Chemical Waste Backyard." *Wall Street Journal,* (May 31).

Reynolds, Lloyd G. 1982. *Labor Economics and Labor Relations.* 8th ed. Englewood Cliffs, N.J.: Prentice-Hall.

Rhodes, Lucien, and Patricia Amend. 1986. "The Turnaround." *Inc.,* (August), 42–48.

Riggs, James L, and K. K. Seo. 1979. "Wa: Personnel Factor of Japanese Productivity." *Industrial Engineering,* (April), 32–35.

Roberts, Karlene, Raymond E. Miles, and L. Vaughn Blankenship. 1976. "Organizational Leadership Satisfaction and Productivity: A Comparative Analysis." In Ervin Williams, ed. *Participative Management: Concepts, Theory and Implementation.* Atlanta, Ga.: School of Business Administration, Georgia State University.

Rout, Lawrence. 1986. "Many Big-Company Executives Leaving For More Responsibility in Smaller Firms." *Wall Street Journal,* (March 13).

Salancik, Gerald R., and Jeffrey Pfeffer. 1977. "An Examination of Need-Satisfaction Models of Job Attitudes." *Administrative Science Quarterly,* 22 (September), 427–56.

Schein, Edgar H. 1968. "Organizational Socialization and the Profession of Management." *Industrial Management Review,* 9, 1–15.

———. 1981. "Does Japanese Management Style Have A Message for American Managers?" *Sloan Management Review,* 23 (Fall), 55–68.

Schelling, Thomas C. 1978. *Micromotives and Macrobehavior.* New York: W. W. Norton & Co.

Schleuning, Neala. 1986. "The Aesthetics of Work." *The Human Economy Newsletter,* 7 (June), 3–8.

Schultz, Theodore W. 1971. *Investment in Human Capital: The Role of Education and of Research.* New York: The Free Press.

Schumpeter, Joseph A. 1961. *The Theory of Economic Development: An Inquiry into*

Profits, Capital, Credit, Interest and the Business Cycle. New York: Oxford University Press.

Sen, Amartya K. 1977. "Rational Fools: A Critique of the Behavioral Foundations of Economic Theory." *Philosophy and Public Affairs,* 6, 317–344.

Shaiken, Harley, 1984. *Work Transformed: Automation and Labor in the Computer Age.* New York: Holt, Rinehart and Winston.

Shen, T. Y. 1981. "Technology and Organizational Economics." In Paul C. Nystrom and William H. Starbuck, eds. *Handbook of Organization Design, Volume 1, Adapting Organizations to their Environments.* Oxford: Oxford University Press.

Shepherd, William G. 1982. "Causes of Increasing Competition in the U.S. Economy, 1939–1980 ." *Review of Economics and Statistics,* 64 (November), 613–626.

Simmons, John, and William Mares. 1982. *Working Together: Employee Participation in Action.* New York: New York University Press.

Simon, Herbert A. 1957. *Administrative Behavior: A Study of Decision-Making Processes in Administration Organization.* New York: The Free Press.

Sobel, Irvin. 1982. "Human Capital and Institutional Theories of the Labor Market: Rivals or Complements?" *Journal of Economic Issues,* 16 (March), 255–272.

Solow, Robert M. 1957. "Technical Change and the Aggregate Production Function." *The Review of Economics and Statistics,* 39 (August), 312–320.

Solow, Robert M. 1960. "Investment and Technical Progress." In K. Arrow, S. Karlin, and P. Suppes, eds. *Mathematical Methods in Social Sciences* (1960), Stanford, Calif.: Stanford University Press.

Sombart, Werner. 1967. *The Quintessence of Capitalism: A Study of the History and Psychology of the Modern Business Man.* Translated and edited by M. Epstein. New York: Howard Fertig.

"Steel Man Ken Iverson." 1986. *Inc.,* (April), 41–48.

Steinherr, A. 1978. "The Labor-Managed Economy: A Survey of the Economic Literature." *Annals of Public and Cooperative Economy,* 49, 129–148.

Stephen, Frank H., ed. 1982. *The Performance of Labor-Managed Firms.* New York: St. Martin's Press.

Stephen, Frank H. 1983. "Review Article: The Economics of Labor-Managed Firms." *Journal of Economic Studies,* 10 (2), 66–71.

Stollenwerk, James H. 1984. "Rexworks: A Case Study of Applied Social/ Economic Justice." Paper presented at Conference on Community Dimensions of Economic Enterprise on June 10 at Marquette University, Milwaukee, Wisconsin.

Svejnar, Jan. 1982. "Codetermination and Productivity: Empirical Evidence from the Federal Republic of Germany." In Derek C. Jones and Jan Svejnar, eds. *Participatory and Self-Managed Firms.* Lexington, Mass.: Lexington Books.

Takeuchi, Hirotaka. 1981. "Productivity: Learning from the Japanese." *California Management Review,* 23 (Summer), 5–19.

Taylor, Frederick W. 1911. *The Principles of Scientific Management.* New York: Harper.

Thomas, Henk. 1982. "The Performance of the Mondragon Cooperatives in Spain." In Derek C. Jones and Jan Svejnar, eds. *Participatory and Self-Managed Firms.* Lexington, Mass.: Lexington Books.

Thomas, Henk, and Chris Logan. 1982. *Mondragon: An Economic Analysis*. London: George Allen and Unwin.

Thomas, R. Roosevelt. 1978. "Managing the Psychological Contract." Boston: Harvard Business School Case Services.

Toffler, Alvin. 1980. *The Third Wave*. New York: Bantam Books.

Tomer, John F. 1973. "Management Consulting for Private Enterprise: A Theoretical and Empirical Analysis of the Contribution of Management Consultants to Economic Growth in the United States." Unpublished Ph.D. Dissertation, Rutgers University.

Tomer, John F. 1977. "Intangible Capital Formation and Economic Growth: The Management Consulting Contribution." Paper presented at the Meeting of the Eastern Economic Association, Hartford, Conn., April 14, 1977.

Tomer, John F. 1980. "Community Control and the Theory of the Firm." *Review of Social Economy*, 38 (October), 191–214.

Tomer, John F. 1981a. "Organizational Change, Organizational Capital and Economic Growth." *The Eastern Economic Journal*, 7 (January), 1–14.

Tomer, John F. 1981b. "Worker Motivation: A Neglected Element in Micro-Micro Theory." *Journal of Economic Issues*, 15 (June), 351–362.

Tomer, John F. 1983a. "Productivity Through Cooperation: The Role of Japanese and Gandhian Development Strategies." Unpublished paper presented at the Third World Congress of Social Economics at Fresno, California on August 18.

Tomer, John F. 1983b. "The Japanese Company: The Challenge for Economists." *Eastern Economic Journal*, 9 (January–March), 57–68.

Tomer, John F. 1984. "Mortgage Redlining Behavior and Antiredlining Policy." *Journal of Business*, 12 (Spring), 10–20.

Tomer, John F. 1985. "Working Smarter the Japanese Way: The X-Efficiency of Theory Z Management." In Paul Kleindorfer, ed. *The Management of Productivity and Technology in Manufacturing*. New York: Plenum.

Tomer, John F. 1986. "Productivity and Organizational Behavior: Where Human Capital Theory Fails." In Benjamin Gilad and Stanley Kaish, eds. *Handbook of Behavior Economics*, Greenwich, Conn.: JAI Press.

Umstat, Denis. 1977. "MBO + Job Enrichment: How to Have Your Cake and Eat It Too." *Management Review*, 66 (February), 21–26.

Vanek, Jaroslav. 1970. *The General Theory of Labor-Managed Market Economies*. Ithaca. N.Y.: Cornell University Press.

Vanek, Jaroslav. ed. 1975. *Self-Management: Economic Liberation of Man*. Baltimore, Md.: Penguin Books.

Vogel, David. 1978. *Lobbying the Corporation: Citizen Challenges to Business Authority*. New York: Basic Books.

Vogel, Ezra F. 1979. *Japan as Number One: Lessons for America*. New York: Harper Colophon Books.

Vroom, Victor. 1976. "Some Personality Determinants of the Effects of Participation." In Ervin Williams, ed. *Participative Management: Concepts, Theory and Implementation*. Atlanta, Ga.: School of Business Administration, Georgia State University.

Walton, Richard E. 1985a. "Toward a Strategy of Eliciting Employee Commitment Based on Policies of Mutuality." In Richard E. Walton and Paul R. Lawrence, eds. *HRM Trends and Challenges*. Boston, Mass.: Harvard Business School Press.

Walton, Richard E. 1985b. "From Control to Commitment in the Workplace." *Harvard Business Review*, 64(March–April), 76–84.

Walton, Richard E. 1985c. "Challenges in the Management of Technology and Labor Relations." In Walton, Richard E. and Lawrence, Paul R. eds. *HRM Trends and Challenges*. Boston, MA: Harvard Business School Press.

Walton, Richard E., and Lawrence, Paul R. eds. 1985. *HRM Trends and Challenges*. Boston, MA: Harvard Business School Press.

Ward, Benjamin N. 1958. "The Firm in Illyria: Market Syndicalism." *American Economic Review*, 48 (September), 566–589.

Weiermair, Klaus. 1984. "Heterogeneity in Production and Organization Design: Comparative Economic Perspectives of Organizational Innovativeness." Paper presented August 30 at the 11th Annual EARIE Conference, INSEAD, Fountainebleau, France.

Weiermair, Klaus. 1985. "Worker Incentives and Worker Participation: On the Changing Nature of the Employment Relationship." *Journal of Management Studies*, 22 (September), 547–570.

Wilkins, Alan L., and William G. Ouchi. 1983. "Efficient Cultures: Exploring the Relationship between Culture and Organizational Performance." *Administrative Science Quarterly*, 28 (September), 468–481.

Williams, Ervin. ed. 1976. *Participative Management: Concepts, Theory and Implementation*. Atlanta, Ga.: School of Business Administration, Georgia State University.

Williamson, Oliver E. 1967. "Hierarchical Control and Optimum Firm Size." *Journal of Political Economy*, 75 (April), 123–138.

Williamson, Oliver E. 1970. *Corporate Control and Business Behavior*. Englewood Cliffs, N.J.: Prentice-Hall.

Williamson, Oliver E. 1975. *Markets and Hierarchies: Analysis and Antitrust Implications*. New York: The Free Press.

Williamson, Oliver E. 1979. "Transaction-Cost Economics: The Governance of Contractual Economics." *The Journal of Law and Economics*, 22 (October), 233–261.

Williamson, Oliver E. 1981. "The Modern Corporation: Origins, Evolution, Attributes." *Journal of Economic Literature*, 19 (December), 1537–1568.

Wintrobe, Ronald. 1981. "It Pays to Do Good, but Not to Do More Good than It Pays: A Note on the Survival of Altruism." *Journal of Economic Behavior and Organization*, 2 (September), 201–213.

Yankelovich, Daniel, 1981a. *New Rules: Searching for Self-Fulfillment in a World Turned Upside Down*. New York: Random House.

Yankelovich, Daniel. 1981b. "New Rules in American Life: Searching for Self-Fulfillment in a World Turned Upside Down." *Psychology Today*, (April), 35–91.

Zaleznik, Abraham. 1985. "Decisions, Coalitions, and the Economy of the Self." Paper presented at the Middlebury College Conference on the Psychological Foundations of Economic Behavior, October 25–26.

Zuboff, Shoshana. 1985. "Technologies That Informate: Implications for Human Resource Management in the Computerized Industrial Workplace." In Richard E. Walton and Paul R. Lawrence, eds. *HRM Trends and Challenges.* Boston, Mass.: Harvard Business School Press.

Zwerdling, Daniel. 1980. *Workplace Democracy: A Guide to Workplace Ownership, Participation, and Self-Management Experiments in the United States and Europe.* New York: Harper Colophon Books.

Index

About the Author

JOHN F. TOMER is currently associate professor of economics and finance at Manhattan College, Riverdale, New York, where he teaches managerial economics, a seminar on the Japanese economy, intermediate macroeconomics, corporate finance, money and banking, and other subjects. His articles have appeared in the *Journal of Economic Issues*, the *Review of Social Economy*, the *Eastern Economic Journal*, the *Journal of Post Keynesian Economics*, the *Public Finance Quarterly*, the *Journal of Behavioral Economics* and *Urban Affairs Quarterly*. His article, "Working Smarter the Japanese Way," appears in Paul Kleindorfer's *The Management of Productivity and Technology in Manufacturing* (Plenum 1985) and his "Productivity and Organizational Behavior" appears in the *Handbook of Behavioral Economics* by Benjamin Gilad and Stanley Kaish (JAI Press 1986).

Tomer hopes to continue research that combines economic analysis with behavioral and humanistic perspectives. It is his hope that his work might influence the United States in particular to adopt a more people-oriented approach to its economic development. He is proud of his family of four including his wife, Doris, and sons, Russell and Jeffrey, now nine and five years old, who reside with him in Troy, New York. Tomer at age forty-four still hopes to actualize some of his unrealized potential in tennis and skiing.